The Management of
Collective Bargaining

Warwick Studies in Industrial Relations
General Editors: G. S. Bain, R. Hyman and K. Sisson

Also available in this series

Conflict at Work
P. K. Edwards

Managing the Factory
P. K. Edwards

Dismissed: A Study of Unfair Dismissal and the Industrial Tribunal System
Linda Dickens, Michael Jones, Brian Weekes and Moira Hart

Consent and Efficiency
Eric Batstone. Anthony Ferner and Michael Terry

Unions on the Board
Eric Batstone, Anthony Ferner and Michael Terry

The Changing Contours of British Industrial Relations
William Brown (ed.)

Profiles of Union Growth
George Sayers Bain and Robert Price

The Social Organization of Strikes
Eric Batstone, Ian Boraston and Stephen Frenkel

Shop Stewards in Action
Eric Batstone, Ian Boraston and Stephen Frenkel

Trade Unionism under Collective Bargaining
Hugh Armstrong Clegg

The Management of Collective Bargaining

An International Comparison

Keith Sisson

Basil Blackwell

First published 1987

Basil Blackwell Ltd.
108 Cowley Road, Oxford, OX4 1JF, UK

Basil Blackwell Inc.
432 Park Avenue South, Suite 1503
New York, NY 10016, USA

British Library Cataloguing in Publication Data
Sisson, Keith
  The management of collective bargaining :
  an international comparison.—(Warwick
  studies in industrial relations)
  1. Collective bargaining
  I. Title   II. Series
  658.3'154   HD6971.5
  ISBN 0-631-13439-5

Library of Congress Cataloging in Publication Data
Sisson, Keith.
  The management of collective bargaining.
  (Warwick Studies in Industrial Relations)
  Bibliography: p.
  Includes index.
  I. Collective bargaining.   I. Title.   II. Series.
  HD6971.5.S57 1987   331.89   87-6642
  ISBN 0-631-13439-5

Typeset in 10 on 11½ pt Times
by DMB (Typesetting), Oxford
Printed in Great Britain by
TJ Press Ltd, Padstow, Cornwall

for Jan

Contents

List of Tables and Figures

Tables

Figures

Abbreviations

Britain

Employers' Organizations

BEC   British Employers' Confederation – amalgamated with FBI and NABM to form CBI in 1965.

BPIF   British Printing Industries Federation – formerly British Federation of Master Printers.

CBI   Confederation of British Industry – the employers'/trade confederation formed in 1965 through amalgamation of the BEC, FBI and NABM.

CIA   Chemical Industries Association.

CMF   Clothing Manufacturers' Federation.

EEF   Engineering Employers' Federation.

FBI   Federation of British Industries – trade confederation which joined with BEC and NABM to form CBI in 1965.

FCEC   Federation of Civil Engineering Contractors.

NABM   National Association of British Manufacturers – trade confederation which joined with BEC and FBI to form CBI in 1965.

NFBTE   National Federation of Building Trades Employers.*

NPA   Newspaper Publishers Association – the employers' organization of the national daily and Sunday newspapers printed in London and Manchester.

* The NFBTE changed its name to the Building Employers' Confederation in 1984. NFBTE will be used in the text rather than BEC, to avoid any confusion with the British Employers' Confederation.

NS   Newspaper Society – the employers' organization of the regional and provincial newspapers.

Trade Unions

ASE   Amalgamated Society of Engineers – forerunner of the Amalgamated Engineering Union.

TUC   Trades Union Congress.

France

Employers' Organizations

CGPF   Confédération Générale de la Production Française/ Confédération Française du Patronat Français – names of the employers'/trade confederation prior to 1940.

CNPF   Conseil National du Patronat Français – employers'/trade confederation (post-1945).

CPF   Confédération de la Presse Française – employers' organization of the provincial newspapers.

FFSPIG   Fédération Française des Syndicats Patronaux de l'Imprimerie et des Industries Graphiques – printing employers' organization.

FNB   Fédération Nationale du Bâtiment – building employers' organization.

FNTP   Fédération Nationale des Travaux Publics – civil engineering employers' organization.

FPF   Fédération de la Presse Française – employers' organization of the Paris (and some provincial) daily newspapers.

PME   Confédération Générale des Petites et Moyennes Entreprises – employers' confederation of small and medium sized firms.

UIC   Union des Industries Chimiques – chemical employers' organization.

UIH   Union des Industries d'Habillement – clothing employers' organization.

UIMM   Union des Industries Métallurgiques et Minières – metalworking employers' organization.

Trade Unions

CFDT   Confédération Française Démocratique du Travail – second largest trade union confederation with socialist tendencies. Originally the Confédération Française des Travailleurs Chrétiens, some of whose members seceded to maintain the CFTC.

CFTC	Confédération Française des Travailleurs Chrétiens – trade union confederation with links with the Catholic church. The term 'maintenu' is used to describe the organization retaining the title following the formation of the CFDT.
CGC	Confédération Générale des Cadres – trade union confederation of supervisors and senior white-collar workers.
CGT	Confédération Générale du Travail – largest trade union confederation with close links with the Communist Party.
CGT-FO	Confédération Générale du Travail-Force Ouvrière – the 'reformist' trade union confederation which seceded from CGT in 1948. Now largely representative of white-collar workers especially in the public sector.
FDL	Fédération du Livre – main printing trade union.

Italy

Employers' Organizations

AIE	Associazione Italiana Editori – employers' organization of weekly newspapers and periodicals.
AIIA	Associazione Italiana Industriali Abbigliamento – clothing employers' organization.
AIIGCT	Associazione Italiana Industriali Grafiche Cartotechnice e Transformatrici – printing and paper products employers' organization.
ANCE	Associazione Nazionale Costruttori Edili – construction employers' organization.
ANIC	Associazione Nazionale dell'Industria Chimica – chemical employers' organization.
ASAP	Associazione Sindacale per le Aziende Petrolchemiche e Collegate a Partecipazione Statale – employers' organization of public sector enterprises in the oil and chemical industries.
CONFAGRICOLTURA	Confederazione Generale dell'Agricoltura Italiana – agricultural employers'/trade confederation.
CONFCOMMERCIO	Confederazione Generale del Commercio Italiano – commercial employers'/trade confederation.
CONFINDUSTRIA	Confederazione Generale dell'Industria Italiana – employers'/trade confederation.
FEDERMECCANICA	Federazione Sindacale dell'Industria Metalmeccanica Italiana – metalworking employers' organization.

FIEG Federazione Italiana Editori Giornali – employers' organization of daily newspapers (and some weekly magazines).

INTERSIND Associazione Sindacale Intersind – employers' organization of public sector enterprises.

Trade Unions

CGIL Confederazione Generale Italiana del Lavoro – main trade union confederation with strong links with the Communist Party.

CISL Confederazione Italiana dei Sindacati Lavoratori – second largest trade union confederation with links with the Christian Democrat Party.

UIL Unione Italiana del Lavoro – third main trade union confederation with links with the Socialist Party.

Sweden

Employers' Organizations

AG Allmänna Gruppen – the so-called 'general' employers' organization which looks after the interests of the chemical employers.

BA Byggnadsämmesförbundet – building employers' organization.

GAF Grafiska Arbetsgivareförbundet – printing employers' organization.

JBF Järnsbruksförbundet – iron and steel employers' organization.

SAF Svenska Arbetsgivareföreningen – the employers' confederation.

SBI Svenska Byggadsindustriförbundet – civil engineering employers' organization.

SIF Sveriges Industriförbund – the trade confederation.

SKF Sveriges Konfektionsindustriförbund – clothing employers' organization.

SVEABUND Svenska Väg-och Vattenbyggarnas Arbetsgivareförbund – bridges and waterways employers' organization.

SVF Sveriges Verkstadsförening – engineering and shipbuilding employers' organization.

TAF Tidningarnas Arbetsgivareförening – newspaper employers' organization.

Abbreviations

Trade Unions

LO   Landsorganisationen i Sverige – the manual workers' trade union confederation.

PTK   Privattjänstemannakartell – the SACO and TCO 'umbrella' organization which negotiates on behalf of white-collar workers in the private sector.

SACO   Sveriges Akademikers Centralorganisationen – the professional workers' trade union confederation.

TCO   Tjänstemannens Centralorganisationen – the white-collar workers' trade union confederation.

West Germany

Employers' Organizations

AC   Arbeitsring Chemie – chemical employers' organization.

AES   Arbeitgeberverband Eisen und Stahl – iron and steel employers' organization.

BDA   Bundesvereinigung der Deutschen Arbeitgeberverbände – the employers' confederation.

BDI   Bundesverband der Deutschen Industrie – the trade confederation.

BDZ   Bundesverband Deutscher Zeitungsverleger – newspaper employers' organization.

BI   Bekleidungsindustrie – clothing employers' organization.

BVD   Bundesvereinigung Druck – printing employers' organization.

Gesamtmetall Gesamtverband der Metallindustriellen Arbeitgeberverbände e.V. – engineering and shipbuilding employers' organization.

HVB   Hauptverband der Deutschen Bauindustrie – civil engineering employers' organization.

VDA   Vereinigung der Deutschen Arbeitgeberverbände – a predecessor of the BDA.

ZVB   Zentralverband des Deutschen Baugewerbes – building employers' organization.

Trade Unions

DGB   Deutscher Gewerkschaftsbund – the trade union confederation.

IG Metall   Industriegewerkschaft Metall – metalworkers' trade union.

Editors' Foreword

The University of Warwick is the major centre in the United Kingdom for the study of industrial relations, its first undergraduates being admitted in 1965. The teaching of industrial relations began a year later in the School of Industrial and Business Studies, and it now has one of the country's largest graduate programmes in the subject. Warwick became a national centre for research into industrial relations when the Social Science Research Council (now the Eeonomic and Social Research Council) located its Industrial Relations Research Unit at the University. Subsequently, in 1984, the Unit was reconstituted as a Designated Research Centre attached to the School of Industrial and Business Studies. It continues to be known as the Industrial Relations Research Unit, however, and now embraces the research activities of all members of the School's industrial relations community.

The series of Warwick Studies in Industrial Relations was launched in 1972 by Hugh Clegg and George Bain as the main vehicle for the publication of the results of the Unit's projects, as well as the research carried out by staff teaching industrial relations in the University and the work of graduate students. The first six titles in the series were published by Heinemann Educational Books of London, and subsequent titles have been published by Basil Blackwell of Oxford.

The Unit is making the role of management in industrial relations a central aspect of its current research programme. This volume, by the present Director of the Unit, is a major part of this endeavour, and presents the results of an ambitious international study. A considerable amount of material, much of it previously unavailable in English, was collected from secondary sources dealing with France, Italy, Sweden, West Germany, Britain, Japan and the USA. Original material was also gathered in a systematic programme of interviews with employers' organization officials and managers in the first five of these.

The book uses this material to present the first thorough comparative account of the role of employers and their organizations in the development and practice of collective bargaining. The starting point is the often-neglected fact that a key characteristic of the structure of collective bargaining is whether employers combine with one another to deal with trade unions. In Britain and Western Europe employers have traditionally dealt with trade unions through the agency of employers' organizations, whereas in Japan and the USA they have preferred to deal with them independently. In Western Europe multi-employer bargaining through employers' organizations continues to be the predominant pattern; in Britain multi-employer bargaining is in decline.

In accounting for the differences in employers' behaviour, the book places considerable emphasis on the origins of and early developments in the structure of collective bargaining. The institutional arrangements which emerged – and which were grounded in the different patterns of industrialization – have had a profound effect on the behaviour of employers as well as trade unions. The argument is developed in a way that makes it possible not only to present a considerable amount of empirical material but also to explain some of the key features of industrial relations in Britain and other countries.

George Bain
Richard Hyman
Keith Sisson

Preface

This study owes a great deal to Hugh Clegg. It was Hugh who first
stimulated my interest in undertaking a comparative analysis of the role
of employers and their organizations. It was Hugh who, along with Jan,
my wife, did so much down through the years to help me keep at it. It
was Hugh who, along with other colleagues at Warwick – and notably
George Bain, William Brown (now at Cambridge), Paul Edwards and
Roy Lewis – read several drafts of the manuscript and made numerous
suggestions for its improvement. The fact that some of the study's conclusions might be seen to be at variance with those of his own work did
not appear to worry him in the slightest.

A considerable debt of gratitude is also due to the large number of
employers' organization officials and managers, in this country and in
France, Italy, Sweden and West Germany, whose willingness to answer
questions frankly not only made the study possible, but also helped to
dispel the myth that their reluctance to talk to researchers was a major
reason for the neglect of management in the industrial relations
literature; to Paul Banfield, Gerry Cronan, Daniel Keohane, the late
Brian Robinson, and Peter Summerfield, all postgraduate students, for
assisting with the fieldwork in Britain; to Jenny Jackson for helping to
produce some of the statistics in the Appendix; to Annemarie Flanders
for helping to produce the list of references and the index; to Connie
Bussman for typing so many drafts that she probably knows the text off
by heart; and to the British Academy and the Wolfson Foundation for
helping to make it possible for me to spend six months of a sabbatical
year in France and Italy doing fieldwork for the study.

Peter 'Jake' Jackson deserves a special word of thanks. Not only was
he responsible, with the financial support of the Unit, for the original
fieldwork carried out in Sweden and West Germany, but he also helped

to shape many of the questions and ideas that went into the design of the project. Had he stayed in the Unit or been able to continue on the project, there is little doubt that his name would have been included on the title page.

The bulk of the fieldwork was undertaken in the second half of the 1970s. The delay in writing up the results is entirely my own responsibility. A heavy teaching and administrative load in the School, and then the demands of being the Director of the Industrial Relations Research Unit contributed. Much more important, however, was the time taken trying to resolve a number of problems that anyone who has done serious comparative research will immediately recognize. In tackling these problems, I have tried to take into account new developments from literature published since the fieldwork was conducted, and I hope that the study has benefited by placing the fieldwork data in their broader context.

Piecing together a balanced picture from extremely superficial, and in some cases non-existent, secondary sources proved to be an exceedingly long drawn out business. Then there was the need to check, and check again, the interpretation to be placed on these sources; views about the logic of collective action by employers and the government of employers' organizations – even those of the most distinguished scholars – turned out to be especially vulnerable to the tendency to see issues simply from the standpoint of one's own country. The attempt to integrate a considerable amount of empirical material theme by theme rather than country by country also proved much more difficult than might be imagined, and explains why the material is divided country by country within four of the eight chapters. Coupled with this was the problem of developing an explanatory framework which was not so general that, in trying to explain everything, it really explained nothing, and which emphasized uniformities from one country to another and yet which took into account the rich diversity of behaviour. Finally, and perhaps most difficult and important of all, there was the problem of capturing the significance for present day behaviour of both the long-term interaction between trade unions and employers and the critical incidents in this relationship – which explains why the study does not follow recent fashion in depicting complex social processes in terms of figures and diagrams.

Keith Sisson

1

Aims and Approach

Ever since the publication *Industrial Democracy* by the Webbs in 1897, collective bargaining has been seen, first and foremost, as a method of trade union action to be compared with mutual insurance and political activity. Admittedly, perceptive observers such as Flanders (1970b: 215) have been at pains to emphasize that there could be no adequate theory of collective bargaining which saw it only in these terms and which overlooked the management interest. For reasons that are not altogether clear, however, especially in view of the attention that managerial strategies towards the control of the labour process have received in recent years (see, for example, Braverman, 1974; Burawoy, 1979 and 1985; and Edwards, 1979), there has been no systematic attempt to explore managerial attitudes and policies towards collective bargaining, even though it is one of the most important methods of settling the conditions of employment in industrialized market economies. Indeed, as Clegg (1976: 119) points out in a previous volume in this series, very little information of any kind is available about the role played by employers and their organizations in collective bargaining. The result is that there has been a widespread failure to appreciate how much this role varies from one country to another, and what the implications are for the conduct of collective bargaining.

The Structure of Collective Bargaining:
Multi-Employer or Single-Employer Bargaining?

The present study sets out to make a contribution towards remedying these deficiencies. It compares and contrasts the role of employers and their organizations in the development and practice of collective bargaining in a number of industrialized market economies: Britain, France, West Germany, Italy, Japan, Sweden and the USA. In particular, it is concerned with one of the key distinguishing characteristics of the structure of collective bargaining, namely whether or not the bargaining is collective on the part of employers. By definition, collective bargaining requires collective action on the part of employees. It does not require collective action on the part of employers; individual employers as well as employers' organizations can be the bargaining agents with trade unions. In other words, collective bargaining can be multi-employer or single-employer. Furthermore, multi-employer bargaining can be national or regional in scope; it can also be single-industry or multi-industry, depending on whether or not the 'peak' employers' organization or employers' confederation is a bargaining agent. Single-employer bargaining can also take place at a number of levels depending on the structure of the firm, although this aspect will not be a major concern in the study. More importantly, the individual employer can be involved in both multi-employer and single-employer bargaining; in this case the latter is usually referred to as workplace bargaining.

To put the subject matter of the study into context, the great majority of the employers in Britain has traditionally negotiated with trade unions through the agency of an employers' organization. Such multi-employer bargaining had developed in many industries at either the district or national level by the end of the nineteenth century and was subsequently reinforced by the recommendations of the Whitley Committee during and immediately following the First World War. The report of the Donovan Commission (1968: 12) described multi-employer bargaining as the 'keystone of the formal system of industrial relations'. According to the Ministry of Labour's evidence quoted by the Commission (1968: 13), there were about 500 separate institutions, many called National Joint Industrial Councils, on which employers' organizations negotiated both substantive and procedural agreements with trade unions for entire industries or sections of industries.

Employers' organizations continue to negotiate multi-employer agreements with trade unions in most industries, but in recent years more and more issues have been covered by collective bargaining that is specific to a single employer. In 1968 the report of the Donovan Commission argued that the workplace bargaining in which employers had increasingly become involved was in many respects in conflict with the formal system of industrial relations. To deal with many of the problems that it saw stemming from this conflict, the Commission argued that employers should negotiate effective single-employer agreements to supplement the multi-employer agreements negotiated by their employers' organizations. Subsequently, the negotiation of productivity agreements, the revision of payment systems, and the introduction of job evaluation and domestic disputes and grievance procedures have achieved some of the objectives desired by the Commission. Yet little has been done to relate these developments to the multi-employer agreements that continue to be negotiated. The result is that multi-employer bargaining has little or no impact on many of the larger employers in manufacturing industry; for them single-employer bargaining has become the predominant pattern. For example, the Warwick Survey (Brown, 1981: 8) suggested that in 1978 less than 10 per cent of engineering employers and 25 per cent of chemical employers regarded multi-employer agreements as the most important level of pay bargaining for manual employees.

It is important to point out, however, that the Donovan analysis was not wholly appropriate to a large number of British employers and its central prescription was not adopted by them. For many employers in industries such as clothing, construction, and printing, multi-employer bargaining continues to be the predominant pattern. For example, the Warwick Survey (Brown, 1981: 8) suggested that, in 1978, 75 per cent of employers in clothing and 69 per cent of employers in printing and publishing regarded multi-employer agreements as more important than single-employer agreements so far as pay bargaining was concerned. In the report of the first Workplace Industrial Relations Survey (Daniel and Millward, 1983: 263) no less than four fifths of employers in construction expressed the same opinion. The same is true of many of the smaller employers in large-scale manufacturing industries. That is to say, the multi-employer agreement negotiated by the employers' organization is likely to be the most important source of increases in pay, as well as decisions relating to other terms and conditions of employment.

By comparison with Britain, multi-employer bargaining in France, West Germany, Italy and Sweden appears to enjoy greater support among employers; in these countries even employers such as Ford, who in Britain has always been regarded as a proponent of single-employer bargaining, are members of employers' organizations and parties to the multi-employer agreement they negotiate. Yet there are important differences between the countries. In some cases the bargaining is multi-tiered. In France, Italy and Sweden, for example, it is not only the 'branch' or industry employers' organizations that are bargaining agents; the employers' confederation also fulfils this role. There are also differences between the three countries in the locus of power. In Sweden the employers' confederation has been the main bargaining agent throughout most of the post-Second World War period. On the other hand, in France and West Germany the local or regional branch employers' organizations are powerful bargaining agents in their own right in many industries, and the negotiation of the rates of pay is their responsibility. There are also significant differences so far as the situation in the workplace is concerned. In each country the larger employers have increasingly been drawn into workplace bargaining but the scope and content vary as does the workers' bargaining agent with which the employer is faced.

The USA and Japan are also included in the study, albeit at a more superficial level of analysis, because they offer yet further contrasts. In the USA, there appears to be a dual structure of collective bargaining. In industries such as clothing, construction, and printing, multi-employer bargaining covering a region or a city is predominant; in large-scale manufacturing industries single-employer bargaining at the enterprise or establishment level is predominant. In Japan, employers' organizations play an important role in collective bargaining but are not normally bargaining agents; single-employer bargaining at the enterprise or establishment level is predominant.

It is with the description, explanation and implications of these aspects of employers' behaviour, then, that the study is concerned. To supplement the limited secondary sources available, the study draws on the results of a systematic programme of interviews with four main groups of employer representatives in Britain and the other Western European countries: officers of the employers' confederations in each country; officers of the most important industry or branch employers' organizations at the national level in five industries (chemicals, clothing, construction, metalworking and printing) reflecting the different behaviour of employers discussed above; officers of some of the regional and local branch employers' organizations in the five industries; and senior managers drawn from individual employers in some of the industries (especially, for reasons which will emerge later, in chemicals and metalworking). Further details about employers in each country, based on official sources, are to be found in the appendix.

Needless to say, any attempt at a comparative study lays itself open to the criticism that it should have included this or that case. The claims of some other countries to be included in the first group are very strong. Australia and the Netherlands are perhaps the best examples. It quickly became apparent, however, that the five countries in this group, plus the USA and Japan, were more than enough to handle. Since the objective was to present the findings as far as possible in an integrated fashion and not country by country, the omission of other countries is perhaps not so important; the conclusions can more easily be subjected to criticism and comment by those with expert knowledge of them. The same applies to other industries.

The Approach of Previous Studies

Surprising as it may seem, the bulk of the recent literature concerned with management's role in industrial relations has little to say about collective bargaining. Most of it is more or less exclusively preoccupied with management–worker relations rather than management–trade union relations. Collective bargaining, if it is considered at all, is largely seen as peripheral or as an example of a strategy of 'responsible autonomy' as opposed to 'direct control' (Friedman, 1977: 78–9). Certainly there is little recognition of the variety or the complexity of what is involved in collective bargaining. It is necessary to return to literature of an older tradition to begin to get any real insights.

The Logic of Collective Bargaining

The most succinct statement concerning the logic of collective bargaining from the employer's point of view is that of Flanders (1974: 355–6). Employers, he argues, do not recognize trade unions for the purposes of collective bargaining simply because they are forced to do so. Collective bargaining serves two employer interests. One is *market* control. By negotiating pay and conditions that are more or less standard, employers effectively take the costs of one of the most important factors of production out of competition. This interest, it needs to be emphasized, is relatively limited in its application. Superficially, market control can be achieved only by multi-employer bargaining; single-employer bargaining cannot contribute to market control because it affects only one employer. Also, if employers experienced no problems in setting pay and conditions collusively, the co-operation of trade unions – at least for the purposes of market regulation – would be unnecessary. As will be argued below, these considerations mean that in practice only those employers in highly competitive industries are likely to resort to multi-employer bargaining in the interests of market control.

According to Flanders, the second interest served by collective bargaining, which finds echoes in the recent work of economists associated with the Harvard school (see, for example, Freeman and Medoff, 1984), is a contribution to *managerial* control. The employer needs explicit rules within which to manage his workforce – substantive rules to establish standards on such matters as payment, hours of work, and manning; and procedural rules concerned with discipline and grievances, and with how the substantive rules are made. Both types of rule introduce a degree of certainty into what would otherwise be a very unstable situation. For example, managers can predict with greater accuracy what their labour costs are likely to be in the immediate future; or, to give another example, both managers and workers know what to expect in the event of a breach of disciplinary rules. Much more importantly, the introduction of rules which are largely impersonal helps to overcome many of the problems associated with direct supervision. In particular, the introduction of such rules provides 'a substitute for the personal repetition of orders by a supervisor' (Gouldner, 1954: 164).

The employer could make the rules unilaterally or rely on governments to make them. The significance of collective bargaining is that it is a process of joint rule – or decision-making with workers or their representatives being involved with managers in making and administering the rules. The important implication is that rules which are jointly made will enjoy greater legitimacy; in processing claims and grievances in an orderly fashion, the representatives also become in Wright Mills' famous phrase (1948: 224–5), 'managers of discontent'.[1] For in many cases it is not enough that workers obey the rules: it is important that they think them fair and feel commitment to them. This is especially so in the case of the enterprise or establishment which employs large numbers of workers. It makes sense to deal with workers who perform like or similar tasks in groups or categories. To attempt to deal with such workers in-dividually and separately is not only time-consuming and costly, but is also likely to lay the employer open to accusations of unfairness with the consequent disaffection of many workers. In brief, then, by providing for rules which are jointly made, collective bargaining is held to con-tribute to managerial control by legitimating rules and by institutionalizing industrial conflict.

Collective Bargaining and Industrial Structure
Attempts have also been made to explain why some employers engage in multi-employer bargaining, whereas others appear to prefer to deal with trade unions independently. For example, Pierson (1961: 41) observes that in the USA multi-employer bargaining appears to thrive in those in-dustries in which 'employers tend to be small relative to their union counterparts, product competition either on a national or local basis is intense, capital requirements relative to labour requirements are low, and profit margins are narrow'.[2] In these conditions, which are to be found mainly in industries serving local markets like printing and building, significant economies of scale are available to the smaller employer in sharing the costs of trained experts and officials to deal with trade unions and to give advice on social legislation and personnel problems generally. More to the point, the small employer is likely to be too weak on his own to withstand pressure from trade unions – in these industries usually craft trade unions – in a competitive market. He also has a vested interest in regulating an important aspect of the competitive market as well as

[1] Henry Mohd, who had a significant influence on ICI's policy towards trade unions, had made the same point as Wright Mills many years earlier: 'the trade unions are extremely useful to us in bringing to our notice matters that we should not otherwise be aware of' (quoted in Reader, 1973: 66).
[2] Another attempt to explain employers' collective bargaining preference in terms of industrial structure is that of Ingham (1974). Unlike Pierson and his colleagues in the USA, however, Ingham does not argue from first principles and so it is difficult to generalize from his framework. Moreover, while Ingham does valuable service in emphasizing the importance of industrial 'infrastructure' at the time the structure of collective bargaining emerges, the argument of the present study, which is outlined in the next section, suggests that he has drawn the wrong conclusions. See Jackson and Sisson (1976) for a more detailed critique of Ingham's approach.

institutionalizing industrial conflict: the regulation of pay and the other terms and conditions of employment by multi-employer bargaining is aimed as much at the pressure for undercutting from other employers as the upward pressure from trade unions.

Pierson (1950: 358) also identifies the circumstances which in his view lead to single-employer bargaining: 'production units tend to be large, capital constitutes an important part of total costs, and is relatively immobile, and product competition is less intense'.[3] Although the larger employer is better able to withstand trade union pressure on his own, there are a number of pressures on him, it can be argued, to recognize the trade union and, more importantly in the present context, to negotiate independently of other employers. Although labour costs may be relatively insignificant overall, many of the jobs are specific to the establishment and training for them takes place within an internal labour market at considerable cost. The employer cannot afford to allow expensive plant and equipment to stand idle because of industrial disputes or allow a small group to disrupt a highly-integrated production process. The larger the number of workers employed, the greater the need of the employer for explicit rules and procedures for its efficient operation. Furthermore, the co-operation of the workforce in upholding these rules and procedures is as essential as is a specialist staff to develop and maintain them.

As Ulman (1974: 275) has argued, product market considerations would also appear to place a premium on independence in the case of the monopolistic or oligopolistic employer. The larger employer can exploit his advantages in terms of the economies of scale and lower unit costs to make concessions which smaller employers cannot afford or to embarrass them as a deliberate act of policy by raising his workers' wages. Alternatively, he might wish to avoid the collusive wages and prices setting of the smaller employers.

At first sight, the explanation that Pierson and Ulman put forward to account for multi-employer and single-employer bargaining in the USA would appear to have general validity. As the details in the appendix show, the industries in which multi-employer bargaining is the predominant pattern in all countries – clothing, construction and printing –

[3] Pierson (1960; 1961) has been quick to point out that the situation facing the larger employer does not preclude multi-employer bargaining. Examples in the USA have included newspapers, motion pictures, ocean transport, paper and pulp, railroads and shipbuilding. It has not been unknown for employers in cars and steel to act together. In some cases – newspapers and motion pictures are good examples – the situation facing the large employer is very similar to that facing the smaller firm; they make more or less homogeneous products, are highly competitive, share a common technology and often are geographically concentrated. In some cases there are special factors to be considered: the relationship with the government as well as a common technology helps to explain the situation on the railroads. In general, however, the larger employers have found their market position much less coercive and so have not joined together to achieve a uniformity of regulation. Rather they have acted together on specific issues or to achieve specific objectives.

are characterized by a large number of small employers and competitive conditions. Second, the chemical and metalworking industries in France, Italy and Sweden, where multi-employer bargaining also continues to be the predominant pattern, have a much larger number of small employers than in Britain, where multi-employer bargaining is declining; the growth of the large multi-establishment enterprise is also more pronounced in Britain than in these other countries.[4] Third, the manufacturing industries in Japan, where single-employer bargaining is the predominant pattern, are dominated by the large *keiretsu* or 'linked groups' such as Mitsui, Mitsubishi, Sumitomo and so on.

Even so, it does not seem possible to explain a number of the important features of employers' collective bargaining behaviour in terms of industrial structure. In particular, there is no immediately obvious reason why, in the age of managerial or monopoly capitalism, most large employers in manufacturing industry in the Western European countries continue to favour multi-employer bargaining. Furthermore, it does not seem possible to explain by reference to industrial structure how the large employer arrives at the rules and procedures that are specific to his own needs. In the countries being studied they can be the result of unilateral action on the part of managers or joint consultation in some form of works council or workshop bargaining with shop stewards.

Collective Bargaining and the Industrializing Elite

A second approach to explaining the collective bargaining behaviour of employers accords a critical role to the industrializing elite that is responsible for initiating industrialization or that emerges during its course. It does not necessarily contradict the first approach. The various configurations of industrial structure, it is pointed out, are themselves the result of human action. So any explanation of employers' behaviour is likely to be inadequate if it does not take into account the attitudes and opinions or, to use the more generic term, the ideologies of the elite groups to which entrepreneurs and managers belong.

At first sight, the distinction drawn by Kerr and his colleagues (1973: ch. 2) between 'middle-class' and 'dynastic' elites would appear to be particularly relevant in understanding differences in the rule-making processes in the countries included in this study. The 'middle-class' elites of Britain, Sweden and the USA are held to be guided primarily by the market mechanism in making decisions. The timing and pace of industrialization, it is said, are largely dictated by the return on capital. The important link between employer and employee quickly becomes the cash nexus; in the words of Mann (1973: 41), the 'middle-class' elite

---

4 The fact that British-owned companies like GEC and ICI have withdrawn from membership of employers' organizations or have 'non-conforming' status so far as the multi-employer agreements are concerned, confirms that North American ownership is not the critical factor.

appears to have been more ready to accept a 'bureaucratic, economically based mode of control'. Pluralism in politics reflects itself in industrial relations. The right of workers to belong to trade unions is accepted and collective bargaining becomes the predominant method of regulating the terms and conditions of employment. The implication is that employers' organizations and multi-employer bargaining are likely to serve essentially *economic* functions, their main purpose being to regulate competition much in the way the discussion in the previous section suggests.

In the case of the 'dynastic' elites, of which Germany and Japan are held to be examples, the market mechanism is said to be less important in the early stages.[5] The timing and pace of industrialization are not determined exclusively by market considerations. The requirements of defence, the need for protection, the desire to maintain some of the traditional values of the pre-industrial society – these considerations were also important. Entry to the ranks of management, for example, is largely determined by family connection. There is a strong sense of class interest generally, which might be thought to lead to employers' organizations assuming greater political importance. In relations with workers great emphasis is placed on traditional values. Paternalism is very strong. Opposition to trade unionism is much more intransigent; the trade union is seen as an external influence which is likely to disturb the family atmosphere, and every effort is made to deny it access to the workplace. Joint consultation is preferred to collective bargaining. True, the market mechanism becomes increasingly important – the growth in the size of enterprises and industrial concentration, for example, weakens the class solidarity of employers – but the traditional values have a lasting influence.

The problem with this approach is that the actual behaviour of the industrializing elites in the seven countries does not match that which is associated with a particular ideal-type. Britain, Sweden and the USA, for example, are all classified as 'middle-class' elites and yet the behaviour of employers and the structure of collective bargaining could hardly be more different in these countries. Germany and Japan are classified as examples of 'dynastic' elites and yet in this case too there are fundamental differences. At the level of aggregation with which this study is concerned,

[5] Kerr and his colleagues do not specifically classify the type of industrializing elite in France and Italy, which are the other two countries included in the study. Here the situation is more complex. As other writers have argued (Mann, 1973, ch. 5; Giddens, 1973, ch. 11), the industrializing elite has not achieved the same degree of hegemony as in other countries. That is to say, employers have not enjoyed the same success in persuading the other groups in these societies to accept their own moral, political and cultural values. Traditional elements such as the church remain a potent force. Industrialization is uneven. Large multi-establishment enterprises have grown up side-by-side with small family-owned businesses; the agricultural interest remains very powerful. The very unevenness of industrialization is held to explain many of the contradictions in these societies. The paternalism of the industrializing elite is matched by the class consciousness of the trade union movement; both are mutually reinforcing. The 'events' of May 1968 in France or the 'hot autumn' in 1969 in Italy, it is suggested, mean that the prospect of convergence with the countries in which the 'middle-class' elite presides over industrialization is extremely remote.

it seems, the very notion of an ideal-type of industrializing elite has little meaning. As will be argued in more detail later, the situation which the industrializing elite in each country faced is different. Moreover, the ideology of the industrializing elite is as much, if not more, a product of experience as it is the property of the early members of the elite.

The Argument of the Present Study

It quickly became apparent that, however useful they were in mapping out the territory, the approaches discussed above could not be allowed to dominate the study. For one thing, it would have been more difficult to satisfy one of the main aims which had prompted the setting up of the project: that of presenting a considerable amount of previously unavailable empirical information. More important, too much of interest would have been left unexplained. Many of the variations observed – in the patterns of organization, levels of collective bargaining, contents of collective agreements and so on – are fundamentally important in their own right in influencing behaviour. They cannot be dismissed out of hand as anachronisms which will necessarily disappear in time; or as irrelevancies even when confronted with the seemingly overwhelming similarities of capitalist societies.

As the project progressed, it became increasingly clear that in order to understand the current behaviour of employers an historical perspective was required. In particular, no explanation could be complete which did not take into account the interaction between employers and trade unions: the fact that to a large extent attitudes and policies were mutually reflecting and reinforcing. Yet this did not mean that no generalizations could be made. A common thread did begin to emerge which offered an opportunity to integrate some of the key elements of the approaches discussed so far with an historical perspective. What follows is an attempt to set out the argument in a relatively straightforward manner without too many qualifications. The remainder of the study supplies the information to support the argument. It also includes the many points of detail which cannot adequately be fitted into a general framework and yet which might help to achieve a better understanding of the role of employers.

The Starting Point
For the most part, the recognition of trade unions for the purpose of collective bargaining has not occurred in a piecemeal and *ad hoc* fashion with individual employers weighing up the advantages and disadvantages of such a decision. Nor is the structure of collective bargaining the result of individual employers and trade unions or, for that matter, governments making rational choices from a range of possible options. Instead, both recognition and the structure of collective bargaining are rooted in

very specific compromises – in most cases struck relatively early in the process of industrialization – involving large numbers of employers more or less regardless of their individual views.[6]

If some employers came to an accommodation with trade unions at an earlier date, in Britain the key date so far as the important group of engineering employers was concerned was 1898; so far as employers in many other industries were concerned it was the period 1917–19. In Sweden the key date so far as engineering employers were concerned was 1905 and for employers more generally 1906. In France, Italy and Germany the periods following the First World War and, to a lesser extent, the Second World War were critical. In the USA and Japan the critical periods were 1933–7 and 1945–8 respectively.

This is not to say, it needs to be emphasized, that the structure of collective bargaining that emerged in each country has been totally fixed and immutable. For example, as previous sections have argued, in the post-Second World War period employers in the larger establishments in Britain and Western Europe, in particular, have increasingly been drawn into forms of workplace bargaining to supplement or even to supplant the rules and procedures provided for in multi-employer agreements. Even so, what might be termed the original structure of collective bargaining has had lasting effect; it has mediated the effects of subsequent economic, political and social changes as well as being affected by them.

The circumstances in which the compromises were struck also reveal a great deal about employers' motives for engaging in collective bargaining. In Britain and Sweden the settlements in engineering in 1898 and 1905 respectively were voluntary. In France, Italy and Germany, the compromises were underwritten by governments with compulsory rules. One reason for this difference is that, although the British and Swedish settlements followed major industrial conflicts, in France, Italy and Germany the conflict was on a much wider scale. Indeed, the very fabric of existing society appeared to be threatened by industrial and political unrest. The situation was also very special in the USA in the mid-1930s and in Japan in the late 1940s; governments, faced with major economic and social crises, were anxious to secure the co-operation of the trade unions that employers hitherto had refused to recognize. It can be concluded that employers and governments agreed to recognize trade unions and to allow them to participate in the process of making and administering

---

[6] The argument here has some similarities with that advanced by Burawoy (1985) to explain patterns of state intervention in four of the countries (Britain, Sweden, the USA and Japan) considered in this study. Burawoy, however, provides only the merest sketch of the interaction between industrialization and the behaviour of employers and unions; and he gives no specific attention to collective bargaining. As against the somewhat mechanical picture presented by Burawoy, wherein each country is taken as an example of an ideal-type and the complexities of interactions are given short shrift, the present study attempts a more detailed reconstruction of employers' and unions' behaviour.

employment rules first and foremost in order to institutionalize industrial conflict, and that they did so in response to circumstances,
without any overall plan.

For governments, the institutionalization of industrial conflict was
usually an end in itself. For employers, however, it was a means to an end:
the maintenance of managerial control. As observed earlier, in explaining
the contribution that collective bargaining makes to achieving this objective, most of the emphasis has tended to be placed on the legitimacy of
employment rules that involve trade unions in their negotiation and
administration. Yet relatively few of these rules were (or have become) the
subject of joint regulation; in most cases only a framework of minimum
pay and conditions was involved. In fact, much more important was the
legitimacy that trade union involvement in the rule-making process gave to
the employers' right to manage. For collective bargaining involves *mutual*
recognition. In agreeing to make some rules subject to joint regulation,
employers were requiring that trade unions should recognize the
employers' right to make the other rules unilaterally. In a number of cases
– engineering in Britain and Sweden are perhaps the obvious examples –
this trade-off was explicit; in both cases trade unions were forced to agree
to the exercise of managerial prerogative as the *quid pro quo* for the
employers' willingness to negotiate over pay and other conditions of
employment.

In view of the common tendency to idealize collective bargaining in
recent years, these points can, for the sake of emphasis, be put slightly
differently. The willingness of employers to recognize trade unions
should not be interpreted as a general commitment to joint regulation.
Equally, it did not mean that employers were any less anxious to
minimize the impact of trade unions.

Here lies the significance of the structure of collective bargaining that
is a major focus of the present study. The structure of collective bargaining defines the nature and extent of trade union involvement in
the rule-making process and so offers employers an instrument with
which to control the activities of trade unions and their members.
As Clegg (1976: 8–10) has argued, it is not simply that the employer's
recognition legitimizes the structure of trade unions (that is, the
coverage of trade unions by industry and occupation) in existence
at the time it is granted. In addition, the extent of collective bargaining and the degree of security afforded to trade unions affect
membership density; the level of negotiations has a major influence on
the distribution of power within the trade union movement; and the level
of negotiations and the status and contents of agreements have a profound influence on the ability of trade unions to mount industrial action.

What of market control? In clothing, construction and printing, where
collective bargaining was generally established without government
intervention before the general waves of recognition, multi-employer

bargaining did help in taking wages out of competition. But even in these industries, it can be argued, market control was a secondary consideration; the mostly small employers involved were too weak on their own to withstand the challenge of craft trade unions which were beginning to exploit their control of labour supply to impose their own rules and regulations.

In chemicals and metalworking, market control was of even less significance. In many cases employers were quite capable of settling wages in collusion with one another without the help of trade unions. Indeed, the control of the market – partly as a result of government tariffs and partly as a result of cartels – helped metalworking employers in France, Germany and Italy to withstand the challenge of trade unions until the First World War; in contrast with Britain and Sweden, where employers were heavily involved in highly competitive markets, there was little to fear from competition in the event of industrial action.

Multi-Employer Bargaining in Britain and Western Europe

It is possible to begin to understand, against this background, why the larger employers in metalworking and chemicals in France, West Germany, Italy and Sweden, unlike their British counterparts, continue to deal with trade unions through the agency of employers' organizations. Multi-employer bargaining is preferred to single-employer bargaining not simply because it makes for economies of scale in terms of time, effort and staff to negotiate a single agreement for an entire industry or because (in some industries) it helps to regulate the market. The irony is that the institution of multi-employer bargaining that trade unions helped to bring about and continue to support is primarily valued by employers because it helps to neutralize the workplace from trade union activity. Multi-employer bargaining in these countries makes it possible to exclude the workplace from hostilities in the sense that the incidence of industrial action experienced by the individual employer in isolation is very rare. It also enhances the discretion that the individual employer is able to exercise in the workplace; the role that the trade union is able to play there is very restricted and, in many cases, the trade union is excluded altogether. In brief, then, multi-employer bargaining serves to maximize the freedom of the individual employer and not to limit it in the way that is often implied (see, for example, Flanders, 1970b: 90).

Patently, multi-employer bargaining in Britain has not given employers a similar framework of control, which is why it is in decline. The unique pattern of unofficial and unconstitutional strikes confirms that the workplace has not been excluded from hostilities. Furthermore, the 'largely informal, largely fragmented and largely autonomous' workplace bargaining that figured so prominently in the Donovan Commission Report (1968) was seriously threatening the employer's ability to manage. It was in order to get control in the workplace that many employers were obliged to shift even further in the direction of single-employer bargaining.

To understand why multi-employer bargaining in Britain did not help employers to neutralize the workplace, it is necessary to appreciate that the contents of multi-employer agreements are very different from those in the other countries. Paradoxical as it may seem, although the relatively sparse coverage of substantive issues allows the individual employer in Britain to settle most issues in the workplace unilaterally, it is the comprehensive and detailed coverage of substantive rules in the other countries that gives the individual employer greater freedom. Contrary to the impression sometimes given, few of the rules are standard; most establish minimum conditions only, or leave considerable flexibility to the employer in their implementation. More significantly in the present context, whereas the coverage of agreements in Britain gives the employer few points of legitimate defence in the event of his unilateral action being challenged, the detailed coverage of the substantive rules in the other countries tends to limit the scope for further negotiations in the workplace, or to ensure that any workplace bargaining that does take place is largely administrative or supplementary. It also means that negotiations are concentrated in time in the period immediately following the settlement of the multi-employer agreement. The result is that the workplace bargaining is much less autonomous than in Britain.

In comparison with the other countries, the legal framework in Britain has also given little, if any, support to the practice of multi-employer bargaining. British employers have never had the positive legal right to belong to employers' organizations or to be represented by them for the purposes of collective bargaining. Above all, the legal status of multi-employer agreements is very different. In Britain multi-employer agreements are 'gentlemen's agreements' binding in honour only. In the other countries multi-employer agreements are legally enforceable contracts, and both the rights and duties of the parties to each other and the substantive conditions have the force of law. The effect is to give multi-employer agreements a significance in the other countries that they have never enjoyed in Britain. Employers, trade unions and governments have a vested interest in their continued existence, even if the interest is not the same.

It will be argued here that the key to explaining these differences in the contents and status of multi-employer agreements lies in the specific circumstances of industrialization in each country. Especially important were developments in the metalworking industries which, because of their size and significance, were to have a determining influence on the overall pattern in each country. In Britain, where industrialization was early and protracted, employers in the engineering and shipbuilding industries were faced with the challenge of craft trade unions in a competitive economy. Attempts to defeat the craft unions met with no lasting success, mainly because their strength lay within the workplace and did not depend on formal recognition by the employer. So it was that, when employers found themselves obliged to come to terms with the craft unions towards the end of the nineteenth century, it was on the basis of procedural rules imposed at the national level. Such arrangements appeared to be the most effective way of controlling the activities of the local district committees that made up the craft unions; they also recognized that a very considerable and complex body of rules was already in existence at the local level.

The pattern of industrialization was very different in the other countries. Both the type of employer and trade union that emerged were very different. At the risk of over-simplification, France, Germany and Italy can be considered together. Here a mixture of very large and very small employers was confronted by the challenge of industrial unions which had little or no presence in the workplace. Protected from competition by government tariffs and cartel arrangements, the large employers in particular, most of which dominated their local communities, did not need to seek an accommodation with trade unions before the First World War. Multi-employer bargaining emerged only in the crisis years of 1918–9 with government support which was quickly followed up by legislation. In short, multi-employer agreements were legally enforceable contracts and codes from the very beginning.

The pattern of developments was different again in Sweden. Unlike Germany and Italy, where industrialization was also late and extremely rapid, the employers that emerged were small in size as well as number. They were quickly confronted by trade unions of skilled workers which were able to take advantage of the employers' heavy involvement in highly competitive overseas trade to force them to come to an accommodation without the direct involvement of government. Unlike the craft unions in Britain, however, the Swedish unions did not have the controls over the supply and use of labour to set pay and conditions unilaterally. In return for a willingness to negotiate a set of national substantive rules then, the employers were able to insist on the principle that the period of a collective agreement should be free from further claims as well as industrial action. In effect, then, although legislation making collective agreements legally enforceable was not introduced until 1928, employers had already laid the foundations for a contractual system of multi-employer bargaining.

Single-Employer Bargaining in the USA and Japan

This argument appears to have little relevance to the USA and Japan where single-employer bargaining is the predominant pattern. Yet in an important sense they are the exceptions to prove the rule. In both countries relatively large individual employers emerged in the manufacturing industries at an early date in the process of industrialization. In the USA, having come to an accommodation with trade unions mostly on a multi-employer basis, these employers were subsequently able to inflict a major defeat on trade unions with the success of the 'open shop' campaign at the turn of the century. In Japan these large employers were successful, to all intents and purposes, in preventing the emergence of an independent trade union movement altogether. In both countries the large employers used 'welfarism', 'internal job ladders' and 'employee representation plans' or company unions to institutionalize industrial conflict. In these circumstances employers and governments did not come under strong pressure to engage in multi-employer bargaining as they had done in Europe. Subsequently, when it did become necessary to reach an accommodation with trade unions, single-employer bargaining was perceived to be the lesser of two evils. In particular, single-employer bargaining meant that employers did not have to unscramble the elaborate systems of internal regulation and that they could continue to deal with their own employees, albeit now organized in independent trade unions, rather than with the external organizations they had struggled so long to avoid. Paradoxical as it may seem, then, it is single-employer bargaining that serves to neutralize the workplace from trade union activity in the USA and Japan.

The Plan of the Study

The plan adopted for writing up the study reflects these emphases. The bulk of the study is concerned with explaining why employers in Britain, unlike those in the other Western European countries, appear to have been unable or unwilling to maintain the system of multi-employer bargaining. Chapter 2 re-appraises the significance of multi-employer bargaining in these countries. Chapters 3, 4 and 5 explore in more detail precisely what it is about multi-employer bargaining in Britain that is different from the other countries: chapter 3 is concerned with the structure and government of the employers' organizations; chapter 4 with the levels at which multi-employer bargaining takes place and chapter 5 with the contents and status of multi-employer agreements. Chapter 6 returns to the origins of multi-employer bargaining in the five countries. Chapter 7 goes on to attempt to explain the different courses of development in the USA and Japan which led to single-employer bargaining. The final chapter reviews the main findings of the study, and the appendix gives details of the employers in the seven countries.

2

Multi-Employer Bargaining in Britain and Western Europe: The Issues Redefined

As chapter 1 has pointed out, the satisfaction of trade union demands for the 'common rule' and the advantages to employers of taking wages out of competition have figured prominently in explanations of multi-employer bargaining. It is perhaps not surprising, against this background, that attempts to assess the effectiveness of multi-employer bargaining have tended to emphasize its success in achieving standard pay and conditions of employment in the workplace. The most notable example is that of the Donovan Commission in Britain in 1968. In discussing the declining effectiveness of industry-wide (multi-employer) agreements, the Commission (14–16) emphasized the significance of the growth over time in the 'gap' between the rates of pay in the multi-employer agreements and actual earnings. In Appendix 5 (338–9) the Commission presented further evidence based on an analysis of the position in five different situations, depending upon the relationship between nationally (mainly multi-employer) determined rates of pay and actual earnings. The Commission (339) concluded that: 'on any reasonable estimate the effective regulation of pay by industry-wide agreement is now very much the exception rather than the rule in Britain and is largely confined to the public sector'.

By itself, however, the existence of an earnings 'gap' says very little about the effectiveness of multi-employer bargaining from the employers' point of view. Most multi-employer agreements, including those in industries such as clothing, construction, and printing, where market control might be supposed an important objective, are quite specific in their provision for *basic* or *minimum* rates of pay. By implication, the intention is not to standardize pay and conditions of employment. Rather it is to establish a floor which employers are free to exceed if they wish. Significantly, too, an earnings 'gap' is not unique to Britain. Indeed, the concept of 'wage drift' originated in Scandinavia, and particularly in Sweden, where the term *löneglidning*, or 'wages-glide', was used in the early 1950s to describe the differential movement in the rates in multi-employer agreements and actual earnings (National Board for Prices and Incomes, 1968: 15). Comparative data also suggested that both the size of the earnings gap and the extent of wage drift were as great, if not greater, in other countries than in Britain (Phelps Brown, 1962).

In what respects, then, is the situation in Britain different from that in the other countries? To begin to answer this question – and to establish the full significance of multi-employer bargaining – it will be necessary to consider the ways in which payments and other rules that are specific to the workplace are arrived at. In particular, it is essential to take into account the nature and extent of any workplace bargaining over these payments and rules in which employers are involved. For example, there may be significant differences in the type of bargaining agent with which the employer has to deal; in particular, the degree to which the activities of the bargaining agent are circumscribed by the law may vary significantly. Or, to take another and related aspect, the workplace bargaining may be primarily concerned with the application of the terms and conditions of the multi-employer agreements or with improvements to them; that is to say, it may be essentially *administrative* or *supplementary*. Alternatively, workplace bargaining may have little or no relationship to the terms and conditions of the multi-employer agreement. In this case workplace bargaining, which might be described as *autonomous*, begins to have close parallels with the single-employer bargaining of Japan and the USA. Because of the complexity of the issues involved, each of the countries will be considered in turn, beginning with Britain.

Britain

In most sizeable workplaces where trade unions are recognized, the bargaining agent the employer deals with is a shop steward or a committee of shop stewards. Shop stewards, who are representatives of trade union members at their place of work, first emerged in the craft-based industries and, in particular, in the engineering and shipbuilding industries where they were already a force to be reckoned with by the First World War. Subsequently their growth throughout manufacturing and, indeed, private services and the public sector was widespread. Thus, by the late 1970s it would appear that shop stewards were all but universal among manual workforces of more than 100 employees in manufacturing (Brown, 1981: 53). This growth, it must be emphasized, has been largely spontaneous. Unlike some of the other countries to be considered, the shop stewards receive no direct support from the legal framework; even multi-employer agreements say relatively little about their rights and activities.

The degree to which shop stewards are organized in committees largely reflects the practice of workplace bargaining. Here an important distinction is to be drawn between industries such as clothing, construction and printing, on the one hand, and chemicals and engineering on the other. As the previous chapter has pointed out, in the first group of industries multi-employer bargaining is likely to be the most important source of increases in pay as well as the decisions relating to the other terms and conditions of employment. For example, the Warwick Survey (Brown, 1981: 8) suggested that 75 per cent of employers in clothing and 69 per cent in printing regarded multi-employer agreements as more important than single-employer agreements so far as pay is concerned. A similar Department of Employment Survey (Hawes and Smith, 1981: 266) suggests that no less than four fifths of employers in construction regarded multi-employer agreements as the more important.

The workplace bargaining in which the employer is involved in these industries is likely to be fairly informal and fragmented; it is likely to involve individual shop stewards or full-time trade union officials rather than a committee of shop stewards. It is not necessarily in conflict with the 'formal' system of multi-employer bargaining or as *autonomous* as the workplace bargaining associated with the chemical and engineering industry discussed below. Rather it is likely to be concerned with the administration of the multi-employer agreement or with the negotiation of supplements to it. The workplace bargaining in which these employers are involved, then, might be described as *administrative* or *supplementary*.

The situation in the chemical and, in particular, the engineering industries is very different. It is not simply that a number of the larger employers, such as Ford or ICI, negotiate independently of employers' organizations. By the late 1960s, to paraphrase the report of the Donovan Commission, many employers – especially in the larger establishments in engineering – were settling matters in their own workplaces in negotiation with shop stewards rather than through multi-employer bargaining. As well as pay, the report instanced the arrangements for dealing with redundancies, sick pay, pension schemes and the circumstances justifying individual dismissal. In relation to multi-employer bargaining, the Commission (1968: 36) suggested that the workplace bargaining in which employers were increasingly involved was 'of equal or greater importance'.

The nature of this workplace bargaining was important too. The Commission, following Flanders (1970b: 169), confirmed that it was 'largely informal, largely fragmented and largely autonomous'. It was informal because of the predominance of unwritten understandings and of custom and practice; it was fragmented because it involved individual shop stewards or relatively small groups of workers; it was autonomous – and this is the important characteristic in the present context – because it rarely involved employers' organization or trade union officials and had little or no relationship to the terms of the multi-employer agreement.

One result was a unique pattern of strikes with more than 90 per cent being unofficial and in breach of the procedure for handling disputes in the multi-employer agreement. By implication, then, these strikes were experienced by employers individually and in isolation rather than collectively at the time of, say, the negotiation of the multi-employer agreement.

Significant changes in the nature of this workplace bargaining, which were already taking place while the Commission was deliberating, were to have a profound effect. Partly in response to the growing climate of international competition and partly in response to the pressure from successive governments, many of the larger employers in engineering and chemicals effectively reconstructed their workplace industrial relations. The main instances of the reconstruction were productivity bargaining, the introduction of formal workplace procedures, the reform of payment systems, and the rationalization of pay structures. In the context of the present discussion their impact had a two-fold significance: much workplace bargaining has become more formalized and there has been a very considerable centralization of workplace bargaining at establishment level.

The largely piecemeal way in which the reconstruction was undertaken also had important implications for the practice of multi-employer bargaining. It is not altogether clear whether the Donovan Commission intended that its proposed factory and company agreements should be supplementary to multi-employer agreements or to supersede them.[1] Be that as it may, one thing is clear: little attempt was made to reconstruct multi-employer bargaining in the light of the changing circumstances. In some cases – engineering is the most notable in 1968 – minimum earnings levels were substituted for basic rates of pay; in other cases guidelines for workplace bargaining were drawn up. Overall, however, things stayed much as before. Consequently, the significance of multi-employer agreements diminished even further.

By the end of the 1970s in most large establishments in the engineering and chemicals industries the 'formal system' – to use the language of the

---

[1] The overriding need for individual employers to negotiate effective factory and company agreements is clearly stated. Yet the Commission appeared to see a continuing role for employers' organizations and multi-employer bargaining. Employers' organizations, the Commission (1968: 46) argued,

> should join with trade unions to consider what amendments may be needed in industry-wide agreements to facilitate effective collective bargaining in the company and the factory, confining industry-wide agreements to matters which they are capable of regulating, providing guide-lines for satisfactory company and factory agreements, and where appropriate granting to agreements which follow these guide-lines exemption from clauses of the industry-wide agreements. Reform on these lines will not diminish the authority of industry-wide agreements or employers' associations. On the contrary, it will give them greater influence in the actual conduct of industrial relations in the factory than they have been able to exert for many years.

Donovan Commission – continued to be the multi-employer bargaining between the employers' organization and the trade union. The employer may have remained a member of an employers' organization – for example, the Warwick Survey (Brown, 1981: 19) suggested that something like three quarters of establishments in manufacturing with more than 500 employees were members. He is likely to follow some of the terms and conditions of the multi-employer agreement such as those that deal with hours, and overtime rates or holiday entitlements, and likely to use the disputes procedure. Besides these issues, however, multi-employer bargaining has little impact. This is especially true of pay. For example, the Warwick Survey carried out in 1978 (Brown, 1981: 8) suggested that less than 10 per cent of employers in the engineering industries and less than 25 per cent of employers in the chemical industry regarded multi-employer agreements as the most important level of pay bargaining.

There might also be said to be a second 'formal' system in these establishments, namely the negotiation between the management and a committee of shop stewards. Moreover, a number of the members of the committee may be full-time; that is to say, even though they continue to be paid by the employer, they spend their time on trade union activities. These negotiations are likely to be the most important source of increases in pay and they may also deal with some of the basic procedural issues such as the handling of disputes, discipline and redundancy. Pay agreements may be for a fixed term, but those covering procedures and other issues are likely to be open-ended. The negotiations are likely to cover significant groups of manual workers, if not all of them. In the case of the multi-establishment enterprise they may cover more than one establishment. Full-time trade union officials may or may not be involved.

There continues to be an 'informal' system in these establishments, but for the most part it is not in conflict with either of the 'formal' systems. The 'informal' system is the more or less continuous bargaining that takes place between managers and individual shop stewards over the administration of the terms of agreements reached at higher levels or over problems that are specific to the individual group. Senior stewards may or may not be involved.

In many of these establishments, then, much of the workplace bargaining in which the employer is involved is more formal and less fragmented than it was at the time the Donovan Commission reported. Overall, workplace bargaining is not in conflict with multi-employer bargaining because it has little or no relationship with the terms and conditions of the multi-employer agreements. It is truly *autonomous* and is best thought of as single-employer bargaining.

To summarize, a dual structure of collective bargaining appears to be developing in Britain which in some respects is similar to that in the USA. That is to say, among employers in clothing, construction and printing the predominant pattern of collective bargaining remains multi-employer; and workplace bargaining is essentially *administrative* or *supplementary*. Among the larger employers, especially in engineering and chemicals, the predominant pattern of collective bargaining is no longer multi-employer; workplace bargaining is to a greater or lesser extent *autonomous* and is in many ways comparable with single-employer bargaining.

Italy

In marked contrast to Britain, where some form of union workplace representation was to be found in most large establishments with union members by the Second World War, in Italy trade unions had little or no presence in the workplace until the late 1960s. Great significance has come to be attached to the decisions of the trade union confederations, CISL and CGIL, in the early 1950s to seek to integrate the workplace into the structure of collective bargaining. If these decisions were important symbolically – they recognized the need to establish a viable trade union organization in the workplace and reaffirmed trade union support for the principle of collective bargaining – they were essentially confessions of weakness. The workplace branches or sections which the confederations attempted to establish were little more than paper organizations, and they never played an important role (Neufeld, 1961: 505). The main vehicle for workplace representation was the 'internal commissions' whose functions were covered by a series of agreements between the trade union confederation and CONFINDUSTRIA, which is the employers' confederation.[2]

[2] An initial understanding on the elections to and the functions of the 'internal commissions' – the Buozzi–Mazzini accord – had been reached as early as September 1943 so far as central and southern Italy was concerned. In the north the situation was more complicated. In a final attempt to take control of the factory occupation movement which was beginning to get under way, Mussolini announced the setting up of joint 'management councils'. Subsequent attempts to put the 'management councils' on a statutory basis were firmly blocked by CONFINDUSTRIA and from the confusion emerged the multi-industry agreement of August 1947 dealing with the 'internal commissions'. Further multi-industry agreements were to deal with the 'internal commissions' in subsequent years. The last of these, in 1966, provided for the election by secret ballot of 'commissions' in all enterprises with more than 40 employees, the size varying with the number employed. In the words of CONFINDUSTRIA (1972), the functions of the 'commissions' were to be as follows:

> negotiation with management to ensure complete observance of legislative regulations relating to social security, health and safety of working conditions, labour contracts, attempting in the first instance to settle any disputes amicably; to study together with management the draft regulations, prior to their implementation, relating to production matters, vacation periods, timetable of working hours; to formulate proposals for the improvement of working methods and to assist in the improved functioning of services such as firms' shops, canteens, health and sanitary facilities, as well as the social services provided by the firm (welfare, assistance, cultural and recreational facilities).

Strictly speaking, workplace bargaining was beyond the powers of the 'commission', but this did not stop employers from exploiting their potential or CONFINDUSTRIA from encouraging them to do so. One study, for example, claims that in more than 50 per cent of the cases of recorded workplace agreements in the period 1953–7 the 'commissions' were the bargaining agent on the workers' side (Guidi *et al.*, 1974: 388). Sometimes employers negotiated with one group of trade union members on the 'commissions' at the expense of the others.[3] Even the widespread development of so-called 'articulated bargaining' following the major conflict of 1962–3 in metalworking flattered to deceive: trade unions won the right to negotiate with employers on certain issues in the workplace, but still did not have a secure base there.[4]

It was only following the upheaval of the so-called 'hot autumn' of 1968–9 that really significant changes took place in the patterns of both workplace trade union representation and workplace bargaining. Beginning in 1968 – the strike at Pirelli is often quoted as one of the first examples – a wave of unrest spread throughout metalworking and other industries. The traditional structure of workplace representation that was centred on the 'internal commissions' began to fall apart: the division of responsibilities implicit in the model of 'articulated bargaining' was simply ignored. Rank-and-file committees and 'factory councils' sprang up, with 'delegates' being elected by workers in their department or by the

---

[3] The tactics of FIAT, to quote one example, were notorious (Edelman and Fleming, 1965: 39–43; Neufeld, 1961: 505). In the early post-war years the management favoured CISL and to some extent UIL, negotiating pay increases with their members on the 'commission' while refusing to do so with those of the CGIL. As the position of CISL began to harden against the principle of 'commission' involvement in workplace bargaining, it too found disfavour in the company's eyes. A schism within CISL membership, which at first appeared in 1952, reappeared in 1958 and was, CISL claimed, largely management-inspired. Only in 1962 during the crisis leading up to the renegotiation of the category agreement in metalworking did FIAT finally agree to negotiate with the trade unions rather than the 'commission' and to stop payment of no-strike bonuses which had been introduced as late as April 1962 in negotiations with members of UIL and the independent FIAT trade union.

[4] The negotiations in metalworking in 1962 marked the first major breach in CONFINDUSTRIA's policy of so-called 'exclusive national bargaining'. Failure to agree a more flexible bargaining structure demanded by the trade unions in metalworking led to a split between CONFINDUSTRIA and the public sector employers represented by INTERSIND and ASAP. (For further details of these organizations, see chapter 3). In return for a commitment 'not to promote and to intervene to avoid action or claims intended to modify, complete or alter what has been the object of agreement at the various levels', INTERSIND agreed to a new negotiating structure. Negotiations were to be allowed at sector and, more importantly, at enterprise level. In the latter case they could cover such issues as piece rates, production bonuses and new job classifications. Although some concessions were made in terms of trade union activity in the workplace, there was no formal recognition of the trade union at that level; the bargaining agent was to be the provincial trade union. In the private sector agreement was not finally reached until February 1963 after further strikes and after enterprise agreements signed by FIAT and Olivetti in October 1962 which further discomforted CONFINDUSTRIA's position. Subsequently, the 'articulated bargaining' introduced by the INTERSIND-ASAP accord was adopted in most other industries, although no provisions were made for sector negotiations. For further details, see Giugni (1965a, b, c; 1971a, b; 1976) and INTERSIND (1968).

workforce as a whole in general assemblies. Sometimes the trade unions were involved in these developments, sometimes not. The same is true of the claims with which employers were subsequently presented and negotiated. It was only in March 1971 that the three metalworking trade union federations formally decided to reconstruct their workplace organization on the basis of the rank-and-file 'delegates' and 'factory councils'.

The confusion of the times is reflected in the legislation, better known as the 'Workers' Charter', which was rushed through in May 1970 to give workers the right to establish 'trade union representation' in each production unit employing more than 15 in industry and services and five in agriculture. If, by implication, the 'Charter' denies legal recognition to the 'internal commissions', it is silent on what form the representation should take. Like the scope of workplace bargaining, on which it is also silent, the legislation leaves the matter to the parties to decide. It simply states that 'trade union representation' may be established on the initiative of the organizations affiliated to the 'most representative' trade union confederations at the national level or by those that are signatories to national or provincial collective agreements. The trade union representation is to have the right to hold works meetings, and referenda, to post notices and collect dues as well as to appoint officers who are to have paid leave of absence. The employer is not to indulge in anti-trade union conduct and a trade union is enabled to secure a judgment from the local magistrate ordering the employer to stop such activity.

A CONFINDUSTRIA study of 1973 describes the pattern of workplace representation that had emerged by June 1972. It found that only 7 per cent of establishments had no form of representation, 45 per cent had only one form and 47 per cent more than one form. Other important findings revealed the position of the 'internal commissions' and the 'factory councils'. There was much evidence for the declining importance of the 'internal commissions'. In metalworking, for example, the 'internal commissions' had been excluded by other forms of representation in some two thirds of the establishments; this had happened in a similar proportion of establishments in the north west, regardless of industry. 'Factory councils', it emerged, had been established in approximately one third of establishments in the north west and north east.

As in Britain, in the 1970s many of the larger employers entered into written agreements to which these representative bodies, usually the 'factory council', are parties. In some of the large multi-establishment enterprises, like FIAT or Olivetti, these agreements were enterprise-wide; and the so-called 'platform of claims' was developed and debated by a body of workers' representatives drawn from the 'councils' of the different establishments – known as the 'union combine' – together with full-time national and provincial trade union officials. The difference in comparison with Britain is that the negotiations usually took place in the period following the negotiation of the multi-employer category or industry agreements and supplemented the terms and conditions of those agreements. Certainly, they have not replaced multi-employer bargaining as the main source of joint regulation. Significantly, too, the negotiations were likely to take place in the offices of the multi-employer territorial employers' organizations that are affiliated to CONFINDUSTRIA; officials from the territorial employers' organization are also likely to participate in the negotiations. Indeed, in 1972 a report by the metalworking employers organization, FEDERMECCANICA, suggested that more than half of the negotiations leading to enterprise and workplace agreements in metalworking in the north took place in the offices of the territorial employers' organizations. It is not only the small employers who are involved. The FIAT negotiations usually take place in the territorial employers' organizations office in Turin.

There have been a number of investigations into the contents of enterprise agreements carried out by CONFINDUSTRIA and its branch employers' organizations. Perhaps the most useful for illustrative purposes is that carried out in the chemical industry and published in 1975; it covers the period 1970–4 and is essentially a qualitative study designed to establish general trends. Three broad groups of contents or issues are identified; firstly, issues that are specifically referred to the workplace by the national category agreement; secondly, issues which are supposed to be exhausted by that agreement and for which there is no explicit reference to the enterprise; and thirdly, issues that are 'extra-contractual' in the sense that they are not covered at all in the category agreement.

Issues covered in enterprise and workplace agreements under the first and second groups, which are considered together, include 'remuneration' – and, in particular, the 'production premium' (which is a straightforward workplace supplement not directly related to output or performance); the classification of personnel within the system of grades that appear in the multi-employer agreement; 'working conditions' and, in particular, the scope of the activities of the special committees for which provision is made under the 'Workers' Charter'; the 'organization of work' which embraced items such as the allocation of hours, night and shift work, transfer, postings and subcontracting; and 'workers' representation', which usually involved an improvement in the hours and facilities available to trade union representatives or the 'factory council' members.

The main issue to fall under the heading of 'extra-contractual' was investment. Many of the larger employers, it seems, had committed themselves to an area of investment (usually the south), the amount of the investment, and the timing and the phasing of the investment over the 5-year period 1974–8. In some cases simultaneous undertakings had been entered into to maintain existing employment levels in the north. Some employers had also given undertakings to make specific sums available for investment in agriculture, fertilizers and preventive medicine.

The workplace bargaining in which Italian employers are involved does not stop with the negotiation of an enterprise agreement. In many of the larger establishments management is intimately involved with the 'factory councils' and the 'delegates' in the discussion of day-to-day problems as well as the negotiations that arise from the administration of the terms of the national category agreement and the enterprise agreement. For example, in one of the establishments visited during the course of the research, there was a 'factory council' with some 20–25 members with a number of subcommittees that met with management to negotiate on specific issues, such as working conditions or social services. The individual 'delegates' were intimately involved in the operation of the payment by results system which was the most widely prevalent payment system, and were also very active in negotiations over the allocation of jobs within the classification system in the national category agreement. All in all, management representatives agreed that negotiation was more or less continuous; if they were not meeting with 'delegates' every day, there was something happening at least once a week that led to meetings either at department level or with the personnel department.

In some respects, then, the scope of workplace bargaining is greater than in Britain. Investment, pollution, social services – these are just some of the issues which have become the subject of agreements. Unlike Britain, however, workplace bargaining has not replaced multi-employer bargaining as the main source of joint regulation. Essentially, workplace bargaining is *administrative* and *supplementary*. Although in the middle 1970s a number of employers in metalworking debated the wisdom of continuing with national category negotiations in their present form, none seems to have seriously questioned the principle of multi-employer bargaining as such.[5] Indeed, as chapter 4 describes in more detail, in 1977, 1983 and 1984 multi-industry bargaining involving CONFINDUSTRIA and the trade union confederations was used to put a brake on workplace bargaining. Employers continue to work through their employers' organizations. This is as true of the large multi-establishment employers

---

[5] For example, in 1974 a senior official of the metalworking employers' organization, FEDERMECCANICA, publicly expressed the employers' misgivings about the role of the multi-employer category negotiations (Mortillaro and Fernex, 1976: 74–8). In the light of the developments in workplace bargaining, the category agreement, detailed though it was, had lost a large part of its function as an instrument of normative and economic regulation. Some people, he went on, argued that the category agreement had more and more assumed the significance of a 'policy document'; it was useful for defining the general lines of industrial relations policy, but had progressively lost the obligatory or normative element associated with its judicial nature. If this was the case, the direct and indirect cost of the agreement in terms of strikes was quite out of proportion to its significance and renegotiation had simply become a 'rite'. Perhaps it would be better to accept reality, regard the category agreement as a policy document with some specific agreements to regulate certain issues like holidays and negotiate on pay only at fixed intervals.

such as FIAT or Olivetti in metalworking and Montedison in chemicals as it is of the smaller employer in clothing, construction and printing. Moreover, the large employers continue to play a pivotal role in the affairs of employers' organizations. For reasons that will emerge as the study progresses, multi-employer agreements remain an important document for large and small employers alike. The trade unions, for their part, seem no more ready than the employers to abandon the practice of multi-employer bargaining.

Sweden

As yet, the developments in workplace bargaining in Sweden have not been nearly so dramatic as in Britain or Italy. Despite their strong attachment to multi-employer bargaining – very few negotiate independently of employers' organizations – Swedish employers admitted trade union representatives into the workplace at a very early date and tacitly admitted that there would be some form of workplace bargaining. The 'Basic Agreement' of 1938 between the employers' confederation, SAF, and the manual trade union confederation, LO, confirms earlier understandings; Article 3 states that negotiation shall 'in the first instance be conducted between the parties at the workplace, with participation of local organizations where they exist'. The notes amplify this article: 'by "local organizations" is understood any organization in relation to which the trade union federation is by statute or establishment practice the next higher instance of negotiation, such as a union, a factory club etc.'. Similar provisions exist in the agreement between SAF and the white-collar confederations.

Despite the lack of statistical surveys, it would appear that the works or 'factory club' has been widely adopted as the nucleus of trade union organization at the workplace (Korpi, 1978b: 356–7). Union rules state that the 'factory club' is to carry out instructions received from the trade union or its branch, and it is 'to prepare, organise, and deal with all demands and relations between workers and the employer'. In the case of LO trade unions, the 'factory club' has a board or executive together with a club chairman. In the larger establishments it is not unknown for the chairman to be full-time and a number of his colleagues on the board or executive may have officially recognized responsibilities for dealing with such matters as safety or work study. Also in the larger establishments there may be an infrastructure of group organization and 'contact' persons at the level of the department or work group on which representation on the board is based. Employers, it seems, have not been opposed to granting appropriate facilities.

So the situation in Sweden appears to be very similar to that in Britain and Italy. It is, however, different in one important respect: the 'factory club' is less independent than a joint shop stewards' committee or a 'factory council'. The 'factory club' is an agent of the trade union. Legally, the 'factory club' chairman and members of the board are subject in the same way as their full-time trade union officials to the 'peace obligation' that is implicit in the multi-employer agreements signed outside the workplace. If they call for or take part in industrial action in support of a workplace issue during the life of the multi-employer agreement, they not only render themselves, but also their trade union, liable to legal action by the employer. It is true that Swedish employers do not always make use of the possibilities that are available under the legal framework; nonetheless, it can be argued, their very existence has been important in shaping attitudes to workplace bargaining.[6]

To date, the scope of the workplace bargaining in Sweden also appears to be more limited than in Britain or Italy. The insistence on upholding managerial prerogatives at the workplace dies hard among Swedish employers. It is enshrined in the famous paragraph 23, subsequently clause 32, of the constitution of SAF that will be discussed in later chapters. For many years it was a prominent feature in the multi-employer agreements negotiated by SAF and LO members. With the passage of the Collective Agreements Act of 1928, managerial prerogative received further legitimacy. By making collective agreements legally enforceable, the Act not only underpinned the 'peace obligation' in the multi-employer agreements with the implications already described. It also, more directly, put the management rights clause in these agreements on a statutory basis. Against this background, it proved very difficult for the 'factory club' to extend the scope of workplace bargaining, which helps to explain why in the 1970s trade unions sought legislative means of extending workplace bargaining into areas previously the preserve of managerial prerogative.

In one of the very rare studies of workplace bargaining in the 1970s (and the lack of such studies is perhaps indicative of its 'non-problem' status) Korpi (1978b: 361) found that wages accounted for something like 69 per cent of the issues in workplace bargaining in the metalworking industries. Only one in eight was concerned with what might be described as the exercise of managerial prerogative; that is to say, manning, task allocation of workers, hirings, lay-offs, work discipline, production and the behaviour of management representatives. Moreover, about one half of unofficial strikes in the establishments in the sample had been concerned with wages, the other half with the issues of managerial authority – indicating that management resistance to negotiating on non-wage issues is considerably greater than on wages. Furthermore, if these strikes are divided by types of issues in dispute, negotiations were held prior to the strike in two thirds of wage disputes, but in only one third of managerial

---

6 Having said this, SAF does seek to ensure that employers exercise their rights under the law. Chapter 3 gives the details. One of the establishments visited during the course of the research took legal action against the strikers. The details are given in chapter 5.

authority issues. Korpi (1978a: 276) concludes: 'it would thus appear that especially issues relating to managerial authority have been less "legitimate" and have tended to be excluded or under-represented in workplace bargaining'.[7] Most of the wage issues concerned the setting of the piece rates which were the predominant form of payment system. In about half of the large and medium size establishments the respondents indicated that some kind of agreement or general understanding existed with respect to how workers should proceed in the event of a dispute. Often, however, they gave varying and not infrequently contradictory opinions on the substance of these understandings. In the other establishments there appeared to be no understandings and the practice appeared to be even more varied. On average, two or three management representatives were present: while the chairman of the 'factory club' was accompanied by members of the board and, in the case of the larger establishments, by representatives of the work groups or departments involved.

The significance of piecework bargaining was confirmed in interviews with management and 'factory club' representatives carried out during the course of the research. It also emerged that negotiations did not stop with individual piece rates. The effect of negotiations between SAF and LO and a relatively tight labour market had obliged the management to negotiate with the 'factory club' over the general level of piece rates. In recent years it had been the practice for the multi-employer agreements in metalworking to allocate a small percentage – known as the low wage kitty – for negotiation at the workplace. The multi-employer agreement was usually signed in February following the SAF-LO agreement that runs from the beginning of the year. The provision for the low wage kitty provided an opportunity for the 'factory club' to negotiate with management on the rates in general as well as the application of other clauses in the multi-employer agreement.

A second set of negotiations took place between the management and the 'factory club' in mid- or late summer, following the negotiation of the other central agreements for white-collar workers and those in the

---

[7] The study of Hart and Von Otter (1973), which is primarily concerned with the process of wage formation at the plant level in the late 1960s, also touches on the issue of workplace bargaining. Their findings are broadly similar to Korpi's. For example, in the case of a paper plant negotiating 'conferences' were conducted 15 to 20 times a year in the period 1967-70. Of the issues dealt with at these conferences more than 50 per cent were directly wage issues. For the most part, these negotiations consisted of a process of applying and interpreting the rules of the collective agreement on piecework, and on wage grades. Hart and Von Otter state that issues such as the length of the working day or overtime were hardly ever taken up by the union. Occasionally questions on the organization of work would arise but in this area the employer retained a free hand in the last instance as a result of paragraph 32. The low level of non-wage (27) as opposed to wage issues (106) was all the more startling because the plant had undergone a drastic restructuring as a result of which the workforce was reduced by 40 per cent. Hart and Von Otter's basic conclusion is that in the main the activity of the local negotiations revolved around applying and interpreting the higher level multi-employer agreements.

public sector. Armed with wage data from the central union, the 'factory club' negotiated what is in effect a 'wage drift agreement', which applies to all piece rates, though usually some attempt is made to improve the relative position of the rates of the lower paid in conformity with trade union policy. The 'club' chairman estimated that over the past two years this second agreement had virtually doubled the increases that resulted from the multi-employer agreements.

In terms of its conduct, workplace bargaining in Sweden is largely informal. In Korpi's (1978a: 275) words,

> negotiations involving top level negotiators from the respective sides are to a very large extent informal. The negotiations are generally initiated through oral agreements to discuss some issues mentioned by the party who asks for the negotiations, but generally with no expectations that discussions will necessarily be limited only to these issues. They generally result in tacit understanding and informal agreement rather than written statements. The degree of formalisation tends to increase with size of firm and depends to some extent on the type of wage system in the firm.

The fact that the workplace bargaining in Sweden is essentially informal does not mean that it is *unofficial*. The widespread use of payment by results and the provision for *minimum* rates in the multi-employer agreements together with the provisions of the 'Basic Agreement', imply that some form of workplace bargaining will take place. Put another way, workplace bargaining is for the most part intended to be *supplementary* to multi-employer bargaining. In contrasting his own analysis to that of the Donovan Commission, Korpi (1978a: 272) himself makes the point that:

> In the Swedish case it is thus not possible to assume *a priori* that workplace bargaining stands in conflict with the industry-wide (multi-employer) agreements. Obviously workplace bargaining is, instead, a necessary complement to the types of settlements contained in the industry-wide agreements.

It remains to be seen how the situation develops and, in particular, whether the spate of legislation[8] culminating in the so-called 'Co-

---

[8] The main laws deal with the National Pension Insurance Fund (1974), board representation (1972 and 1976), the work environment (1974, 1976 and 1978), security of employment (1974), the position of trade union workplace representatives (1974), time off for training of workplace representatives (1974) and co-determination (1978).

Under the Co-Determination Act, the employer is obliged to take the initiative in beginning negotiations before decisions are made on major issues including closure, re-organization and expansion as well as changes in the position of individual employees. The employer is also required to negotiate on any other issue if the trade union requests it. In the event of a failure to reach agreement locally, the trade union can refer the issue to higher levels. The employer is supposed to postpone the implementation of any changes until the discussions are concluded. For further details, see Forseback (1980: 41–2).

Determination Act' of 1977 makes any material difference to the nature and extent of workplace bargaining. As things stand, however, it can be argued that workplace bargaining is not as well developed as in either Britain or Italy. It is not simply that it is largely *administrative* or *supplementary*. To date, its coverage in terms of subject matter would appear to be less comprehensive than the other two countries. Furthermore, in as much as the 'factory club' is regarded as the legal agent of the trade union and subject to the 'peace obligation', trade union workplace representatives are less independent than shop stewards in Britain and 'delegates' in Italy.

West Germany

Like their counterparts in Italy and Sweden, few employers in West Germany negotiate independently of employers' organizations. A major exception is Volkswagen which is in part publicly owned and so debarred from membership of the metalworking employers' organization. Significantly, Ford, which in Britain has always been regarded as a proponent of single-employer bargaining, is an extremely active member of the North Rhine Westphalia metalworking employers' organization and a party to the agreements it negotiates. To make the contrast with its behaviour in Britain even more striking, Ford joined the employers' organization in 1963 when it was faced with the prospect of industrial action on the part of the metalworkers' trade union, IG Metall, in support of demands for a company agreement.[9] Other notable members of employers' organizations include the three chemical giants, Bayer, BASF and Hoechst, each of which employs more than 50,000 people.

The main difference between West Germany and the countries so far considered lies in the extent to which the legal framework impinges on the nature and extent of the workplace bargaining in which employers are involved. It is not simply that the Works Constitution Acts of 1952 and 1972 provide for the setting up of 'works councils' in establishments with at least 100 employees (the 1952 Act) and subsequently five employees (the 1972 Act).[10] These Acts also deal with the substance of workplace bargain-

---

[9] The circumstances in which Ford decided to join the metalworking employers' organization rather than negotiate directly with IG Metall are described in more detail in chapter 5.
[10] Any employee over the age of 18 may make nominations to the 'works council', providing the nomination is signed by one tenth of the labour force or 100 employees, whichever is the smaller. Membership provisions cover both wage and salary groups. The current provisions range from one 'works councillor' in establishments with between 5 and 20 employees to 15 in establishments with more than 2000 employees; thereafter the number of works councillors is to increase by one for each additional 200 employees.

Works councillors must be given time off to carry out their duties and may indeed work full-time on them. Again, the number of full-time councillors allowed is determined by the size of the enterprise. The range is from 1 full-time councillor for enterprises with 300 to 600 employees, to 11 full-time councillors for those with between 9000 and 10,000 employees.

ing. Indeed, they grant the works council rights of co-determination, consultation and information.

The issues subject to co-determination are extensive. Broadly speaking, they may be divided into four main areas: social welfare, personnel policies, individual matters, and economic issues (Commission on Industrial Relations, 1974b: 24). Among the more important of these matters are the determination of the forms and principles of methods of wage payment, especially in the case of incentive systems; regulation of working time and overtime; personnel changes and dismissals; arrangements of the physical workplace; setting of bonuses and premiums (above basic wage rates); and all fringe benefits. The works council has rights of joint consultation in respect of safety regulations, construction equipment, manpower and production planning, training and planning the arrangements of the workplace. Finally, it has rights of information: the employer must keep the works council, or its economic committee informed on plans for new buildings and equipment, proposals for job procedures, works site layout, personnel and manpower planning, and must provide a quarterly report on the economic affairs of the company.

If, in the larger establishments especially, the provisions of the Works Constitution Acts ensure that workplace bargaining is not insignificant, they also help to explain why such workplace bargaining is very much subordinate to multi-employer bargaining; why, to use the terms introduced in the opening section of this chapter, it is essentially *administrative* and *supplementary*. First, the legislation imposes an important limitation on the scope of workplace bargaining. Subsection 1 of section 77 does not allow works agreements to be concluded on issues that are already the subject of a collective agreement except where that agreement specifically makes provision for them. Second, it subjects works councillors to a general clause requiring them to perform their duties in a spirit of 'trustful co-operation' (section 2). Third, it binds works councillors by a 'peace obligation' not to call or take part in industrial action in pursuit of their demands (section 74.2). If they do so, they lay themselves open to the risk of legal action by the employer. In the event of a failure to agree, resort must be had to conciliation or the labour court. Fourth, it provides that, where the employer is covered by a multi-employer agreement, the trade union has no legal right to interfere in the workplace; that is to say, in most cases neither the works councillors nor the 'trustmen' (workplace trade union representatives)

In situations where the works council has nine members, it may elect a 'works committee'. A 'company council' must be formed in the case of multi-establishment enterprises. Each works council is to nominate two members to represent wage and salaried workers and voting strength depends on the number of employees in the plant. The company council can conclude company-wide agreements on behalf of the works councils, but it cannot enforce its decision on them.

can call on the trade union for support in the same way that shop stewards in Britain or 'delegates' in Italy can.

For many years the full significance of the implications of the legislation did not become apparent. Early fears raised by trade unions about their formal exclusion from the workplace and other implications of the Works Constitution Act of 1952 soon gave rise to a much more complacent approach.[11] Their ability to organize election slates effectively guaranteed trade union members a preponderance of works council seats. For example, in the case of IG Metall the average proportion of works councillors who are trade union members has been above 80 per cent since the data were first collected in 1957 (Miller, 1978: 340). The works councils also appeared to be effective bargaining agents. As in the other countries, in the 1950s and early 1960s employers found it necessary to offer pay supplements in order to bring the basic rates in the then regional multi-employer agreements up to the going rate in the district. Sometimes employers unilaterally introduced cost of living increases or productivity bonuses or Christmas annual bonuses, and sometimes they negotiated these payments with members of the works council in a so-called 'second wage round' (Müller-Jentsch, 1984: 200). For example, in 1954 IG Metall (1955: 235 and 31, quoted in Miller, 1978: 339) estimated that time workers in the industries that it covered were earning as much as 26.6 per cent above the regional basic rates; in the iron and steel and automobile industries the earnings 'gap' was as much as 50 per cent.

The relative weakness of the works councils only became exposed during the economic downturn of 1966–7. Not only did many employers react to the recession by reducing manning levels, but also by reducing bonus and other supplementary payments. In some cases there was considerable resistance and the level of unofficial strikes increased significantly, culminating in the more widespread unrest of 1969. In general, however, the works councils proved singularly unsuccessful in combating the cuts introduced by employers. Perhaps even more significantly, a study by Krusche and Pfeiffer (1975: 183, quoted in Miller, 1978: 342) found that in a sample of 1378 works councillors some 86 per cent had agreed to reduce supplementary payments and 69 per cent said that the move was justifiable.

Subsequent attempts to overcome the so-called 'company-mindedness' of works councillors proved only marginally successful. Greater recognition was given to workplace trade union representatives[12] in both

[11] At the time the Works Constitution Act of 1952 was seen as a major defeat for the trade unions. They had sought direct influence over works council policy and the removal of the 'peace obligation' from the legislation. They were disappointed on both counts. Ironically, the trade unions had themselves contributed to their exclusion from the workplace by their decision in the late 1940s to base their local organization not on the then legally independent works councils but on the geographical district.

[12] Although the *Vertrauensmann* or 'trustman' is the subject of collective agreements in a

multi-employer agreements and union organization. The trade unions also won greater control over the activities of the works councils as a result of the 1972 Works Constitution Act.[13] Paradoxical as it may seem, however, this made trade unions more dependent on works councils – a process encouraged by employers who have in some cases been prepared to allow them to establish 100 per cent trade union membership as a means of consolidating a good working relationship (Streeck, 1978: 21–4).

Those within the trade unions who argued for a 'plant-level wages policy' also suffered a defeat. The opposition of employers plus the reluctance of trade union executives to do anything that might threaten the position of their members in the smaller undertakings meant that there was no move away from multi-employer bargaining. Instead, the trade unions embarked upon a strategy of negotiating regional agreements that took into account workplace conditions. One way in which the attempt was made involved the negotiation of so-called 'opening clauses' that make it possible for the employer and the works council to adapt the regional agreement at the workplace. Attempts were also made to extend the regional agreements to cover issues that previously had been left to determination at the workplace. Perhaps the best example of this is the productivity bonus that will be referred to in chapter 5, which deals with the contents and status of multi-employer agreements.

IG Metall did not meet with a great deal of resistance from the metalworking employers in its attempts to achieve some decentralization of multi-employer bargaining. Such decentralization, it can be argued, was a small price to pay to avoid negotiations with trade unions at establishment level. The vigorous pursuit of regional multi-employer bargaining does present difficulties, but these are not insurmountable. As chapter 4 on the levels of multi-employer bargaining describes in more detail, the metalworking employers' organization, Gesamtmetall, in particular, has been able to co-ordinate the bargaining policies of the regional metalworking employers' organizations with some degree of success. Furthermore, the attempt to extend the coverage of regional bargaining was seen as bringing positive advantages. In particular, it meant a reduction in scope for workplace bargaining by works councillors and an increase in basic wages without adding to the employer's wage bill. Significantly there was a reduction in the size of the earnings gap in the

---

number of industries, he is not formally recognized by the Works Constitution Acts. Essentially, he provides an information link between the trade union and its members in the workplace.

[13] By increasing the number of works council members – particularly those who are full-time – the 1972 Act effectively increased the number of trade union activists who were given protected status by the law. The Act also gave trade union officials greater access rights to the works council and entitled works councillors to participate in trade union training courses at the employers' expense. Furthermore, works councils were obliged to co-operate in 'good faith' with the trade union.

years that followed (Miller, 1978: 348). Indeed, in one of the establishments visited during the course of the research it was found that no supplementary payments were being made which were not provided for in the regional metalworking agreement.

Compared with Sweden and Italy, then, the law plays a much more important part in determining the nature of the workers' bargaining agent and the scope of workplace bargaining in West Germany. In particular, the legal framework severely restrains the activities of works councillors; it also obliges trade unions to operate through the works councils. On the face of it, workplace bargaining takes place on a broad range of issues. Even so, it appears not to pose any serious threat to the system of multi-employer bargaining. It is largely *administrative* and *supplementary* in form.

France

France is the most complex case. As in West Germany, there are statutory provisions for workplace representation. Indeed, the legal framework provides for no less than three forms of workplace representation, reflecting the intense struggle between employers and trade unions over the issue. Historically, the first of these were the 'employee delegates'[14] introduced by the Matignon Agreement in 1936 at the height of the 'Popular Front' and subsequently given legal backing by the law of 16 April 1946. The second were the 'works committees'[15] introduced in the aftermath of the Second World War by the Ordinance of 22 February 1945 and the subject of further legislation in 1966. They were to be established in enterprises employing more than 50 people, with the number of representatives varying from 3 in the case of enterprises with from 50–75 employees to 11 in the case of those with more than 10,000. The third form of workplace representation is the 'union section'.[16] The

[14] 'Employee delegates' are elected annually by a ballot of colleges of workers in establishments with more than 10 employees. Candidates are nominated on lists in the first instance by the most 'representative' trade unions, but employees who are not in a trade union may propose candidates on the second ballot if less than half the electorate voted in the first. The number of employee delegates ranges from 1 in the case of establishments with from 11 to 25 employees to 9 in the case of establishments with more than 1000 employees; each one is to have 15 paid hours per month to spend on their work, which is to represent individual workers in disputes with management. The chief executive must also meet them once a month and at their request on urgent matters.

[15] In the case of multi-establishment enterprises there is a central committee as well. The system of ballots is very similar to that in the case of the employee delegates, except that there is an additional college for technical and managerial staff. The distribution of seats is to be governed by collective agreement, or failing that, by the inspector of labour. Each 'representative' union may appoint a non-voting member.

[16] The 'union section' can collect subscriptions, display and distribute information, and meet once a month within the workplace outside working hours. The number of union 'delegates' which each section can nominate ranges from 1 in the case of establishments with between 50 and 1000 employees to 4 in the case of establishments with more than 6,000

law of 27 December 1968, which was passed in the wake of the events of May of that year, allows 'representative'[17] trade unions to set up a 'union section' to represent the interests of its members in establishments with more than 50 workers.

By comparison with West Germany, until the passage of the so-called 'Auroux Laws'[18] of 1982, the obligations which the legislation imposed on French employers to engage in workplace bargaining were virtually non-existent. The rights accorded to the employee delegates and the union delegates were strictly those of representation. Although the works committee was to meet each month under the chairmanship of the chief executive, its rights too were limited. It had rights of co-determination or decision only in matters of social welfare. In the important matter of work rules its rights were limited to consultation only; in matters of finance and economic affairs they were limited to information. If the legal limitations on the activities of the delegates and the members of the works committee appeared to be correspondingly small – they were not, for example, debarred from calling or taking part in industrial action – they were nonetheless important. The employer could quote the letter of the law in refusing to negotiate on certain issues. He could also insist that the number of delegates and the time available to them, both of which are hardly generous by comparison with the provisions of the Works Constitution Acts, conformed to the legislation.

Notwithstanding their opposition to a trade union presence in the workplace[19] French employers have had an ambivalent attitude to

employees: delegates in establishments with less than 150 employees have no paid hours to perform their activities, those in establishments with between 150 and 300 have 10 hours per month and those in establishments with more than 300, 15.

[17] There are five trade union confederations which are regarded as 'representative' for the purposes of negotiating collective agreements at the national level and for setting up trade union 'sections' at plant level. The term is a legacy of the law of 24 June 1936. In the debates which led up to the passage of the law the Prime Minister, Blum, is said to have interpreted the relevant clauses to mean that no more than one trade union would be regarded as representative in each case. But the subsequent circular from the Ministry of Labour to the labour inspectorate implied that more than one could be regarded as representative in each case in order to avoid giving the reunited CGT a monopoly to the exclusion of the Catholic trade union confederation, the CFTC (Sturmthal, 1951: 288ff). The issue came to the fore again after the Second World War in 1945 with the formation of the CGC and then again in 1947 and 1948 with the split within the CGT. It was then that a list of representative organizations was drawn up at the national level, though the Minister of Labour can add to the list at the regional or local level providing the organization fulfils the criteria, which include membership, dues income, 'experience and seniority', together with 'patriotic attitude during the occupation' (Lorwin, 1954: 205ff).

[18] The Auroux Laws, so named after the Minister of Labour from 1981 to 1983, deal with 'workers' rights in the enterprise', the 'expansion of representative institutions', the promotion of collective bargaining and the settlement of collective labour disputes, and committees to deal with health, safety and working conditions. For further details, see Caire (1984), Delamotte (1985) and Eyraud and Tchobanian (1985).

[19] Significantly, of the 32,972 enterprises subject to the law relating to the trade union sections in 1972 only 35 per cent had an establishment section, though more than 90 per cent of the enterprises employing more than 1,000 had one (CIR, 1974b: 50). The picture is

workplace bargaining. In the 1950s, for example, it looked as if France was about to anticipate the pattern that was to develop later in Italy. In 1955 and 1956 a number of the larger employers followed Renault's lead in negotiating enterprise or workplace agreements with full-time trade union officials (International Labour Office, 1960; Reynaud, 1975a: 191–2). In the great majority of cases these agreements were supplementary to the multi-employer agreements and dealt with actual rates of pay and provided for consultation before industrial action was taken in the event of disputes. Significantly, many of the employers involved – in cars, aircraft manufacture, shipbuilding, electrical and mechanical engineering, chemicals and food – were already paying well above the rates of pay in multi-employer agreements. The larger French employers, it seems, were not immune to the pressures which their counterparts in the other countries were experiencing. Reynaud (1975a: 193–4) sums up the objectives which these employers had in negotiating enterprise and workplace agreements as follows:

> The suppression of strikes improves the possibilities of planning; the advantages which followed increased the stability of personnel; the regular increases are more easily absorbed and can even lead to more efficient management. In short, the contractual engagement is better suited to those who can and must plan for the medium and long term.

Although the employers involved, including Renault, continue to negotiate enterprise and workplace agreements, the practice begun in 1955 and 1956 did not have deep roots. A change in the economic climate in 1957 made it more difficult for a number of the employers to commit themselves to long-term agreements. Nor did the agreements achieve the hoped-for social peace; the trade union confederation, the CGT, became increasingly reluctant to put its signature to agreements which included a peace obligation. The attitudes of other employers were important too. The confederation of small and medium employers, the so-called PME, complained about the 'tyranny' of the larger enterprises. The metal-working employers' organization, UIMM, was no less concerned about the implications of the negotiation of enterprise and workplace agreements; by introducing competition between enterprises on the North American pattern, it was argued, such agreements threatened employer solidarity (Reynaud, 1975a: 194).

---

not dissimilar in the case of the works committees introduced in 1946; figures supplied by the Ministry of Labour suggested that only 9,000 enterprises had introduced committees out of 24,000 subject to the law (CIR, 1974b: 49). It also seems that the enterprises in which individual delegates do not accumulate a number of duties is the exception (Bachy *et al.*, 1974: 264). Sometimes this is because of the desire to maximize the number of credit hours available to an individual representative. More often than not, it seems that this is because of a shortage of people willing to take on the responsibilities.

Despite a brief flurry of activity in the period immediately following May 1968, enterprise and workplace agreements continued to be the exception rather than the rule throughout the 1970s. In a study of 48 enterprises Bachy and his colleagues (1974: 152) found that relatively comprehensive workplace agreements existed in only 14, and partial agreements in another 20. Overall, they found that only 14 per cent of a range of issues to do with the organization and conditions of work involved any form of negotiation. In the larger sample drawn from the Rhône-Alpes region, Bunel and Saglio (1976: 445) found that only 30 per cent of enterprises had signed workplace agreements. These included, the authors were careful to point out, not only agreements which conformed to the requirements of the law, but the sum total of the agreements – informal as well as formal. Both studies confirmed that workplace agreements were more likely to be found in the larger enterprises, those where trade union membership, especially among the CGT and the other major trade union confederation, the CFDT, is higher, and those where there had been some form of industrial action leading to the agreement.

The attitudes expressed by the personnel director of a large multi-establishment enterprise during the course of the research are fairly typical of employers more generally. The company had never had an enterprise agreement and quite clearly did not want one. The personnel director stressed the danger to employer solidarity of negotiating agreements whose terms and conditions were superior to those of the regional multi-employer agreement in metalworking. He also added that the vast amount of recent legislation, together with the multi-industry agreements negotiated by the CNPF and the trade union confederations, had really left little scope for formal workplace agreements.[20] He went on to argue that the management had nothing to gain by negotiating an enterprise agreement. By definition, such agreements would mean superior contractual terms and conditions to those of the legislation and multi-employer agreement. These, he argued, might prove to be embarrassing if the economic situation became worse. And what would be the benefits? He argued that it would not be a guarantee of social peace. Far from it. He believed that its negotiation – and subsequent renegotiation – would simply provide a focal point for agitation by the trade unions.

The passage of the 'Auroux Laws', obliging employers to engage in negotiations each year with workplace trade union representatives, would appear to have made little difference in the short run. According to a

[20] This is a very common and time-honoured argument of employers in France. See, for example, Waline (1951: 25) and Chotard (1976: 20).
In 1974 Bachy (1974: 152) and his colleagues observed:

> for the average enterprise, the renewal of negotiations at the inter-industry level seemed to play the same role as the development of legal rules: the rapid progress of negotiation at the summit tended to encourage employers to be prudent so as not to accumulate hastily rules whose generalisation imposed supplementary changes above all on the small and medium size enterprises.

Ministry of Labour report (quoted by Delamotte, 1985: 23), during the first 16 months of the operation of the legislation, there had been negotiations in only 42 per cent of enterprises. Even more significant was the fact that the negotiations had led to agreements in only 16 per cent of cases. The agreements were also relatively limited in their scope involving mostly wages (87 per cent), hours of work (47 per cent) and the organization of working time.

The legal framework, the content of higher level agreements, the reluctance of employers, and the ideologies of the trade unions all work against the negotiation of formal workplace agreements. To conclude from this, however, that workplace bargaining does not take place in France would be a great mistake. The negotiation of formal agreements represents only the very tip of the iceberg. Much of the workplace bargaining that takes place is informal and involves the administration of the legal regulations or the higher level collective agreements; much of it takes place between first line supervisors and the delegates. The following quotation from Reynaud (1975a: 195–6) gives some of the flavour of what happens:

> discussion and compromise take place often not on a global text which claims to cover the relations and rules of work in their entirety, but piece by piece: one day on a rise in wages, and then on a formula for holidays, and then on the amount of work and the forms of remuneration. This piecemeal negotiation does not have the ambitions of a comprehensive regulation or a signed contract. But it corresponds better to a changing situation where the pressure of demands cannot be anticipated and where it is better to be able to regulate fairly quickly the incidences of conflict which appear even if it is in the heat of the moment.

Perhaps the main difference between France and the other countries is that these issues are rarely the subject of oral let alone written agreements. On the face of it, the vast majority of decisions relating to employment is taken unilaterally by the employer. Yet these decisions are not taken in a vacuum. Certainly, there is evidence to suggest that many *militants* or trade union activists believe the influence they exert is not inconsiderable. The bargaining, to borrow the term from Batstone (1978), is at 'arms length' with both *militants* and managers more or less constantly seeking to structure attitudes to their own advantage. As Batstone (1978: 82) puts it:

> the use of power is less institutionalised than in many other countries so that what happens at the bargaining table is of far less significance than a more direct demonstration or indication of force. Consequently, particularly for management, the subtle game of taking hints and cues is dependent far more upon understanding what is happening at the point of production rather than upon the statements of union negotiators. At the same time, both parties

concentrate their efforts upon a longer term strategy of influencing the militants of the workforce and the position of the unions.

Clearly, then, a process of accommodation has been reached that helps to explain why the rhetoric of French industrial relations can be very different from the reality. Trade unions are able to claim the credit for any improvement in pay or conditions without compromising their longer term objectives by signing agreements that might thought to be supporting the *status quo*. For their part, employers are able to maintain an impression of making decisions unilaterally. They are not called upon to cultivate a bargaining relationship with trade unions in the workplace. Indeed, there is every incentive to seek to deny the trade unions any advantage. More importantly in the present context, the principle of multi-employer bargaining is not threatened. Any workplace bargaining that takes place involves the legally-constituted delegates or works committees. Such workplace bargaining is also largely *administrative* or *supplementary*.

Conclusions

A considerable body of evidence suggests that workplace bargaining, like the earnings 'gap', is not a phenomenon unique to Britain. Employers, especially in the larger establishments, are involved in workplace bargaining in each of the other four countries. Moreover, it is possible to identify a number of common factors underpinning its development. Briefly, to repeat the argument in chapter 1, they are: an increase in size and industrial concentration; leading on the one hand to economies of scale and a greater ability to pay; and, on the other, the development of more bureaucratic and decentralized forms of management. The result is that the larger employers have increasingly been forced to develop what might be described as internal systems of job regulation. By this it is meant that they have been obliged to develop rules and procedures specific to their own needs: rules that cannot be catered for in an agreement applying to a larger number of different situations. Workplace bargaining develops because the acquiescence, if not the co-operation, of the workforce in upholding these rules and procedures is as essential as a specialist staff to develop and maintain them.

It must be equally clear, however, that the nature and extent of the workplace bargaining in which employers are involved are very different from country to country. First, there are differences in the type of bargaining agent employers have to deal with. In Britain employers negotiate with shop stewards who are more or less independent of their trade unions. In the other countries the workers' bargaining agents tend to be much less independent. In France and West Germany the main bargaining agents are essentially non-trade union bodies. Although trade union influence is considerable, the activities of the delegates and the works' committees in France and the works councils in West Germany are circumscribed by the legal framework. Sweden fits into a second category. The 'factory club', which is the main bargaining agent, is a trade union body. Yet it is much less independent than a joint shop stewards' committee. Legally, it is regarded as an agent of the external trade union; and the external trade union can be called to account for its activities. Only in Italy is it possible for the workers' bargaining agents in the establishment, the delegates and factory councils, to act as independently as in Britain; even here industrial unionism and the centralization of much of the bargaining at enterprise level makes independent action less likely in practice.

Second, and dependently, there are differences in the relationship between workplace bargaining and multi-employer bargaining. In many large establishments in Britain workplace bargaining has replaced multi-employer bargaining as the main source of joint regulation. Furthermore, it is not a question of this workplace bargaining administering or supplementing the terms and conditions of the multi-employer agreements employers' organizations continue to negotiate. The workplace bargaining has little or no relationship to these agreements. It is now truly *autonomous*. In effect, even if the multi-employer agreements continue to have some importance, this is single-employer bargaining and is to be compared with the single-employer bargaining in Japan and in large-scale manufacturing industry in the USA.

There are few signs in the other countries of even the very large employers moving in a similar direction to their British counterparts. Much of the workplace bargaining they are involved in, it has been argued, might be described as *administrative*. By this it is meant that the bargaining is about the application of the terms and conditions of the multi-employer agreements; a good example might be the bargaining over the positioning of a specific job under the job classification scheme in the multi-employer agreement. A second category, which is very much related, has been described as *supplementary*. In this case the workplace bargaining the employer is involved in adds to or improves upon the terms and conditions of the multi-employer agreements. Examples might be the negotiation of a workplace supplement or superior facilities for workplace representatives. In both cases the negotiations often take place in the wake of multi-employer agreements reached by employers' organizations and trade unions, thereby emphasizing their relationship to these agreements. In some respects, then, it is not dissimilar to the workplace bargaining in clothing, construction, and printing in Britain where multi-employer bargaining remains the predominant pattern.

The comparison, which is summarized in Table 2.1, not only draws attention to the main differences between the five countries. It also makes it possible to develop a better understanding of the significance of

TABLE 2.1

Types of Workplace Bargaining

Status of Workers' Bargaining Agent	Statutory	Dependent	Independent
Nature and Extent of Workplace Bargaining			
Administrative Supplementary Autonomous	{ France ⎩ West Germany	{ Sweden	{ Italy Britain

multi-employer bargaining. As chapter 1 pointed out, there are strong *a priori* grounds for expecting employers in clothing, construction and printing to engage in multi-employer bargaining. Not only are the small employers who tend to dominate these industries less capable of dealing with trade unions on their own. Multi-employer bargaining also facilitates the regulation of competition in both their labour and product markets. These are the reasons, it can be argued, why British employers in these industries continue to engage in multi-employer bargaining. In the case of the larger employers in metalworking and chemicals, however, the material structure is much less coercive. Indeed, there are *a priori* grounds for expecting the employer to prefer independent to collective action. In short, there must be reasons other than market control to explain why employers in the metalworking and chemical industries outside Britain continue to engage in multi-employer bargaining.

These reasons, which are implicit in the comparison made in this chapter, are largely to do with the significance of multi-employer bargaining in maintaining *managerial* control. The argument can perhaps best be developed by reinterpreting the shift from multi-employer to single-employer bargaining on the part of British employers in the larger establishments in engineering and chemicals. The shift took place, it can be argued, not so much because these employers preferred independence to collective action; or because multi-employer bargaining did not determine actual terms and conditions of employment in the workplace. Rather in the post-Second World War period multi-employer bargaining in Britain was proving incapable of fulfilling what for employers was its major attraction over single-employer bargaining, namely the neutralization of the workplace.[21] The unique pattern of unofficial

---

[21] In view of the developments in Britain in such industries as engineering, which will be considered in chapter 6, it is surprising that the significance of multi-employer bargaining in contributing to the neutralization of the workplace has received little or no attention from British observers. Perhaps Phelps Brown (1959: 124) comes closest to recognizing the

and unconstitutional strikes confirms that the workplace had not been excluded from hostilities. Furthermore, the 'largely informal, largely fragmented, and largely autonomous' workplace bargaining was seriously threatening the employer's ability to manage. To get control in the workplace, British employers were obliged to engage in productivity bargaining, to change their payment systems and introduce job evaluation, and to reform their domestic procedures in the way the report of the Donovan Commission prescribed. Yet each of these activities could effectively be undertaken only by the individual employer and so exaggerated the shift to single-employer bargaining.

The argument holds in reverse for the larger employers in metalworking and chemicals in the other countries. Despite the differences between the countries, these employers show no signs of abandoning multi-employer bargaining. This may make for some economies of scale in terms of time, effort and personnel. It may put a floor under competition; in the case of industries such as clothing, construction, and printing it may help to regulate the market. Above all, however, multi-employer bargaining – supported in France, Sweden and West Germany by the legal framework – makes it possible to neutralize the workplace. Not only is the incidence of industrial action experienced by the individual employer on his own very rare. The discretion which the individual employer is able to exercise in the workplace is enhanced by multi-employer bargaining; the trade union is, in effect, excluded from the workplace or the role it is able to play there is severely restricted.

These conclusions provide the immediate, but not the full, explanation for the decline of multi-employer bargaining in much of manufacturing industry in Britain and the support which it continues to enjoy in the other four countries. To provide the full explanation, it will be necessary to explain more precisely what it is about multi-employer bargaining in Britain that is different from the other countries. In particular, it will be necessary to explain why multi-employer bargaining in Britain proved incapable of neutralizing the workplace as it appears to have done in the

---

potential of multi-employer bargaining in this regard. In listing the possible advantages of multi-employer bargaining to British employers he points out that

> those (employers) who had little love for the union were still willing to meet it to negotiate a rate, because of all union activities this interfered with them the least. They could hotly resist any encroachment on their prerogatives as managers of their own business, but collective bargaining only meant that they were paying the same price as their competitors for one factor of production.

By contrast, the objective of neutralizing the workplace – and, in particular, of excluding the trade union from the workplace – figures prominently in the discussion of employers' strategies in France by Sellier (1960; 1961). It is also revealed in the extremely frank exchange of views in Italy in 1961 between Sulla, the Minister of Labour, and Costa, President of CONFINDUSTRIA, at the height of the dispute in metalworking over trade union demands to be involved in workplace bargaining. For further details see Ammassari (1976: 105–8, 332–9).

other countries. To this end, the next three chapters explore in some detail the structure of multi-employer bargaining in the five countries; that is to say, the structure and government of the organizations which are the employers' bargaining agents, the levels at which multi-employer bargaining takes place, and the contents and status of multi-employer agreements.

3

An Anatomy of the Employers' Organizations

Employers' organizations are one of the most important private interest groups in the five countries. The reason for giving special attention to them in the present study, however, is that they are the agents of employers in multi-employer bargaining with trade unions.[1] As such, employers' organizations would appear to be faced with special problems in mounting collective action. The employers they represent are independent organizations in their own right; many are in direct competition with one another in both the labour market and the product market. Following Olsen (1969: 14–16), there would also appear to be no rational reason why, if he is able to enjoy the benefits of the 'collective good' achieved by the activities of the majority, the individual employer should make sacrifices in the interests of that 'good'.[2] Prima facie the ability of employers' organizations to surmount these problems would appear to depend on their structure and membership coverage, their internal organization, their legal status, their financial arrangements, the range of their activities, and, perhaps above all, their government. It remains to be seen if this is so.

[1] For further details of the activities of employers' organizations in the five countries, see Armstrong (1984) on Britain, Bunel and Saglio (1984) on France, Bunn (1984) on West Germany, Skogh (1984) on Sweden, and Treu and Martinelli (1984) on Italy.
[2] Offe and Wiesenthal (1980) are not entirely convinced by this argument. They suggest that employers' organizations have fewer problems than trade unions in making decisions. Crucially, unlike trade unions, employers' organizations, they say, are not involved in the simultaneous but partly contradictory processes of framing and expressing the common interest. The individual employer remains an independent organization and the key unit of decision-making so far as investment and employment are concerned. The range of issues for which the employers' organization is responsible is therefore limited; the commitments and obligations which membership require of the individual employer are also relatively marginal. Indeed, membership of an employers' organization serves to hide the very existence of the individual employer and is valued mainly from that point view. See also the summary discussion of both Olsen's, and Offe's and Wiesenthal's views in Schmitter and Streeck (1981).

The Structure of the Employers' Organizations

The term 'structure' is used to describe the membership coverage of trade unions by occupation and industry. The term can be similarly applied to describe the membership coverage of employers' organizations. For the purpose of analysis, it will be useful to distinguish between the employers' confederations and the employers' organizations in the five industries or branches of activity.

The Employers' Confederations

It will be seen from Table 3.1 listing the employers' confederations in the five countries and giving details of their membership coverage, there is nothing exceptional about the membership coverage of the CBI. Like the BDA and SAF, the CBI lays claim to membership in more or less every sphere of business activity in the private sector.[3] Membership coverage of the CNPF is only marginally less; it covers manufacturing and commerce, but agricultural employers are separately represented. CONFINDUSTRIA has the most restricted membership coverage; CONFAGRICOLTURA and CONFCOMMERCIO are the peak organizations of employers in agriculture and commerce respectively.

From time to time reference has been made to the significance of the competition which the CBI faces for the allegiance of the small employer.[4] But the CBI is not unique in experiencing such competition. If anything, the competition which the employers' confederation faces in some of the other countries is far greater. The CNPF in France is perhaps the most obvious case. Indeed, the Confédération Générale des Petites et Moyennes Entreprises lays claim to represent the majority of small and medium-sized employers; 120,000 in industry and 800,000 in commerce and services.[5] In Italy too size has proved to be a common point of reference. Like the CBI, CONFINDUSTRIA has gone to considerable lengths to provide adequate

[3] It is interesting that both the CBI and SAF have expanded their membership out of manufacturing into the other sectors in recent years. A particularly strong fillip was given to CBI membership by the campaign which it successfully fought against the proposals of the Bullock Committee of Inquiry into Industrial Democracy in 1977. In the case of the SAF in Sweden the most significant development in the process of expansion was the merger between SAF and the Handelns Arbetsgivarorganisation in 1964–5. Until the date HAO had been a separately functioning employers' confederation in the general area of commerce and trade with a fairly diverse membership beyond that. In 1976 employers in forestry, agriculture and shipping swelled the ranks of SAF.
[4] See, for example, the discussion in Grant and Marsh (1977: 96–9). When the CBI was established, a number of small employers refused to join and set up the Society of Independent Manufacturers. This organization subsequently changed its name to the Smaller Business Association and then the Association of Independent Businesses. The Association of British Chambers of Commerce and the National Chamber of Trade also stress their ability to look after the interests of small business.
[5] The so-called 'PME' is famed in France for the direct action of its members. For further details, see Brizay (1975: 275), Lefranc (1976: 221) and Reynaud (1975a: 41).

TABLE 3.1
The Employers' Confederations

Country	Abbreviation	Membership Coverage
Britain		
Confederation of British Industry	CBI	Agriculture, manufacturing and commerce
France		
Conseil National du Patronat Français	CNPF	Manufacturing and commerce
Italy*		
Confederazione Generale dell'Industria Italiana	CONFINDUSTRIA	Manufacturing
Sweden		
Svenska Arbetsgivareföreningen	SAF	Agriculture, manufacturing and commerce
West Germany		
Bundesvereinigung der Deutschen Arbeitgeberverbände	BDA	Agriculture, manufacturing and commerce

Notes:
* The enterprises with state participation are represented by the Associazione Sindacale Intersind (INTERSIND) and the Associazione Sindacale per le Aziende Petrolchemiche e Collegate a Partecipazione Statale (ASAP). See text for further details.

representation for small employers. Nonetheless, it faces competition for the allegiance of these employers from the Confederazione Fra Le Associazonie Autonome dei Piccoli Industriale. CONFAPI, as it is known, claims a membership of some 18,000 employers.

Perhaps the only distinguishing characteristic of the CBI's membership coverage is the position of the nationalized enterprises. Since 1969 the CBI has admitted these enterprises into full membership.[6] Indeed, they constitute one of the five full member categories. In the other countries the employers' confederations exclude the nationalized enterprises.[7]

It is difficult to argue that the unique position of the nationalized industries in Britain is significant in the context of the present study. The CBI, it must be remembered, was only formed in 1965 as a result of the amalgamation of the British Employers' Confederation (BEC), the Federation of British Industries (FBI), and the National Association of British Manufacturers (NABM).[8] Like the employers' confederations in the other countries, the BEC also excluded the nationalized enterprises from membership.

Far more important is the position of the nationalized enterprises in Italy. Following their *distacco* or separation from CONFINDUSTRIA in 1956, the enterprises with state participation were required to develop separate channels of representation so far as industrial relations matters are concerned. Subsequently, separate employers' organizations were set up to act as bargaining agents of these enterprises. INTERSIND was set up to represent the interests of the enterprises which came under the jurisdiction of the Istituto per la Ricostruzione Industriale (IRI) and ASAP those which came under the jurisdiction of the Ente Nazionale Idrocarburi (ENI).[9] As later chapters will argue, these developments were to have a decisive impact on the conduct of collective bargaining in the private as well as the public sector in Italy.

The Branch Employers' Organizations

It will be seen from Tables 3.2 to 3.6, giving brief details of the membership coverage of the main employers' organizations in the five industries

[6] Nationalized enterprises had been granted associate membership on the formation of the CBI in 1965. For further discussion of the position of the nationalized industries within the CBI, see Grant and Marsh (1977: 99–102).

[7] Strictly speaking, nationalized enterprises in France are admitted to membership of private sector employers' organizations provided, like Renault, they do not have a monopoly. But they are unable to affiliate directly to the employers' confederation; they belong to their respective branch employers' organization.

[8] The FBI and the NABM were essentially trade organizations. Both have their origins during the First World War.

[9] IRI had been set up in 1933 to protect the shareholders of Italy's largest banks, then in difficulties because of sizeable industrial holdings. At the time of the *distacco* in 1956 IRI employed about 0.25 million people in a wide range of industries and services: engineering, shipbuilding, steel, radio, television, banking. Today the number is probably more than twice that figure. ENI, the other main state-holding company, was set up in 1953. It is involved in refining, transportation and distribution of petroleum products as well as the control of the output of natural gas.

TABLE 3.2
The Branch Organizations in Chemicals

Country	Abbreviation	Membership Coverage
Britain[a]		
Chemical Industries Association	CIA	General chemicals
France[b]		
Union des Industries Chimiques	UIC	General chemicals
West Germany		
Arbeitsring Chemie	AC	General chemicals
Italy[c]		
Associazione Nazionale dell'Industria Chimica	ANIC	General chemicals
Sweden[d]		
Allmänna Gruppen (General Group)	AG	General chemicals

[a] There are separate employers' organizations in gelatine and glue; in paint; in soap, candle and edible fats; surgical dressings; and match manufacture. Each is a bargaining agent in its own right.

[b] Employers in such specialist activities as perfumery, margarine and photographic products are separately organized, but are signatories of the national agreement for the chemical industry.

[c] The pharmaceutical employers are separately organized, but signatories of the national agreement for the chemical industry.

[d] The General Group, which was established in 1920, looks after the interests of those employers whose number is too small to warrant a separate organization. Two bargaining units are involved so far as the chemical employers are concerned.

or branches of activity, that the fragmentation often associated with employers' organizations in Britain is not unique.[10] For example, it is true that in metalworking there is one main employers' organization in France and Italy, whereas historically in Britain there were three. But in Sweden and West Germany, employers involved in the production of metals are separately organized from those involved in its transformation.[11] In West Germany the smaller employers in the metal crafts are separately organized; in Sweden employers in garages and welding are separately organized.

The situation in Italy is deceptive too. The membership of ANIC in chemicals and FEDERMECCANICA in metalworking does not include the

[10] See, for example, the discussion in the CBI's evidence to the Donovan Commission (1965: 13).

[11] As in Britain, separatism born of a long history dies hard. In West Germany, however, there is an additional complication. The BDA, which is the employers' confederation, requires that its member organizations must be totally independent of other interests. Under the Co-Determination Law of 1951 there is a provision for trade union representatives to be elected as the labour managers of enterprises in the iron and steel industry. In effect, this means the BDA cannot represent the iron and steel employers.

TABLE 3.3
The Branch Organizations in Clothing

Country	Abbreviation	Membership Coverage
Britain[a]		
Clothing Manufacturers' Federation	CMF	Ready-made and wholesale bespoke tailoring
France		
Union des Industries d'Habillement	UIH	General
West Germany		
Bekleidungsindustrie	BI	General
Italy		
Associazione Italiana Industriali Abbigliamento	AIIA	General
Sweden		
Sveriges Konfektionsindustri forbund	SKF	General

Note:

[a] As is pointed out in the text, the Commission on Industrial Relations (1974a: 14) identified no less than 21 employers' organizations which had the right to nominate representatives to the statutory wages councils in the clothing industry. But one was the Co-operative Union, two represented retail employers only, and seven represented employers in hat-making. Recently a number of the larger employers' organizations have come together to form the British Clothing Industry Association.

[b] An organization representing building co-operatives is also a signatory of the national agreement.

enterprises in which the state has a major holding. In the case of metalworking especially, this is not an insignificant sector; the total number of enterprises with state participation is not far short of 1,000 and they employ nearly 250,000 workers. They include ITALSIDER, which accounts for the major proportion of steel output, and Alfa Romeo; there are also significant state holdings in cast-iron production and ship-building. The enterprises with state participation in chemicals and metalworking are members of the state employers' organizations ASAP and INTERSIND respectively. They constitute separate bargaining units and ASAP and INTERSIND negotiate separately from their private sector counterparts.[12]

One of the most striking aspects is the similarity which exists between the countries. In four of the countries there are separate organizations of employers in building, on the one hand, and civil engineering on the

[12] There are also enterprises with state participation in clothing, construction and printing. In contrast to chemicals and metalworking, however, the state employers' organizations negotiate jointly with the private sector employers' organizations.

TABLE 3.4
The Branch Organizations in Construction

Country	Abbreviation	Membership Coverage
Britain[a]		
Federation of Civil Engineering Contractors	FCEC	Civil Engineering
National Federation of Building Trade Employers	NFBTE	Building
France[b]		
Fédération Nationale du Bâtiment	FNB	Building
Fédération Nationale des Travaux Publics	FNTP	Civil Engineering
Italy		
Associazione Nazionale Costruttori Edili	ANCE	Building and civil engineering
Sweden		
Byggnadsammesförbundet	BA	Building
Svenska Byggnadsindustriförbundet	SBI	Civil engineering
Svenska Vag-och Vattenbyggarnas Arbetsgivareförbund	SVEABUND	Bridges and waterways
West Germany		
Hauptverband der Deutschen Bauindustrie	HVB	Civil Engineering
Zentralverband des Deutschen Baugewerbes	ZVB	Building

Notes:

a The Federation of Master Builders, which represents small and medium-size employers, has recently negotiated a separate national agreement with the Transport and General Workers' Union. Previously, it had confined its activities to those of a trade organization. There are also a number of separate employers' organizations in such specialist activities as electrical contracting, heating and ventilation, demolition, etc. Each is a bargaining agent in its own right.

b An organization representing building co-operatives is also a signatory of the national agreement.

other. In all five countries employers in printing[13] and newspapers have several separate organizations; and in three countries employers in newspapers are further divided between national and provincial interests.

Further study of Tables 3.2 to 3.6 makes it possible to draw another significant conclusion. In Britain the fragmentation appears to be

13 The employer's organization in printing in Sweden (the GAF) was formed only in 1970 as the result of amalgamation. Previously, there had been four separate organizations representing employers in book-binding, typographic printing, lithographic printing, and paper-packaging respectively.

TABLE 3.5
The Branch Organizations in Metalworking

Country	Abbreviation	Membership Coverage
Britain[a]		
Engineering Employers' Federation	EEF	Engineering
British Iron and Steel Federation (dissolved in 1967)	—	Iron and steel
Shipbuilders' and Repairers' National Association (dissolved in 1977)	—	Shipbuilding
France		
Union des Industries Métallurgiques et Minières	UIMM	Engineering, iron and steel, shipbuilding
Italy[b]		
Federazione Sindacale dell'Industria Metalmeccanica Italiana	FEDERMECCANICA	Engineering, iron and steel, shipbuilding
Sweden[c]		
Sveriges Verkstadsförening	SVF	Engineering and shipbuilding
Jarnsbruksförbundet	JBF	Iron and steel
West Germany		
Gesamtverband der Metallindustriellen Arbeitgeberverbände e.V.	Gesamtmetall	Engineering and shipbuilding
Arbeitgeberverband Eisen and Stahl	AES	Iron and steel

Notes:

[a] Employers in iron and steel and in shipbuilding left in the private sector are organized in the Independent Steel Employers' Association and the Shipbuilders' and Shiprepairers' Independent Association respectively. The National Metal Trades Federation represents employers involved in the production of castings and domestic appliances. There are two regional organizations of iron and steel employers in the Midlands and one in South Wales. There are also separate national organizations of employers in cable-making; jewellery; locks, latches and keys; oil and chemical plant construction; specialist vehicle building; and wire and wire products. There are also regional organizations of employers in cutlery and hand tools based in Sheffield. Each of the organizations is a bargaining agent in its own right.

[b] An organization representing heating, sanitary and ventilation employers is also a signatory of the national agreement.

[c] Welding employers are separately organized.

TABLE 3.6
The Branch Organizations in Printing

Country	Abbreviation	Membership Coverage
Britain[a]		
British Printing Industries Federation	BPIF	Printing
Newspaper Society	NS	Provincial and metropolitan London newspapers
Newspaper Publishers Association	NPA	National newspapers
France[b]		
Confédération de la Presse Française	CPF	Provincial newspapers
Federation de la Presse Française	FPF	Paris daily newspapers and some provincial dailies and periodicals
Fédération Française des Syndicats Patronaux de l'Imprimerie et des Industries Graphiques	FFSPIG	Printing
Italy		
Associazione Italiana Industriali Grafiche Cartotechnice e Transformatrici	AIIGCT	Printing and paper products
Associazione Italiana Editori	AIE	Weekly newspapers and periodicals
Federazione Italiana Editori Giornali	FIEG	Daily newspapers and some weekly magazines
Sweden		
Grafiska Arbetsgivareförbundet	GAF	Printing Newspapers
West Germany		
Bundesvereinigung Druck	BVD	Printing
Bundersverband Deutscher Zeitungsverleger	BDZ	Newspapers

Notes:

[a] The national and local newspapers in Scotland have separate employers' organizations. Each is a bargaining agent in its own right. There are also separate employers' organizations in publishing and ink manufacture.

[b] There is a separate artisans' organization for small employers in printing.

greatest in those industries where multi-employer bargaining continues to be the predominant pattern. This is true of building and civil engineering. It is true of printing and newspapers. Above all, it is true, until 1981, of the clothing industry in which no less than 21 employers' organizations were identified in 1974 on the basis of seats held on wages councils (CIR, 1974a).[14]

[14] Many of these employers' organizations amalgamated in 1981. The new umbrella organization is known as the British Clothing Industry Association.

On reflection, these findings are perhaps not surprising. Very rarely does the fragmentation of employers' organizations involve overlap of and competition for membership. Other things being equal, then, the presence of a number of organizations in the same sector is not necessarily incompatible with effective multi-employer bargaining. Setting aside the significance of their historical development, a separate existence makes it possible to represent the particular interests of specific groups or to tailor agreements to suit their circumstances. Nor need the presence of a number of organizations lead to a fragmented approach. The organizations may come together for the purposes of multi-employer bargaining as they tend to do in building and civil engineering. If one or two of the organizations are dominant, they may be able to set the pattern in matters of common interest. Until the 1981 amalgamation, the CMF in clothing in Britain was a good example.[15] If one single organization covers an entire sector, this may inhibit cohesion; it may be difficult, for example, to reconcile the interests of employers in different product markets.

Primary or Secondary Organizations?

So far as their relationship with the individual employer is concerned, two main types of employers' organization may be identified. Under the first, which might be described as *primary*, the individual employer affiliates directly to the national organization. Under the second, which are essentially federations or *secondary* organizations, the individual employer affiliates indirectly through the intermediary of one or more levels of local organizations.

The Employers' Confederations

It will be seen from Figure 3.1 that the organization of the CBI is very different from that of its opposite numbers. Of the five employers' confederations, the CBI is the only one whose membership is open directly to individual employers as well as employers' and trade organizations. The other four are federations of employers' organizations and trade organizations. The members of the SAF are vertical or single-industry organizations. The memberships of the BDA, CNPF and CONFINDUSTRIA are composed of both vertical and horizontal organizations. The vertical ones are single-industry organizations. The horizontal organizations are multi-industry in coverage and represent a geographical area usually defined by the administrative unit into which the countries are divided, namely, the *départements, Länder,* and *provincie.*

---

[15] The CMF also provided the secretariat for some of the smaller employers' organizations in the clothing industry.

How significant is the CBI's membership structure? Certainly, it has made for considerable complications in the CBI's constitutional arrangements as a later section will illustrate. It can also be argued that the admission of individual employers into membership has served to undermine the authority of the branch organizations; that it has put the employers' confederation in a position of competing for authority with the branch organizations with some inevitable duplication of function and activities. Against this, it can be argued that the membership structure better suits the growth in the number of large multi-establishment enterprises which may not be a member of the relevant branch organizations. Nor does the lack of multi-industry employers' organizations at local level pose problems. Like the SAF in Sweden, the CBI has its own regional offices. Last, but not least, it must not be forgotten that the CBI was formed only in 1965. Significantly, the British Employers' Confederation, which had been the peak organization of employers from 1919 to 1965, had been structured very similarly to the employers' confederations in the other countries; that is to say, membership was restricted to organizations of employers only.[16]

The Branch Employers' Organizations

The details of the internal structure of employers' organizations below the national level in the five branches are set out in figures 3.2 to 3.6. The relationship with trade organizations and local multi-industry employers' organizations is also shown where these are separate. Again, Britain does not appear to be exceptional. It is the similarities between the countries that stand out. For example, in metalworking and building the main branch organizations are essentially federations or *secondary* organizations in all five countries. In clothing and printing they are *secondary* organizations in Britain, France and West Germany; in chemicals, on the other hand, the main branch organizations are *primary* or unitary organizations in Britain, Italy and Sweden.

Like the organizations at the national level, in the great majority of case the local *primary* organizations are also single-industry in their

---

[16] The fact that the CBI is both a primary and a secondary organization is explained by the membership composition of its predecessors which joined together in 1965. The Federation of British Industry had originally been established in 1916 by some of the leading manufacturing companies. Trade associations were only admitted after some considerable debate. The National Association of British Manufacturers too had individual companies as well as trade associations in membership. Incidentally, the great majority of the individual companies in the NABM were small in size, some 74 per cent employing fewer than 100 workers in the penultimate year of its life. Only the British Employers' Confederation excluded direct company membership. In 1964 it had 53 national employers' organizations in membership, mainly but not exclusively manufacturing-based. Had the CBI attempted to reform its membership structure along the lines of its counterparts in the other countries, it would have risked alienating those companies that had enjoyed direct membership of its predecessors. This is especially so in the case of those companies that were not members of their relevant BEC branch organizations.

56

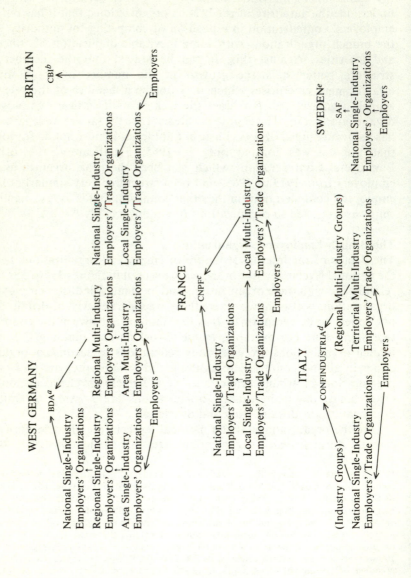

FIGURE 3.1 The Employers' Confederations

Notes:

a The BDA's membership is made up of some 40 vertical organizations which are usually based on an industry or branch of activity; these are national single-industry or branch organizations, which are further subdivided into 366 regional and area organizations. Then there are 12 horizontal organizations roughly corresponding to the 11 *Länder* or Federal Government regions; these are multi-industry employers' organizations which are further subdivided into general organizations in the regions.

b The CBI has more than 6,000 companies in direct membership as well as some 200 trade and employers' organizations.

c The CNPF's membership is made up of slightly more than 80 vertical organizations most of which are based on an industry or branch of activity. Many of them are themselves federations of employers' organizations which represent a narrower branch of activity. The great majority of these vertical or branch organizations are also trade organizations.

d In total there are more than 140 horizontal or multi-industry organizations, now linked in 21 regional organizations to reflect recent changes in the French administration. There is usually one or more in each of the 95 *départements*, depending on the level of activity, and some are further subdivided into more local organizations.

CONFINDUSTRIA's membership is made up of more than 90 vertical organizations which are usually based on an industry or branch of activity; of these the Federazione Associazione Industriali is a grouping of 12 individual organizations with miscellaneous interests. In the great majority of cases the branch or category organizations have both a social and an economic competence. Following the publication of the Pirelli report in 1970, category organizations have been regrouped into 20 broad product market units, leading in at least one case – that of textiles and clothing – to the setting up of a federation of organizations.

There are more than 100 horizontal or territorial multi-industry organizations and their boundaries roughly correspond to the provinces into which Italy is divided. Following the publication of the Pirelli report, the territorial organizations too have been regrouped into broader units. Again, these are 20 in number and conform more or less to the regions into which administration has been divided since the early 1970s.

e SAF's membership is made up of some 40 organizations including the General Group which caters for the interests of those employers which do not fit neatly into specific occupational structures or whose number is too low to warrant a separate organization.

58

FIGURE 3.2 The Branch Organizations in Chemicals

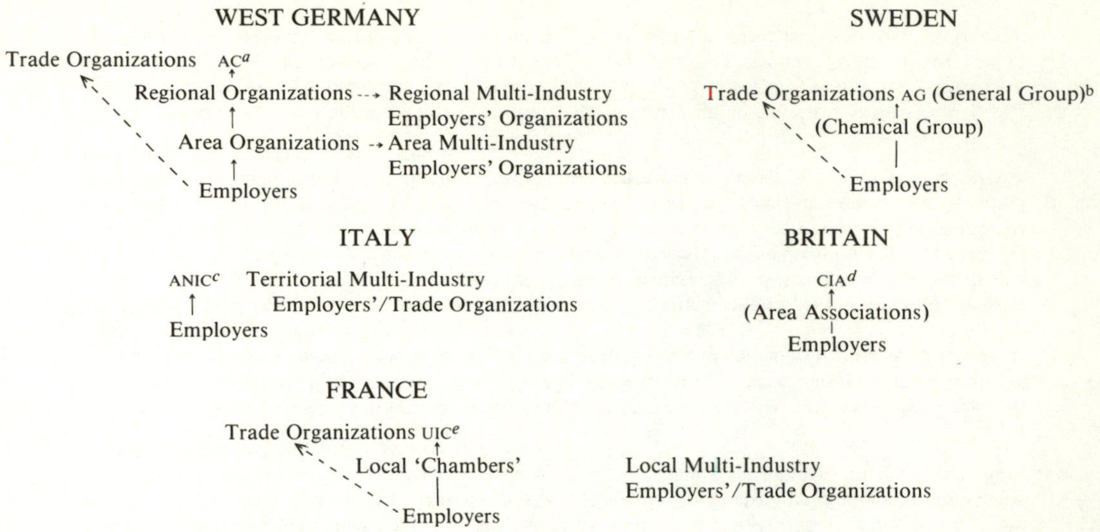

WEST GERMANY

Trade Organizations AC[a]

Regional Organizations --→ Regional Multi-Industry Employers' Organizations

Area Organizations --→ Area Multi-Industry Employers' Organizations

Employers

SWEDEN

Trade Organizations AG (General Group)[b]

(Chemical Group)

Employers

ITALY

ANIC[c] Territorial Multi-Industry Employers'/Trade Organizations

Employers

BRITAIN

CIA[d]

(Area Associations)

Employers

FRANCE

Trade Organizations UIC[e]

Local 'Chambers'

Local Multi-Industry Employers'/Trade Organizations

Employers

Notes:

[a] AC follows the same pattern as other branch organizations in West Germany in as much as its members are the regional or *Land* organizations.

[b] The chemical employers are the largest single section within AG.

[c] ANIC is a primary or unitary organization to which the individual employer adheres directly. It has no separate local or territorial organizations of its own, relying on the territorial organizations affiliated to CONFINDUSTRIA for this purpose.

[d] CIA is formally a primary or unitary organization, and its division into nine areas is largely for administrative purposes.

[e] Strictly speaking, UIC in France is a federation of employers' organizations. Its membership is composed of both vertical and horizontal organizations. The first group comprise some 50 trade associations which are based on products or product groupings. The second group comprises the regional organizations of UIC itself of which there are 28.

FIGURE 3.3 The Branch Organizations in Clothing

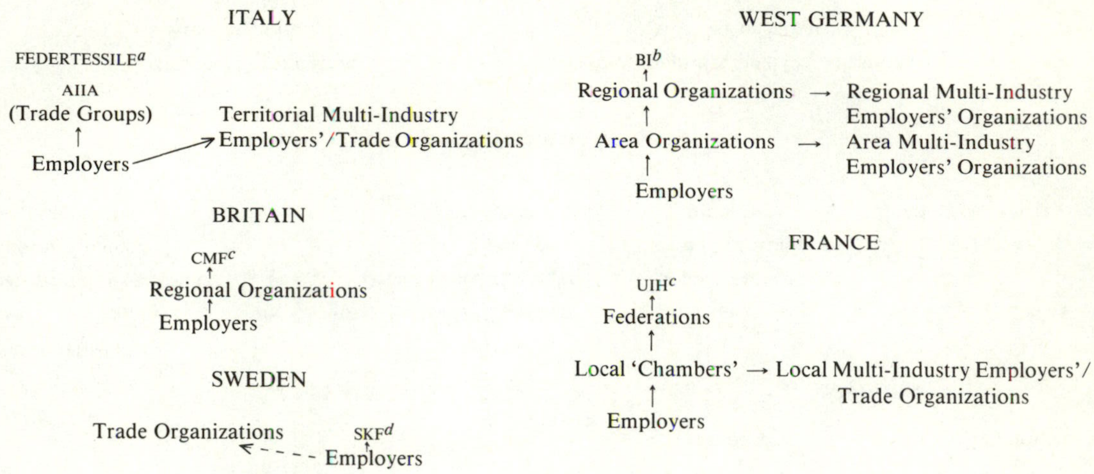

ITALY

FEDERTESSILE[a]
↑
AIIA
(Trade Groups)   Territorial Multi-Industry
↑   Employers'/Trade Organizations
Employers ——————→

WEST GERMANY

BI[b]
↑
Regional Organizations → Regional Multi-Industry
↑   Employers' Organizations
Area Organizations →   Area Multi-Industry
↑   Employers' Organizations
Employers

BRITAIN

CMF[c]
↑
Regional Organizations
↑
Employers

FRANCE

UIH[c]
↑
Federations
↑
Employers

Local 'Chambers' → Local Multi-Industry Employers'/
                   Trade Organizations

SWEDEN

SKF[d]
↑
Trade Organizations
← – – – Employers

Notes:

[a] FEDERTESSILE is a new grouping of employers in clothing and textiles. AIIA itself is divided internally into a number of sectors or groups covering the different branches of activity, but individual employers adhere directly to the national association. Local organization for the AIIA is provided by the territorial organizations affiliated to CONFINDUSTRIA.

[b] BI is structured very similarly to the other branch organizations in West Germany. Individual employers affiliate directly to area organizations of clothing employers; these area organizations are then grouped together in regional or *Land* organizations.

[c] CMF is composed of nine regional organizations of clothing manufacturers which are based on the major centres of the trade. The regional organization based on Leeds is the largest.

[d] SKF is a unitary organization. Like AIIA in Italy, it has close ties with the textile employers' organization.

[e] UIH is essentially a confederation of employers' organizations, grouping together five federations covering menswear, women's fashions, lingerie, corsets, and diverse activities. In the case of the first three confederations individual employers adhere through the intermediary of a number of regional organizations. The corset federation has a mixture of national and regional organizations. The remaining federation is composed of a number of organizations catering for specialist sectors.

60

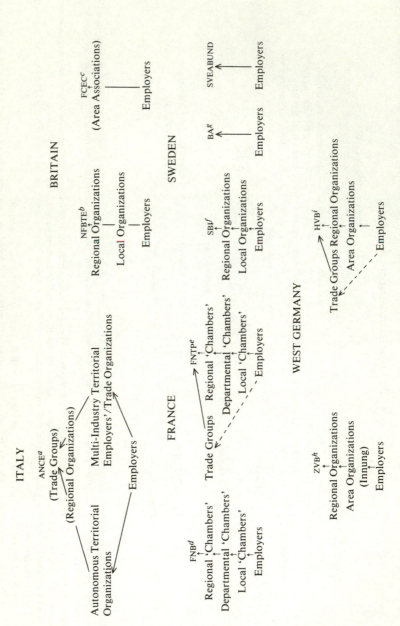

FIGURE 3.4 The Branch Organizations in Construction

Notes:

a In Italy ANCE is fairly unique so far as employers' organizations are concerned. In most cases individual employers adhere through the intermediary of the construction groups, sections or *sindacati* of the territorial organizations or of the territorial organization itself. But there are a number of territorial organizations of building/civil engineering employers which are autonomous; they maintain close links with the territorial organizations proper, but they are separate organizations and adhere directly to ANCE. The provinces of Milan, Rome and Turin are among those with autonomous territorial organizations. Provision has also been made for the setting up of structures on a regional basis in the light of an introduction of the 20 economic regions in 1971, but their competence is mainly if not exclusively economic.

b The internal structure of NFBTE in Britain has undergone considerable change in recent years. Prior to 1973 the NFBTE was formally a 'federal union of employers in the building industry, composed of regional and area or local groups'. The ten regions plus the Scottish organizations were divided into more than 250 local associations. In 1973 the NFBTE became 'an organization of employers in the building industry, having regions and local associations'. The regional and local or area organization now operate as branches of the national federation rather than as semi-autonomous organizations. One consequence has been a considerable reduction in the number of local associations.

c FCEC is essentially a primary or unitary organization, although membership is divided into eight areas.

d Individual employers adhere to FNB through the intermediary of the departmental 'chambers' of which there is one for each of the *départements*. In some cases there are more local 'chambers' each based on a town or district which might even be restricted to a particular trade such as masonry or carpentry. In recent years many of the responsibilities of the departmental 'chambers' in social affairs have been taken over by the regional 'chambers'. These roughly correspond to the regional areas designated by the government and originally had an economic competence only.

e In the case of FNTP in France the vertical organizations represent a number of product groups covering specialized processes, such as road, railway construction, electrical power distribution. The FNTP shares with the FNB the substructures of departmental 'chambers' and regional 'chambers' although in some areas there are local civil engineering associations and local associations of the specialist groups.

f Currently, the members of SBI are organized into some 30 local organizations of master builders which are grouped together into four regional organizations.

g BA and SVEABUND are essentially unitary organizations.

h ZV is composed of 23 regional organizations. This is significantly larger than the number of regions or *Länder* because in some cases craft associations have retained their autonomy and independence. The lowest level of organization within the ZVB remains the *Innung* and it is to this that the individual employer belongs. The *Innung* was the organization to which all employers in building in pre-First World War Germany had to belong in order to comply with government regulations on the control and supervision of apprenticeships and training.

i HVB has about 12 product groups

62

FIGURE 3.5 The Branch Organizations in Metalworking

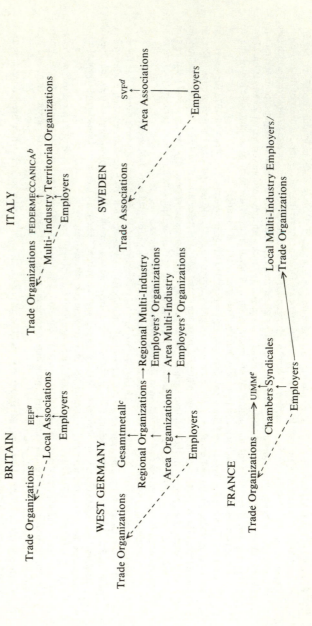

Notes:

a In the case of EEF in Britain, amalgamations – many of them fairly recent – have reduced the number of local associations to less than 20; on the formation of the EEF in 1896 there were 57. As in the case of UIMM and Gesamtmetall, the individual establishment belongs to the local organization. The largest local associations in terms of members are based on London and the West Midlands.

b Individual employers are affiliated to FEDERMECCANICA through the intermediary of the metalworking groups or sections of the territorial organizations which are affiliated to CONFINDUSTRIA or in cases where the metalworking group does not have its own identity, of the territorial organization itself. By far the largest concentration of metalworking employers is to be found in Turin and Milan. The situation in Turin is unique in that the metalworking employers have their own separately constituted organization, the Associazione Industriali Metallurgici Meccaniche Affini, which is affiliated to the territorial organization. Within ASSOLOMBARDA which is the territorial organization for the province of Milan, the employers in metalworking are organized into a Sindacato Metalmeccanici with a number of district or zone organizations.

c In the case of Gesamtmetall in West Germany two tiers are involved. Gesamtmetall's immediate members are the 15 regional or *Land* organizations of metalworking employers. Each of these regional organizations is then in turn composed of a number of area organizations of metalworking employers to which the individual establishment adheres directly. The largest concentration of metalworking employers is to be found in the North Rhine-Westphalia region; within this region there are four area organizations of which the largest has its headquarters in Cologne.

d Currently, SVF is divided into five area organizations: the north, south, east, west and Stockholm areas. Each has an area office in the main town of the area except for the north, whose area office is also in Stockholm. Within each area there are a number of 'co-ordination' groups which are the immediate point of contact for the majority of member employers.

e Membership of UIMM in France is composed of vertical and horizontal organizations. The vertical organizations are the trade associations whose membership is coterminous with that of the UIMM. The horizontal organizations are the regional or local 'chambers' which have an exclusively social competence like that of UIMM itself. With the important exceptions of the iron and steel industries in the north and Lorraine, where there are two separate organizations, the 'chambers' cater for employers involved in both production and transformation of metals. In principle each 'chamber' covers the area of a *département*, but there are exceptions. Also the number of establishments and workers covered by the different 'chambers' varies enormously. At one extreme there is the Paris region which in the late 1970s had some 6,500 establishments employing three quarters of a million workers, and at the other the Lot 'chamber'which in 1976 had only nine members employing 1,400 workers.

FIGURE 3.6 The Branch Organizations in Printing

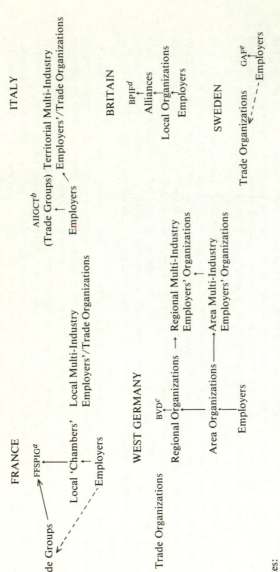

Notes:

a The constitution of FFSPIG makes provision for the affiliation of organizations which specialize in particular printing processes, but it is a condition of membership that these companies belong to the local *chambre syndicale*. In principle there is a local organization or *chambre syndicale* in each of the 95 *départements*.

b AIIGCT is essentially a unitary organization. It relies on the territorial organizations affiliated to CONFINDUSTRIA for its local organization.

c The structures of BVD and BDZ are similar to that of the other branch organizations in West Germany; they are divided into regional organizations which in turn subdivide into a number of area organizations.

d BPIF in Britain is made up of 14 member organizations, 10 of which are regional organizations, known as Alliances, the Society of Master Printers of Scotland and three Irish associations. The regional organizations or Alliances are then in turn made up of a number of local and district associations of which there were more than 100 in the late 1970s.

e GAF in Sweden has regional offices in Gothenburg and Malmö as well as Stockholm coverage; that is to say, their members come from the same branch of activity. The major exceptions to this generalization are the branch organizations in Italy. Local single-industry organizations are rare. Local organization in all five branches is provided by the multi-industry territorial organizations which are affiliated directly to CONFINDUSTRIA. In building/civil engineering and metalworking the memberships of ANCE and FEDERMECCANICA are composed of the territorial organizations; in clothing, chemicals and printing, membership of the national or category organization is composed of individual employers. One implication – and an indication of their relative standing – is that many employers in these three industries affiliate only to the territorial organization.

So far as explanations for the general pattern are concerned, the structuring of the branch organizations along horizontal as well as vertical lines is something which three of the countries have in common. These are France, Italy and West Germany. The common factor is the division of the country for administrative purposes. The primary organizations to which the individual employer is directly affiliated – both vertical and horizontal – more or less correspond with these divisions: in France with the *départements*, in Italy with the *provincie*, and in West Germany with the *Länder*. The introduction of a smaller number of economic regions in France and Italy in the early 1970s helps to explain the addition of a second tier of organizations in these countries.

In these and the other countries historical developments help to explain why employers' organizations in four of the industries tend to be *secondary* rather than *primary*. In most cases the immediate *primary* organizations pre-date the formation of the national organization or there is a long history of local organization.[17] In many cases too this primary organization assumed the responsibilities of a bargaining agent before the national organization. This is true of the multi-industry territorial organizations in Italy as well as the single-industry organizations in the other countries.

Another factor is the geographical location of employers. The development of local *primary* organizations of employers in industries such as building and metalworking reflects the widespread geographical distribution of employers. By contrast, employers in chemicals tend to be more concentrated geographically. This helps to explain why the employers in chemicals in Britain, Italy and Sweden are organized in essentially national *primary* organizations; why in France UIC only has 28 local 'chambers'; why in West Germany some of the regional or *Land* organizations are not further subdivided into area organizations.

---

[17] The major exceptions to this generalization are the local 'chambers' affiliated to UIMM in France. The national organization, UIMM, came first. The development of the local 'chambers' was subsequently sponsored from the centre.

Membership Density

It is difficult to be accurate about the membership density of employers' organizations. In some cases the internal organization discussed in the previous section makes the collection of membership data less than satisfactory; in building, printing and clothing, in particular, most employers are very small and in some sectors come and go quickly. There are also problems associated with the choice of measure. The proportion of the number of employers in membership to the total of those eligible is one measure, but the absence of a small number of large employers can detract from its significance. If the density of employment is used, there is the danger that a large number of employers may be ignored. The proportion of output or sales due to member employers are other measures which are sometimes used, but suffer from similar limitations to the density of employment. In view of these problems, the discussion which follows only seeks to give some idea of the relative density of membership.

The Employers' Confederations
The density of membership of the CBI is similar to that of the employers' confederations in the other countries. With some 80 per cent of employers in manufacturing in membership, the density of the CBI is about equal to that of CNPF and CONFINDUSTRIA. The membership density of the BDA and SAF is only slightly higher at approximately 90 per cent. Significantly, too, in Britain many of the employers who do not belong to their respective branch organizations are members of the CBI. One notable example is Ford which has never been a member of the EEF.

The Branch Employers' Organizations
In metalworking, it is safe to conclude that the density of membership of the EEF is considerably less than its counterparts in the other countries. The EEF estimates its members employ something like two thirds of those working in the engineering industry. This compares with the membership of FEDERMECCANICA in Italy estimated to be between 70 per cent and 80 per cent of employers eligible, and Gesamtmetall in Germany, SVF in Sweden and UIMM in France, all of which are believed to be over 90 per cent. It is significant too that some of the larger employers in engineering are not members of the EEF, whereas in the other countries the great majority of the larger employers are members of their employers' organization.[18]

The situation is not dissimilar in chemicals. The CIA in Britain estimates its membership among employers with more than 150 workers to be of

---

[18] Other examples of non-members of the EEF are International Business Machines (IBM), Massey-Ferguson, Talbot (formerly Chrysler), and Vauxhall. In 1979 GEC and Philips resigned from membership. Of the 25 engineering employers among the hundred largest employers in Britain in 1983, 19 remain in membership.

the order of 43 per cent, although these account for more than 80 per cent of sales. ANIC in Italy and UIC in France claim a membership density of approximately 80 per cent, and AC in Germany and SAF's General Group in Sweden more than 90 per cent. Again, some of the large employers such as ICI[19] were for many years significant by their non-membership of the employers' organization; with the formation of the CIA in 1965, by the merger of the Chemical and Allied Employers' Association with the Association of Chemical Manufacturers, many of these large employers assumed non-conforming status so far as the multi-employer agreements are concerned.

In building the membership density of the NFBTE, which is of the order of 60 per cent of total employment, is about the same as that of ANCE in Italy. It is exceeded in the three other countries. At about 95 per cent the density of the ZVB in Germany is especially high given the large number of small employers. This is to be explained by the fact that the local organizations of building employers, the *Innungen*, have quasi-statutory powers so far as apprenticeship and training are concerned.

In the other industries it is probably true to say that membership density in Britain is more nearly equal to that in the other countries. In civil engineering, for example, membership density is more or less complete in all five countries. With 90 per cent of output, the BPIF compares favourably with printing employers elsewhere, although the membership density of the BVD in West Germany and GAF in Sweden is even higher. In clothing, membership density of employers' organizations is probably less than 50 per cent as it is in the comparable organizations in the other countries.

One immediate conclusion this comparison prompts is that a high membership density is not a necessary condition for multi-employer bargaining any more than a single employers' organization. In building and clothing in Britain density is less than in engineering and yet these are the industries in which multi-employer bargaining is the predominant pattern.

There is another point to be made. The membership density of employers' organizations in metalworking and chemicals in Britain may be less than in the other countries, but the decision of the large employers such as Ford not to be a member of their employers' organization cannot simply be explained in terms of a preference for independence or opposition in principle to multi-employer bargaining. The same goes for employers such as ICI who have withdrawn from membership of their employers' organization. Significantly, many of these employers have not been

[19] In fact, Mond, who was a major figure in the emergence of ICI, had also been a founder member of the chemical employers' organization in 1918. ICI subsequently withdrew from membership in 1935, but remained in membership of the separate trade organization. Hence the introduction of non-conforming status to allow employers such as ICI to remain in membership without an obligation to honour the multi-employer agreement on the amalgamation of the employers' organization and the trade organization in 1965.

reluctant to join employers' organizations and to engage in multi-employer bargaining in the other countries. The case of Ford in West Germany has already been quoted in chapter 2. Massey-Ferguson is an example in France. So it would appear that their decision depends on the practice of multi-employer bargaining in each country.

Legal Status

Prior to the passage of the Industrial Relations Act 1971, most employers' organizations in Britain came within the definition of a trade union under the 1871 and subsequent Trade Union Acts. In practice, this meant they were given special immunities for activities which previously would have been regarded as in restraint of trade. As employers' organizations, they did not have corporate status, however, although some of them obtained it by registration under the various Companies Acts. Like membership of trade unions, membership of employers' organizations was entirely voluntary. The Industrial Relations Act 1971 gave individual workers the right to belong to a registered trade union but it did not extend the right of association to employers. Similarly, the 1971 Act did not extend to employers' organizations the recognition rights accorded to registered trade unions. It simply required employers' organizations to register separately from trade unions. The same distinctions were maintained by the Trade Union and Labour Relations Act of 1974 and the Amendment Act of the same name in 1976; employers' organizations were given a separate definition from trade unions and an option between corporate and unincorporated status.

In two respects the legal status of employers' organizations in the other countries is not dissimilar. First, employers' organizations enjoy some form of recognized corporate status; that is to say, they can own property and can sue and be sued in their own name. Second, the membership of employers' organizations is voluntary; employers are free to join or not to join.[20]

---

[20] It is important to point out that this discussion reflects the situation in the post-Second World War period. Prior to 1945 the legal framework in France, Germany and Italy dealt very differently with the relationship between employers and their organizations. The legal framework gave employers' organizations *de jure* or *de facto* the exclusive right to represent the interests of individual employers. In Imperial Germany the trade organizations from which employers' organizations emerged had legal support in many industries for their *cartel* activities: in building/civil engineering membership of the *Innungen* or local organizations of employers was compulsory. When the Nazis came to power, employers' organizations dissolved themselves, but trade organizations were reorganized and membership made compulsory by the Law of 27 February 1934. In Italy the Law of 3 April 1926 gave exclusive legal recognition to six groups of employers in the private sector including CONFINDUSTRIA. Strictly speaking, employers' organizations in France were dissolved by the Vichy government, but the Law of 16 August 1940 gave their representatives a position of dominance on the 'organization committees' which were set up to run industry.

The major difference concerns the rights of the individual employer *vis-à-vis* employers' organizations and will be discussed in more detail in the next chapter. In France, Sweden and West Germany, the various statutes dealing with collective bargaining recognize the right of individual employers to belong to employers' organizations and to be represented by them in collective bargaining with trade unions; it would be unlawful for a trade union to seek to deny this right just as it would be unlawful for the employer to seek to deny individual workers the right to belong to a trade union. The situation in Italy is only slightly different. There has been no specific legislation in the post-Second World War period dealing with collective bargaining. Nonetheless, the right of association, which applies equally to employers and employees, is set out unequivocally in the 1948 Constitution.

The Costs of Membership

The bulk of the revenue of employers' organizations to cover recurrent expenditure comes from subscriptions. Some require the payment of an entry fee on joining, but this makes a relatively small contribution. Again, the arrangements are broadly similar. The great majority relate subscriptions to some formula which depends on the wage bill of the members; in some cases there are separate calculations for manual and non-manual workers, but usually the total wage bill is used. Some organizations collect subscriptions on a per capita basis. FEDERMECCANICA of Italy does this as did the CMF in Britain. A third group bases subscriptions on both the labour and capital employed. The CIA in Britain is an example; and the UIC in France levies its national trade association members on their turnover, but its local 'chambers' according to their wage bill. Finally, a number of organizations operate a sliding-scale formula in order to taper-off the contribution of the large employers; SVF in Sweden and the BPIF in Britain are examples.

Many employers' organizations set the rate of subscription annually. Because of this and the complexity of the arrangements for collecting subscriptions, it is difficult to give the precise details on any comparable basis. Overall, however, the total subscription paid to employers' organizations rarely exceeds 0.5 per cent of the wage bill. It is difficult to believe, then, that the costs of membership are a major consideration in themselves in the decision of individual employers to affiliate.

Comparatively, the report of the Commission of Inquiry into Industrial and Commercial Representation (1972: 74) estimated that in 1972 the income of the CBI was roughly equal to that of the CNPF in France in 1972. It was slightly more than that of the BDA in West Germany, but it was only about half as much as the total income of the BDA and the BDI (the trade confederation). Notwithstanding that CONFINDUSTRIA has a very much smaller membership, the Commission estimated that its income was twice as much as the CBI's. So far as the branch employers' organiz- ations are concerned, the report (74–5) concluded that 'the British organizations generally enjoy incomes at the best at a level of two thirds though more generally, nearer one half of their nearest continental counterparts'.

Taking all things into consideration, however, it is difficult to believe this difference in income is of major significance in the context of the present study. Apart from mutual aid schemes, which are separately funded, there are no obvious items of expenditure to distinguish the employers' organizations in Britain from those in the other countries. It could be argued that the quality of service is inferior. But the resources of employers' organizations cannot be measured in strict financial terms only. As a subsequent section points out, employers' organizations rely upon the willingness of individual employers to provide representatives for a wide range of time-consuming posts of responsibility. There is no real evidence available one way or the other, but it could be that the con- tribution of British employers is higher on this count.[21] Finally – and perhaps most importantly – the sums of money involved have to be kept in proportion. For the individual employer the costs of membership are relatively insignificant. Had the role and activities of the branch organizations in Britain justified higher subscriptions, the money would probably have been forthcoming.

Range of Activities

Representation is one of the major activities of the employers' organizations in all the countries. In this respect the employers' organizations in Britain are no different from those in the other countries. The interests represented may be individual or collective. The target may be central or local government, trade unions or the public at large. The representation can also take many forms; a telephone call, lobbying, publicity campaigns, financial support for individuals and groups willing to act on the members' behalf. Employers' organizations are also a major source of recruitment for the numerous permanent and *ad hoc* representative bodies which have proliferated in the post-war period due largely to government intervention in the management of the economy.

There is one difference between Britain and the other countries which is perhaps significant. In the other countries the restriction of membership of

[21] Clearly, it is difficult to give precise details about the amount of time that representatives spend on the activities of employers' organizations. Some small indication comes from the following estimates made by Unilever in Britain in respect of the food industry which comprises about a quarter of their business. Unilever representatives held 15 committee chairmanships, 12 seats on main policy-making boards, and 44 committee seats (Grant, 1983: 14).

the employers' confederation to employers' organizations helps to ensure that individual employers have to use these organizations as their representative in the first instance. In Britain, on the other hand, membership of the employers' confederation has been open to individual employers as well as employers' organizations since the formation of the CBI in 1965. This means that the individual employer has direct access to the employers' confederation; he does not have to be a member of the relevant branch organization. Evidently, the relatively recent origins of this development mean that it cannot be counted a significant factor in the decline of multi-employer bargaining in Britain. It could be argued, nonetheless, that it has served to undermine the authority of the branch organizations.

As well as representation, employers' organizations provide a wide range of services for their members. For the purposes of discussion, the significance of these can be considered under two main headings.

Trade Organization Activities

Overall, there is little evidence to suggest that trade organization activities are significant one way or the other from the point of view of the present study. Unlike the BDA in West Germany and SAF in Sweden,[22] the CBI is both a trade organization and employers' organization. But it is not the only body to have this dual purpose: the CNPF in France and CONFINDUSTRIA in Italy also have it. Moreover, at the branch level there are marked similarities between the countries. In all five countries the main organization in metalworking is an employers' organization concerned exclusively with social affairs. In building/civil engineering, on the other hand, social affairs and trade and commerce are the responsibility of the same organization in all five countries. In the other three industries there is no uniform pattern of organization. The branch organizations are both employers' and trade organizations in Britain, France and Italy; whereas Sweden has separate employers' and trade organizations in all three industries and West Germany has separate organizations in chemicals and printing, but a combined employers'/trade organization in clothing.

In the case of metalworking and building/civil engineering the explanations for the similarities between the countries seem fairly straightforward. In metalworking the materials are more or less common and so too is the technology, but the products are very different. It would

---

[22] In West Germany, the Bundesverband der Deutschen Industrie is the peak organization so far as economic and commercial affairs are concerned. The counterpart of the BDI in Sweden is the *Sveriges Industriforbund*. In both cases separate representation has a long history. In Germany the ZDI and BI – both essentially trade associations – had been responsible for establishing separate employers' confederations in 1904. The division was repeated after the Second World War. However, relations between BDA and BDI are close and it has not been unknown for the same person to head both organizations simultaneously. In Sweden SAF was formed in 1902 in the wake of the strike over the political suffrage. Subsequently, there was a proposal that the organization be divided into two sections, one dealing with industrial relations and one with other matters of common interest. But nothing came of this, and SIF was formed in 1910.

be unrealistic to expect one organization to cover the different – in some cases conflicting – trade and commercial interests of the many product groups. To quote an example, the membership coverage of UIMM in France divides up into more than 150 national trade associations.

In building and civil engineering the situation offers a strong contrast. Clearly, within the two broad categories of building and civil engineering the nature of the product or service is much less diverse than in metal-working. But there are other important factors. It is difficult to separate the negotiations of rates of pay from agreed arrangements for tendering. Also issues of training and safety spill over into public accountability. Building employers in West Germany, for example, have to belong to the *Innungen* in order to comply with government regulations on the control and supervision of apprenticeships and training. Membership of an employers' organization in civil engineering is one important way of offering a guarantee of acceptable standards of performance and it is thus almost obligatory.

In the case of the other three branches there is no obvious explanation for the differences between the countries. It is tempting to look for one in the fact that in Sweden and West Germany there exist separate employers' and trade confederations. But, given the situation in building and civil engineering in both countries, where there are combined employers'/trade organizations, it is not as convincing as it seems.

Employers' Organization Activities
Besides the negotiation of multi-employer agreements, which will be the subject of the following chapter, employers' organizations are engaged in a wide range of activities on behalf of their members in their capacity as employers. At the risk of over-simplification, these may be considered under two main headings: management services and mutual aid.

Management Services. In principle, there is no difference between employers' organizations in Britain and the other countries so far as the provision of management services is concerned. These services are provided whenever members decide that they are in the common interest. The main difference is to be found in the particular services provided. In the other countries – and in France and West Germany especially – a major activity of employers' organizations is the analysis and dissemination of information relating to legislation and legal decisions. Indeed, given the links that exist between the multi-employer agreements and statutes it is often difficult to distinguish the interpretation of the one from the other. Again, to give one example only, most of the departments into which the headquarters staff of UIMM in Paris is divided concentrate on giving specialist advice in such matters as contracts of employment and collective agreements, regulation of work and collective disputes, workers' representation, social security and pensions, and health and safety.

This is not to suggest employers' organizations in Britain do not provide advice on the implications of legislation. Legislation dealing with the contracts of employment, redundancy, training, unfair dismissal, sex and race, health and safety has had a major impact. Nearly 80 per cent of establishments in the Warwick Survey (Brown, 1981: 21) reported that their branch organization offered advice on labour law matters; nearly 60 per cent said they had made use of it.

The point is, in Britain, the advisory and consultancy services tend to be available across a broader front, largely reflecting the shift in emphasis from multi-employer to single-employer bargaining that has taken place. Employers' organization officials not only give advice on the application and interpretation of multi-employer agreements. They are often intimately involved in the negotiations which arise from the invoking of the disputes procedure in the multi-employer agreement. Indeed, responsibility for the operation of the disputes procedure continues to be a major activity – and a major reason for membership – even in those industries, such as engineering, in which the effectiveness of multi-employer bargaining on substantive issues has declined. For example, the Warwick Survey (Brown, 1981: 20) carried out in 1978 suggested that on average employers had made use of the disputes procedure just over twice in the previous two years; compared with five years previously, about a quarter reported an increase in usage and only 8 per cent a reduction.

The Warwick Survey (Brown, 1981: 21) also confirmed most employers' organizations in Britain provided a wide range of services – on recruitment, education and training, work study and bonus schemes, job evaluation, local pay levels – as well as legislation. It also suggested there had been a considerable increase in the use of these services over the past five years; some 37 per cent of establishments in the survey reported an increase, and only 2 per cent a decline. Contrary to what might have been expected, demand also tended to be greater among the larger employers. There can be little doubt that provision of these services is a major factor in explaining why membership remains relatively high considering the decline in the effectiveness of multi-employer bargaining; and why there has been an increase in membership especially among medium-sized and smaller employers. Paradoxically, it also means that in some cases employers' organizations probably exercise greater influence over workplace industrial relations in Britain than ever before.

Mutual Aid.   The provision of mutual aid in the event of industrial conflict is one of the oldest functions that employers' organizations have performed for their members; in many cases such provision pre-dates the development of collective bargaining. It can take many forms: an agreement not to offer employment to strikers or trade union members; an understanding that in the event of industrial action there will be no poaching of customers from members or that raw materials or other supplies will be pooled or that the payment of bills will be postponed; and a scheme, either *ad hoc* or permanent, for the provision of financial assistance to the members who are involved in industrial action.

It is with the permanent financial schemes that this section is primarily concerned. At the risk of over-simplification, two main types may be identified. The first takes the form of a mutual insurance policy. It is essentially passive in operation. The employer pays into a fund on a regular basis and is compensated in the event of suffering from industrial action. Under the second type of scheme the employer also pays into a fund on a regular basis. The fund is not only used, however, to compensate the employer who suffers directly from industrial action. It is also used to finance a sympathetic lockout on the part of employers who are not immediately experiencing such action. In other words, the scheme is used offensively to raise the level and, more importantly, the cost of the industrial action to the trade union and its members.

At the time of the research, there did not appear to be any examples of either type of scheme in Britain. The EEF had operated mutual insurance schemes for many years, but the most recent was terminated in 1976. There did not appear to be any examples at all in Italy.

In France the only example which was found was in metalworking. Like the EEF, UIMM has operated mutual insurance schemes since the early 1900s. The most recent scheme was introduced in 1972. It requires members subscribing to it to pay 0.2 per cent of their wage bill each year. Subject to stringent criteria, the subscriber subject to industrial action can claim an amount equal to two thirds of the wages not paid during the dispute.

In Sweden and West Germany employers' organizations have extended the mutual insurance scheme to cover the financing of sympathetic lockouts. In Sweden, SAF – the employers' confederation – has been the main repository of funds to finance sympathetic lockouts since its formation in 1902. The details are described in the footnote below.[23] In

[23] The scheme revolves around the unique relationship which exists between the individual employer and SAF. The individual employer is not only a member of the relevant branch organization affiliated to SAF; he is also a 'partner' or *delegare* of SAF. The annual subscription which he pays to SAF is designed to cover operating expenses and to produce a surplus for the insurance fund which is used to compensate those employers who suffer industrial action. Additionally, the individual employer pays an annual 'liability sum' into a 'guaranty' fund for use in emergencies. Otherwise, the money remains with the individual employer. In fact, the 'guaranty' fund, which stood at some 875 million crowns in 1974, has not been called upon since the 1920s. The money in the insurance fund appears to have been equal to its task. The employer who experiences loss due to industrial action is entitled to compensation at a standard rate of the wage and salary bill for each day of the strike or lockout. Significantly, however, payment of compensation is subject to a number of conditions which serve to give SAF very considerable powers in its relationship with individual employers. For example, Article 31 of the constitution allows the Board of SAF to exceed the minimum levels of compensation 'in proportion to the direct loss which the partner has sustained'. In practice, this usually occurs when only a small number of employers are involved. Section 3 of Article 31 states that no compensation is paid out if the strike or

West Germany, mutual insurance funds existed prior to the First World War and were re-established in a number of industries in the early 1930s. A policy decision to re-establish them again was taken in 1956 at the Annual General meeting of the BDA. The fund was constituted in 1964 and covers Gesamtmetall and eight other branch organizations.

The schemes in Sweden and West Germany do not simply exist on paper. As recently as 1980, SAF initiated a lockout in Sweden following industrial action by members of LO and PTK in support of a pay claim. In 1978 and 1978–9 in West Germany the employers' organizations in printing and steel respectively ordered sympathetic lockouts of sections of their members; the engineering employers did so in 1984. Significantly, the disputes involved issues over which the BPIF and the EEF in Britain suffered embarrassing setbacks in 1979; the introduction of new technology in printing and a reduction in the 40-hour week in engineering.[24].

So how significant are these schemes in the context of the present study? Certainly the ability of employers' organizations in Sweden and West Germany to finance sympathetic lockouts gives them advantages their British counterparts do not possess. Although the effect of the deterrent on the trade union is incalculable, the level and the cost of industrial action to the trade union are raised considerably. At the same time, the effectiveness of the employers' organization is demonstrated to the individual employer. He, in turn, becomes more strongly bound by its decisions. Having said this, it has to be remembered that UIMM's is the only current example of a mutual insurance scheme in France and no such schemes exist in Italy.[25] It also has to be remembered that for many years the EEF in Britain operated a scheme similar to UIMM's. Whatever their significance in Sweden and West Germany, then, mutual aid schemes are not a necessary condition for multi-employer bargaining.

Government

A reading of the relatively few studies of decision-making in employers' organizations would suggest there are significant differences in the

---

lockout does not last longer than eleven days. Furthermore, if the employer has 'taken unjustified measures' against his employees which prolong the action there is no right of compensation. In practice the Board has also established two further conditions for compensation in the event of unlawful or wild-cat strikes:

(a) that no concessions are made to strikers which undermine SAF's authority and the strength of the national agreements; and

(b) that compensation is only paid when the unconstitutional/illegal strikers are sued in the national Labour Court by the employer.

[24] The lockouts in West Germany are discussed in Butler (1980). For the dispute in the engineering industry in Britain, see Rice (1980).
[25] In France and Italy the legal framework is especially important so far as the sympathetic lockout is concerned. For further details, see chapter 5.

machinery of their government. British commentators (Wigham, 1973 on the EEF and Grant and Marsh 1977 on the CBI, have tended to emphasize the difficulties which employers' organizations have in reconciling the interests of their complex memberships. In contrast, West German commentators (Schmölders, 1965; Buchholz, 1969; and Noé, 1970) emphasize the relative ease with which employers' organizations are able to develop a community of interest.[26] There are differences of interest between the large and small employers, it is pointed out, but they are rare and usually quickly resolved. Particular attention is given to the important leadership role of the small number of large employers, while the majority are involved indirectly through participation in the ratification process at the *Land* level and, more generally, at area level.

Certainly the unique membership structure of the CBI appears to have imposed an extremely unwieldy set of constitutional arrangements. In particular, the problems associated with determining the appropriate balance between employers' and trade organizations, on the one hand, and individual company members on the other, more or less obliged the CBI to adopt the constitutional arrangements of the FBI. This means the CBI is governed by a Council of no less than 400 members which meets every month. By comparison, the constitutional arrangements of the employers' confederations in the other countries are relatively straightforward. Like most of the branch employers' organizations discussed below, they have a hierarchy of annual general meetings, general councils, and executive or management committees, together with consultative or standing committees.

In practice, however, the significance of the differences is not as great as may at first appear. Again, it has to be remembered that the CBI is of relatively recent origin; the constitutional arrangements of the British Employers' Confederation were very similar to those of the employers' confederations in the other countries. Also the president's committee set up in 1974 performs much the same function within the CBI as the small executive or management committees in the other countries. Constitutionally, the president's committee is one of the CBI's standing committees. Yet it has much wider terms of reference than the other standing committees; its task is 'to advise the president on major policy issues; and to keep the CBI's public position and overall strategy under review'. Its members also include the chairmen of the other most important standing committees such as employment policy and the small firms' council.

A comparison of the constitutions of the branch employers' organizations suggests a great deal of similarity from one industry to another and one country to another. For example, most local primary organizations usually hold an annual general meeting or general assembly that elects an executive

26 Interestingly enough, the French and Italian literature also stress the difficulties which employers' organizations have in maintaining a common front. See, for example, Brizay (1975), Ammassari (1976) and Collida *et al.* (1972).

council or management board. The executive council is responsible for the day-to-day government of the organization and for the election of the chairman or president who is the chief officeholder; it is also responsible for the appointment of the members of the secretariat. The organizations at the national level also have annual general meetings and executive committees. In addition, a number – especially those which are federations or secondary organizations – may have a general council that fits in between the two. In this case the general council may elect the chairman or president: it may in effect subsume the responsibilities of the annual general meeting. Some national organizations also have a smaller management or president's committee whose members are drawn from the executive committee.

Most national organizations, and the larger local organizations, also make provision in their constitutions for consultative or standing committees. Their task is to advise the executive committee on matters of policy and detail. Most are functional and deal with such matters as collective bargaining or education and training; some may have the responsibility for advising on the interests of employers in specific sectors or of the smaller employers in general.

There is also a basic pattern of representation. In many local *primary* organizations every member is entitled to take part in the annual general meeting. In the organizations at the national level – especially those which are federations or secondary organizations – representation of the *primary* organizations is determined by the amount of the subscription or the number of employees or the size of the wage bill or some combination thereof. Similar formulae are used to determine representation on the general council and the executive committee. In some cases, however, membership of the executive committee is mainly *ex-officio*; it is composed of the chairman or president of the local primary organizations. For example, the executive committee of Gesamtmetall in West Germany comprises the chairman of the 15 *Land* or regional organizations; that of SVF in Sweden comprises the chairmen of the five area committees. Most members of the consultative or standing committees are appointed on the basis of their specialist expertise.

Variations on this basic pattern are largely to be explained in terms of the complexity of membership. For example, small employers are in the great majority. Inevitably, however, representation which is based on the amount of the subscription or the number of employees or the size of the wage bill gives a relative advantage to the large employers. So too does the provision that the executive committee should be composed of the chairmen or presidents of the primary organizations, for it is unlikely that the small employers can supply candidates for such time-consuming posts of responsibility. This imbalance is often offset by putting a ceiling on the representation that the number of employees or the size of the wage bill might otherwise justify. In other cases small employers are given direct representation on the executive committee. Most of the branch organizations in Italy do this; so does the SVF in Sweden. In the case of the branch organization in Italy the representatives come from the specially-constituted consultative committees that look after the interests of the small employers.

To take another example, the branch organizations may have members in a wide range of product markets and the secondary organizations may be founded on national trade associations as well as local employers' organizations. In some cases – the UIC in France and the HVB in West Germany are examples – the national trade associations or trade groupings have direct representation on the executive council. In others there are specialist consultative or sector committees which look after the interests of specific trade groups; here the chairman or president of these committees may be *ex-officio* members. ANCE in Italy is an example.

The constitutional arrangements of UIMM in France are perhaps one of the best examples of the attempt to accommodate members with wide-ranging interests. The structure of the decision-making bodies is intended to deal with the two fundamental problems of the organization: first, the division of competence between UIMM and the national trade associations; and, second, the diversity of member employers so far as size, specialism, and geographical situation are concerned. Under the general assembly, which consists of the presidents and vice-presidents of the member organizations, there are two managing bodies. There is a metal production council for the primary metals industries which are characterized by a high degree of concentration both geographically and in terms of a number of multi-plant companies; it has some 40 members. Then there is a metal manufacturers' council which represents most of the small- and medium-size employers in the engineering industry generally; it has 120 members, one quarter of whom come from the national trade associations and three quarters from the regional organizations or local 'chambers'. Linking the two councils, there is a common board which has the job of formulating the policy of the two sections; it has 28 members appointed in equal numbers from the two councils. Like them, it meets every month. The common board, and hence UIMM itself, is headed by a president elected for a two-year period. In recent years this office has been filled in rotation by the presidents of the two councils largely because of the tensions between the two sectors.

In these and other cases, the representatives involved are very rarely members of the full-time secretariat of the employers' organizations. The representatives may spend a considerable amount of time on its affairs. Indeed, they may in effect be full-time. Invariably, however, they are senior executives of the member enterprises. Senior offices are likely to be filled by the chairmen or managing directors of the more important member enterprises. In the collective bargaining committee mentioned above these officers are likely to be senior personnel executives. By implication, the relationship between lay representatives and full-time officials of an employers' organization is very different from that in a trade union. Essentially, full-time officials are there to provide a secretarial service. They may be able to exercise considerable influence over policy, but have no power base of their own, and very rarely are in a position where they can exercise leadership. They must work through and with lay representatives.

The finding that employers' organizations share a common pattern of government should not come as a surprise. Employers' organizations are faced with a common problem, namely that of accommodating the often conflicting interests of members that are essentially independent organizations in their own right. If an analogy between the government of employers' organizations and trade unions is wanted, the most appropriate would be with the trade union confederation. Special provision may be made for voting arrangements dependent on the kinds of formulae already discussed in respect of representation. For the most part, however, decisions have to be arrived at by consensus. This is not to say that there are no sanctions available to bring recalcitrant members into line. For example, in the event of industrial action, the larger employers may be able to bring suppliers who are members of the same organization into line by threatening to cut off future business. But there are limits to what can be done. Certainly, employers' organizations cannot stand too many expulsions or resignations. As well as the psychological impact such action may have, especially during negotiations with trade unions, the ability of the individual employer to deal separately with trade unions poses a major threat to those who remain in membership.

In the final analysis the only thing that binds the members of employers' organizations together is a sense of common interest. If that is lacking, no amount of constitutional drafting and re-drafting will improve matters. Issues that might prove to be divisive have to be avoided at all costs. Critically important here is the experience of the members. For example, if collective action has been demonstrably successful in the past, it may become an accepted course of action. If there is no such record, then collective action will represent a leap in the dark. It may not be possible even to raise it as an issue for debate. It is perhaps this sense of common interest or, rather, the lack of it, that distinguishes employers' organizations in Britain from those in the other countries. That said, the ability to generate or sustain a sense of common interest would appear to have little, if anything, to do with the structural characteristics of employers' organizations investigated in this chapter. The logical conclusion must be that it is, instead, a reflection of the practice of collective bargaining. In short, collective action is largely a thing of the past in Britain because of the decline of multi-employer bargaining; the more distant its experience, the more difficult it becomes to contemplate.

Conclusions

Overall, then, there would appear to be a number of similarities in the structure and government of employers' organizations in the five countries. The membership coverage of the CBI and the branch employers' organizations is similar to that of their counterparts in the other countries. Likewise the membership density of the CBI and the branch employers' organizations in clothing, construction, and printing is broadly comparable with that of the parallel organizations in the other countries. Furthermore, whether or not an employers' organization also fulfils the functions of a trade organization would appear to be a reflection of the industry. It is true that, unlike its counterparts, the CBI accepts individual employers as members and this affects its constitutional and financial arrangements. Yet these are relatively recent developments; the British Employers' Confederation, which preceded the CBI, was structured in exactly the same way as the employers' confederations in the other countries. Employers' organizations in general, it has been argued, are confronted with a common problem, namely that of accommodating the often conflicting interests of members which are independent organizations in their own right. It is this that moulds their constitutions to a common pattern.

As well as aspects of the legal framework, which will be discussed in more detail in chapter 5, only one significant difference has emerged in the comparison of the structure, activities and government of employers' organizations in Britain and the other countries. Membership density in the chemical and metalworking industries in Britain would appear to be considerably lower than in the other countries. In particular, a number of the larger employers in Britain, such as Ford or ICI, are not members of their branch employers' organization or are non-conforming members so far as multi-employer bargaining is concerned. The intriguing point is that in the other countries these same employers are members of employers' organizations and a party to the multi-employer agreements for which they are responsible. It seems not unfair to conclude, then, that membership and, indeed, the sense of common interest that employers' organizations in the other countries appear to generate, are reflections of the practice of multi-employer bargaining.

4

Centralized or Decentralized Negotiations?

This chapter compares and contrasts the levels at which multi-employer bargaining takes place. The first section deals with the situation in the five industries or branches of activity, and the second with the role of the employers' confederations. In view of a number of apparently contradictory findings, the third and final section discusses the overall significance of the levels of multi-employer bargaining.

The Level of Negotiations within the Branches

Other things being equal, the hierarchy of branch employers' organizations described in the previous chapter means in many industries it is possible for multi-employer bargaining to take place at a variety of levels. It might be expected on *a priori* grounds, however, that multi-employer bargaining at the local level would have stronger appeal for employers than at higher levels. Multi-employer bargaining at this level makes it possible to tailor agreements to suit the particular circumstances of the local labour market, if not necessarily to standardize pay and the other conditions of employment. It also means employers who are close competitors will be affected more or less equally in the event of industrial action being taken by trade unions. It remains to be seen what happens in practice.

Britain
Although in Britain multi-employer bargaining first developed in the five industries on a local or regional basis, since the end of the First World War it has taken place at the national level, albeit in chemicals and printing there are a number of national bargaining units. As Clegg and

his colleagues (1964: 133–68) have argued, much of the impetus for the shift of negotiations from local or regional to national level came from employers themselves. The object was to impose some form of control over the unilateral regulation of craft unions by the introduction of procedures for handling disputes. This was successfully achieved in engineering in 1898 with the introduction of the 'Provisions for Avoiding Disputes'. In building, a national conciliation board was introduced in 1908. In printing, employers were less successful in controlling the activities of craft unions through the use of procedures; the emergence of bargaining agents in the Linotype Association, the forerunner of the Newspaper Society, and the then British Federation of Master Printers was bound up with the negotiation of pay and conditions and the hours question respectively.

Even so, the main impetus for the shift in the level of negotiations came not from employers, but from government. It is sufficient to note here that the passage of the Trade Board Act of 1909, which provided for statutory minimum wages in specified industries, led to the setting up of the clothing industry's first national employers' organization; that the setting up by the government of the Committee of Production in February 1915 and other arbitration bodies led directly to bargaining over pay at this level in industries such as engineering and chemicals;[1] and that the implementation of the recommendations of the Whitley Committee consolidated the trend and extended national bargaining to the other basic terms and conditions of employment. In short, multi-employer bargaining at the national level was firmly established during and immediately following the First World War, although it took many years in some cases to phase out differences between districts and regions.[2]

There has never been any serious attempt on the part of employers to change this situation. The issue of district versus national negotiations was debated at some length by engineering employers in the early 1920s, but they decided to stay with national negotiations (Wigham, 1973: 116). National negotiations made it possible to restrain the more prosperous districts that might otherwise establish embarrassing precedents; and

[1] The rising cost of living during the first two years of the war meant wages had to be adjusted frequently. In engineering there had been two rounds of wage increases, mostly in the form of war bonuses, brought about by a number of local claims, dealt with through the engineering procedure or by reference to the Committee of Production, which had been established in February 1915, and other arbitration bodies. The Amalgamated Society of Engineers complained about the delay involved in claims going through the procedure and then to arbitration and so started to send claims directly from District Conferences to the Committee of Production. On the suggestion of Askwith, Chairman of the Committee of Production, the two sides met to decide whether future applications could be dealt with on a uniform basis. Out of these discussions emerged the National Wage Agreement early in 1917 which provided for the Committee of Production to meet at four-monthly intervals to consider what adjustments in wages were to be necessary. These adjustments were then to be applied across the board. For further details, see Wigham (1973: 86–94).

[2] For a discussion of some of the problems in achieving a truly national wage structure in the engineering industry, see Wigham (1973: 142–3).

during the years of depression they provided the machinery through which wage cuts could be imposed with the minimum of fuss. The fear of leap-frogging lay behind the opposition to later proposals for the fragmentation of the engineering industry into different sectors and the setting-up of a separate organization representing the motor manufacturers (Wigham, 1973: 143, 198–206). Increasingly in the 1960s and 1970s the debate about the most appropriate levels of multi-employer bargaining has given way to that about developments in workplace bargaining. The question which must be asked then, is whether the shift in the level of negotiations from local to national level was a major factor in the decline in the effectiveness of multi-employer bargaining in Britain?

Italy

The evidence from the other countries suggests not. Britain is not unique in having branch negotiations at national level. The most important branch negotiations take place at this level in Italy too. The common factor in each country is the involvement of government. Prior to the First World War any multi-employer bargaining which took place in Italy was very much a local affair and was conducted by the multi-industry territorial organizations or a constituent group.[3] Multi-employer bargaining at the national level emerged only in the immediate post-war period. Against the background of food shortages and mounting social unrest, considerable pressure was put upon employers by the Giolitti government to concede trade union demands for an 8-hour day. This was done by the metalworking employers in the north in February 1919. A national agreement was signed in building a year later and in chemicals in 1920. In each case the agreements encompassed other issues as well as the 8-hour day (Olivetti, 1922).

Under the fascist regime the employers' confederations assumed the responsibility for the negotiation of collective agreements. Even so, national agreements were used as the vehicle for enforcing the regulations of the Charter of Labour of 1927 and subsequent legislation and royal decrees. Only wage scales were set at provincial level in the light of the cost of living.

In the immediate post-Second World War period single-industry category organizations affiliated to CONFINDUSTRIA assumed the responsibilities for the negotiation of the procedural or normative aspects of collective agreements at branch level. Negotiations on pay took place between CONFINDUSTRIA and the then unified trade union movement and set basic rates by industry together with sex, age and provincial differentials. Only with the *conglobamento* or 'package' agreement of 1954 did the category organizations assume the responsibility for pay negotiations; the provincial differentials were finally phased out by an

[3] The early developments in collective bargaining in Italy are discussed in Giugni (1957).

agreement between CONFINDUSTRIA and the trade union confederations in 1968.

Currently, the only branch in which multi-employer bargaining does not take place exclusively at national level is building/civil engineering. Here there are negotiations at national and provincial level. National negotiations between ANCE and the building unions determine a basic framework, but they also empower the local employers' organizations to negotiate with the provincial trade union organizations on such matters as working time, holiday arrangements, payment for special tasks, together with a percentage addition to the rates of pay in the national agreement. These two-tiered negotiations are to be explained largely in terms of the significance of local conditions in this industry and, in particular, the difference in conditions between some of the larger concentrations of population in the north and parts of the south. The existence of a number of autonomous provincial organizations of building/civil engineering employers has also tended to reinforce demands for local autonomy.

Sweden
Branch negotiations take place at the national level in Sweden too.[4] As in Britain and Italy, multi-employer bargaining developed first on a local basis. In contrast to these two countries, however, the move to national level had little to do with government intervention. Essentially, it reflected the desire of employers to maximize their bargaining power. The pattern was largely set in metalworking. From its reconstitution in 1902 in the wake of the general strike, the employers' organization (SVF) adopted a highly centralized constitution. This was partly due to the sparse geographical coverage of metalworking employers in some areas and partly because of the decision to use the sympathetic lockout to counter industrial action mounted by the metalworkers' union.[5] The ability of SVF to wage a successful sympathetic lockout – it did so in 1903 to force the national union to call off a number of local stoppages – was an important factor in bringing about the first national agreement in 1905. SVF agreed to negotiate minimum terms and conditions of employment with the metalworking unions in return for union recognition that employers would be free to manage in their workplaces. Also, instead of devolving the negotiation of minimum rates of pay to area level, where the employers were much weaker, it was agreed that regional differentials should be negotiated at national level.

France
France appears to offer a sharp contrast to the countries so far considered. Of the five industries, multi-employer bargaining takes place

---

[4] Centralized negotiations in the building industry did not emerge until the early 1950s.
[5] The early developments in collective bargaining in the engineering industry in Sweden are discussed in Stryman (1946) and Norgren (1941).

exclusively at the national level only in chemicals[6] and clothing,[7] where in both cases it is a product of the 1950s. In building/civil engineering[8] and printing multi-employer bargaining is two-tier. In both cases negotiations at the national level set a framework of terms and conditions that includes a detailed system of job classifications; in printing, which has a long history of national agreements dating back to 1895, these negotiations also set national minimum wages. Local negotiations then set basic rates of pay for each 'chamber'. In building/civil engineering there has been a tendency for these negotiations to shift from the local 'chamber' to the regional organizations. In printing the local 'chamber' remains the bargaining agent.

The most interesting case is that of metalworking. Apart from an agreement dealing with the 8-hour day in 1919, there were no negotiations at national level until 1968. Forced to concede the principle of collective bargaining as a result of the Matignon 'agreement' of 1936, its employers' organization (UIMM) nonetheless set its face against national negotiations. Nearly four years of discussions between 1946 and 1949 also proved abortive. Only in May 1968 did UIMM agree to national negotiations on 'specific subjects'. The number of these, it must be emphasized, has been limited. As well as an agreement covering the senior white-collar workers (1969), there have been agreements dealing with the intensity of work (1968), security of employment (1969) and staff status (1970). There is also an agreement on job classifications of 1975. Significantly, however, this does not include minimum rates of pay. As with other issues not covered in the national agreements, these are arrived at in negotiations between the local 'chambers' affiliated to UIMM and their trade union equivalents. Although not every of UIMM's 'chambers' is a separate bargaining agent, more than 70 are.

The advantages claimed for regional or territorial negotiations seem real enough. As in the case of building/civil engineering, it is argued that

[6] Collective bargaining had scarcely developed in the chemical industries before the Second World War (Conseil National Économique, 1934: 187). After the war, and when it became possible to talk meaningfully about collective agreements following the law of 1950, the employers had initially favoured local negotiations on the metalworking pattern. But circumstances were against them. The great diversity which existed between chemical enterprises was especially marked at local level. With few exceptions, local organization was also inadequate on both the employers' and the trade unions' side. The employers had little choice, then, but to negotiate a national agreement. Though the possibility of local discussions is provided for, it seems that there have been no agreements at this level.

[7] The only recorded local agreements involve the Région du Nord and the Région Rhone-Alpes which includes the important clothing manufacturing centre of Lyons. In the case of the latter region, which has a long history of collective bargaining, the agreement provides for an enhanced guaranteed minimum wage.

[8] With the exception of a national agreement of 1919 regulating the introduction of the 8-hour day, the negotiations which took place prior to 1950 were exclusively local or regional in character, although the FNB already had the power to co-ordinate and control what happened. The employers' organizations, the FNB and FNTP, resisted national negotiations following the passage of the law of 1950, fearing that they would result in the levelling up of conditions across the board.

agreements can be tailored to suit the particular circumstances of the local labour market and that workers can move from one local employer to another and find comparable terms and conditions of employment. Since many of the basic operations are similar, even though the product might be different, local uniformity is particularly valued. In some cases the advantages are much greater. Many branches of metal production or transformation are concentrated geographically. Steel is concentrated in the north and Lorraine, shipbuilding is located in the Loire-Atlantique region at Brest and St Nazaire, aircraft manufacture is based on Toulouse. Local negotiations in these cases, it is argued, make it possible to deal with the special problems of each branch of activity. The fact the negotiations take place at this level also means local employers are intimately involved in the process of drawing up terms and conditions that will affect them. Indeed, UIMM officials argue that there has been a strong reaction from the 'chambers' to a further increase in the power and authority of UIMM headquarters following the national negotiations since 1968; if the process was to go too far, they say, it could lead to the loss of UIMM's general authority.

In metalworking, then, negotiations take place predominantly at local level. But the situation is not quite as simple as this. UIMM's lay members and officials spend a great deal of time and energy in seeking to co-ordinate the outcomes of the negotiations between local 'chambers' and trade unions. As well as using the negotiations in the Paris region as the 'pilot', headquarters' staff draw up model agreements and clauses for the use of 'chambers'. Headquarters staff also include a number of so-called 'regional delegates' who report directly to the secretary-general. The job of the 'regional delegates' is to ensure effective liaison between headquarters and 'chambers'; they are advised of trade union claims and have the responsibility for seeing that the 'chambers' are fully conversant with UIMM policy on the issues involved. Each one has a responsibility for a given geographical area and they travel extensively to local meetings as well as meeting regularly in Paris with senior 'chamber' representatives.

The fact of the matter is that UIMM insists on local negotiations largely for tactical reasons.[9] Not only do these reasons give an important insight into the practice of collective bargaining in France, they also confirm the significance of the level of collective bargaining to employers in a situation where the procedural regulation of collective agreements is weak or non-existent. The union confederations, particularly CGT and CFDT, are much stronger at national level than they are regionally or territorially, because they would be able to bring to bear their limited resources on one set of negotiations and to appeal to a wider class interest. Negotiations would thus become political; and the size and significance of metalworking in the French economy would make it the perfect 'key' bargain.

---

[9] For a further discussion of UIMM's strategy, see Sellier (1960; 1961; 1970).

Not only are the trade unions much weaker at the local level in terms of the number and experience of officials; it is also possible to get away from political questions, to localize issues, to concentrate on the 'bread and butter' ones. UIMM also fears the consequences of the bidding-up which would take place if the level of negotiations was raised. There are wide differences in earnings between the regions, which have gradually reflected themselves in the minimum rates. Once a levelling-up had taken place, argue UIMM officials, it would be natural to expect trade unions to exploit differences in the ability to pay to start the process off again.

It is in this context that the co-ordination of the outcomes of the local negotiations undertaken by UIMM officials at headquarters has to be understood. Evidently, there have to be some differences between local agreements, otherwise it would be difficult to justify the resistance to national negotiations. On the other hand, UIMM cannot allow its 'chambers' complete autonomy. If it did, there is the danger that the differences between the local agreements would become too large. In that event, the trade unions would almost certainly seize the opportunity to play off one 'chamber' against another and it is likely that the implications of this would be even more damaging to the employers' interests than national negotiations. In short, UIMM is obliged to engage in a very delicate balancing act.

West Germany

The situation in West Germany is the most complex. As early as the 1880s, there had been a shift from local to national multi-employer bargaining in printing and building. In the chemical and metalworking industries, however, there was little or no multi-employer bargaining at any level until the First World War. As chapter 6 will explain in more detail, in the wake of the Legien-Stinnes agreement of 1918 and subsequent legislation, multi-employer bargaining at the national level became the predominant pattern in these and other industries. It remained so throughout the Weimar period. Under the Nazis, there was little attempt to maintain the fiction of collective bargaining; the so-called Trustees of Labour were given the responsibility for setting minimum wage levels in fourteen geographical areas.

In 1948 there was a fairly immediate return to the Weimar pattern of national negotiations in printing. Indeed, the three main types of collective agreement which are to be found in West Germany,[10] namely 'framework

---

[10] Framework agreements or *Manteltarife* normally apply for three to four years or longer and contain statements of agreed policy as well as setting out general conditions of work, such as hours, conditions of shift work, grievance procedures and so on. Additionally, there might be separate agreements on specific topics such as wealth formation – a form of save-as-you-earn scheme involving obligatory deductions from wages at source – a 13-month payment scheme, which provides a means of paying an extra month's wages at Christmas, trade union representatives, training, rationalization, and conciliation and

agreements', 'wage framework agreements' and 'wage agreements', are negotiated nationally in printing. In building/civil engineering and clothing *Land* or regional negotiations prevailed in the immediate post-Second World War period; national negotiations were resumed only in the 1960s.

Similarly, in chemicals and metalworking negotiations at *Land* level predominated in the 1950s. Towards the end of that decade and during the early 1960s a similar process of centralization to that in other industries appeared to be taking place. In 1969, however, it came to an abrupt halt. Since then the predominant pattern has been *Land* or regional bargaining between the affiliates of the employers' organizations, Gesamtmetall and AC, on the one hand, and the regional committees of the trade unions, on the other. In the case of the 'wage agreements', for example, there have been national negotiations only twice in chemicals and once in metalworking in recent years.

As in metalworking in France, however, things are not quite what they seem. Although negotiations on the great majority of issues in chemicals and metalworking take place at *Land* or regional level, there is a great deal of co-ordination from the centre. The procedure adopted by Gesamtmetall in the early 1960s has more or less set the pattern for the chemical employers' organization (AC) and other branch organizations.[11] The collective bargaining committee, which is composed of the members of the executive council and the heads of the negotiating commissions of the regional organizations, is charged with the responsibility for working out a common policy. The executive council then decides whether this policy will take the form of 'recommendations' or 'binding guidelines'. If sufficient unity in the basic principles of the proposed policy cannot be achieved, then it may be decided that several of the *Land* organizations should negotiate in concert. This would usually involve the largest organizations or those whose agreements run concurrently. If a united approach is agreed, a 'core' commission is established, which is made up of individuals drawn from both the collective bargaining committee and the executive council. The 'core' commission is empowered to attend and participate in the negotiations in each *Land*. In each case the 'core' commission, which is bound by the decisions of the collective bargaining committee, constitutes at least one third of the employers' representatives. It is in this way that Gesamtmetall has been able to ensure that

---

arbitration. Wage framework agreements or *Lohnrahmenabkommen* normally apply for similar periods of time and contain policy agreements relating more directly to pay. These are likely to include standard occupational classifications and wage categories, general conditions of piecework payment, and the method of calculating piecework prices. Wage agreements or *Lohntarife* normally last for one year only and contain schedules of minimum hourly earnings for the different occupational classifications and wage categories.

[11] For further details of the procedural arrangements introduced by Gesamtmetall in 1961 and 1962, see Noé (1970).

wage increases in recent years have been of a uniform percentage amount.

The effect, then, is not dissimilar to that in metalworking in France. The explanation, however, is very different. The trend towards national negotiations which can be identified in the late 1950s and early 1960s was not halted by the employers, but by the trade unions. Indeed, it was the employers who had been forcing the pace so far as centralization was concerned.[12] As chapter 2 has already pointed out, in the late 1960s the leadership of IG Metall in particular was criticized for its excessive centralization and its involvement in 'concerted action'. This criticism intensified in 1969: an 8 per cent wage settlement was rejected by members and there was widespread unofficial industrial action in September which resulted in the negotiators returning to the bargaining table and increasing the level of settlement to 11 per cent. Thereafter IG Metall decided regional negotiations would be more appropriate in future. In this way the leadership hoped to meet the demands for more membership participation and a more decentralized wage policy. It was also argued that regional negotiations would allow a more active policy to be pursued: attempts could be made to achieve a breakthrough in the more profitable regions, and those where IG Metall membership was strong, which could then be imposed on the other member organizations of Gesamtmetall.[13]

For their part, the employers did not feel able to reject trade union demand for regional negotiations. Other things being equal, they would prefer negotiations at the national level.[14] The vigorous pursuit of

[12] There had been growing unease within Gesamtmetall about developments in regional bargaining for some time. For example, the strike by IG Metall members in Schleswig-Holstein had proved particularly embarrassing; the 40-hour week and improved sick pay schemes which were won from the Gesamtmetall member organization in that region were extended into the other regions. Largely at the insistence of the employers, the subsequent negotiations on the reduction in hours were tied to nationally negotiated pay increases which were then incorporated into the regional agreements. Subsequently national negotiations – with the results incorporated into the regional agreements – became the predominant pattern throughout the 1960s. Indeed, of the ten sets of pay negotiations between 1956 and 1969, seven were conducted nationally. The employers had maintained the impetus by simultaneously terminating the wage agreements in 1961 and by formulating the strategies for negotiations described in the text. In 1963 they carried their initiative a stage further. Attempts by IG Metall to take advantage of full employment and increasing productivity to seek a redistribution of income to the benefit of their members were firmly rebuffed. The strike in Baden-Württemberg was met with a lockout by the Gesamtmetall member organization in the region and only government intervention helped to save the face of IG Metall. The long-awaited agreement on conciliation was also negotiated nationally in 1964.

For further details of the employers' strategy during this period see Krusche and Pfeiffer (1975). For details of the dispute in Baden-Württemberg in 1963, see Noé (1970).

[13] The trade unions in the other industries, it seems, have not been persuaded of the virtues of a policy of decentralization. In the case of building/civil engineering there are also special reasons. The high mobility of labour has placed a premium on the operation of the central Sozialkassen or insurance funds covering such matters as pensions and holiday pay; there are also quasi-legal responsibilities for carrying out training.

[14] For the metalworking employers' preference for centralized negotiations, see Bergmann and Müller-Jentsch (1975: 247).

regional bargaining does present problems and necessitates the detailed co-ordination described above. IG Metall, on the other hand, was under a great deal of pressure from its members to decentralize negotiations to the workplace. Regional negotiations, it can be argued, were a relatively small price to pay in order to maintain the effective exclusion of the trade union from the workplace. As chapter 2 pointed out (p. 34) regional negotiations had also been not without other advantages for the employers. In some cases it meant an increase in the basic rates of pay without adding to the employer's wage bill. It also meant a reduction in the scope for bargaining by works councillors.

Conclusion

It might have been supposed that the shift in the level of negotiations from local to national level was a major factor in explaining the relative ineffectiveness of multi-employer bargaining in Britain. A comparison with the other countries, however, would seem to suggest that this is not the case. Britain is not unique in having these multi-employer negotiations at national level. Branch negotiations take place at this level in Italy and Sweden too. It is true that branch negotiations take place at local or regional level in France and W. Germany. But in both cases there is also considerable co-ordination from the centre which means that the substantive effect is not dissimilar to national negotiations. Furthermore, the contexts are very different. In France the employers are the protagonists of decentralized negotiations; in W. Germany they accept them reluctantly.

The Role of the Employers' Confederations

An employers' confederation may act as a bargaining agent on behalf of a group of employers from one branch. In Italy CONFINDUSTRIA did so on behalf of the metalworking employers for many years. More generally, however, the collective bargaining in which an employers' confederation is involved is likely to be not only multi-employer in its coverage but multi-industry as well. By definition, a wide range of labour and product markets will be involved. Be that as it may, how does the role of the Confederation of British Industry (CBI) compare with that of the other employers' confederations?

Britain

The role of the employers' confederation in Britain has essentially been that of a pressure group: neither the CBI nor the British Employers' Confederation which preceded it has ever been involved as direct bargaining agent with the Trades Union Congress (TUC). Significantly, too, with the exception of the Joint Statement of Intent of December

1964, the employers' confederation has never been a party to the various understandings reached by post-war Labour governments with the TUC on pay. The most recent example is the Social Contract of 1974–9. Formal meetings between employers and TUC representatives have been rare; even the Mond–Turner talks of 1927–8 took place outside the formal structure of the BEC until the final stages. For the most part contact between the employers' confederation and the TUC has been maintained indirectly through the intermediary of the government or in the various tripartite bodies which have existed. The best example of the latter is the National Economic Development Council which was established in 1962 and which involves regular meetings of representatives of the CBI and the TUC. In recent years there have also been fairly regular informal meetings between CBI and TUC officials. But this is about as far as it goes.

There was a short period in the early 1970s when it looked as if the CBI might develop a more important role. For example, in 1971–2 the CBI was able to persuade its members to hold down prices voluntarily in the hope of creating a better climate for pay restraint. The CBI was also involved in the tripartite discussions with the TUC which Edward Heath's Conservative government initiated before introducing a statutory prices and incomes policy in late 1972. Later under the same government, it was involved in informal discussion with the TUC in an attempt to resolve the miners' dispute of 1973–4. Thereafter, it drew back from so-called 'tripartitism'. In the view of Sir John Methven, who was appointed director-general in 1976:

> The great difference between now and 1974 is that we have learnt that secret trilateral negotiations between unions, employers and Government don't work for us. They don't work because we are the weakest of the three. The TUC is master of arguing in public and negotiating in private. In our case, negotiating in private is like water off a duck's back. We have to argue the public case, to provide a national voice for industry that will influence public opinion and help to shift the Government that way.
>
> (*The Observer*, 5 November 1978, quoted in Grant, 1979: 4).

Like the TUC, the CBI and its predecessor have not had the power to commit their members. Unlike the TUC, however, there is no evidence of attempts to establish common policies in collective bargaining[15] or to become involved in individual disputes. Significantly, for example, the CBI's proposals for changes in pay bargaining outlined in *The Future of Pay Determination* (1977) and *Pay: The Choice Ahead* (1979) – including

---

[15] The CBI set up a pay data-bank and instituted a regular series of 'presentations' on pay trends for its members in the late 1970s. The main aim of those initiatives would appear to have been to persuade members to adopt a more 'enterprise specific' approach to pay determination rather than a co-ordinated one.

a rationalization of bargaining units and the compression of the pay round – met with considerable criticism from many members. Also the attempt in 1980 to put some meaning into the notion of employer solidarity by the introduction of a mutual insurance fund met with failure. In short – and for reasons which will be explored in chapter 6 – the role of the employers' confederation in collective bargaining is very limited; any influence it has is exercised through advice and exhortation.

Sweden

The situation in the other countries is very different. Perhaps Sweden offers the sharpest contrast. The role of the employers' confederation (SAF) has been central to collective bargaining since its formation in 1902.[16] With the negotiation of the 'December Compromise' in 1906 and the 'Basic Agreement' in 1938, SAF and the trade union confederation (LO) set the ground-rules for the development of collective bargaining in Sweden. Subsequently, SAF negotiated multi-industry agreements with LO on safety (1942), training (1944), works councils (1946), time and motion study (1948), a joint female labour council (1951), rationalization (1961) and group life insurance (1966). More recently, in the early 1970s SAF negotiated a spate of multi-industry agreements which complement legislation on pensions, board representation, the work environment, security of employment, the position of trade union representatives, time off for training and co-determination at work.

On pay SAF initiated discussions with LO about the most appropriate form which wage reductions in the five main export industries should take in 1932 on the onset of the Depression. In 1940 SAF entered into an agreement with LO which introduced a sliding scale relating changes in wages to changes in the index of retail prices which was to last for the duration of the war. SAF agreed in 1944 that there should be no downward adjustment in the event of prices falling on condition that collective agreements in the most important industries be concluded at the same time as the revision of the escalator clause.

After an experimental agreement in 1952 SAF and LO have negotiated a series of multi-industry agreements on pay setting out the size of the annual global increase as well as the method of allocating this among the various industries. SAF has reached similar agreements with the central white-collar trade union organizations – TCO, representing white-collar workers generally, and SACO, representing professional workers. With the arrival on the bargaining scene in 1973 of PTK, an umbrella organization representing members of TCO and SACO, there has been an almost com-

---

[16] For a general discussion of the development of multi-industry bargaining in Sweden, see Johnston (1962). For the early developments in the negotiation of the so-called Saltsjöbaden Agreements, see Kugelberg (1953) and Lohse (1958). For developments in multi-industry pay bargaining, see Anderman (1967); Edgren *et al.* (1973); ILO (1959a, b); Mouly (1967); Roberts (1958). For a view on more recent developments, and especially the implications of LO's resort to legislation in the 1970s, see Fulcher (1976).

plete mirror image of negotiating levels and structure within the Swedish private sector for manual (SAF–LO) on the one hand, and non-manual (SAF–PTK) workers, on the other.

Negotiations between SAF and the trade union confederations over the central cost framework have become the cornerstone of collective bargaining in Sweden and have followed a broadly similar pattern on each occasion. During the summer there have been informal exchanges of views on the priorities for the following year. The representative assemblies of the trade union confederations have then met in the autumn and decided their claims. Further informal exchanges have taken place and there has usually been an autumn debate in the Riksdag based on the report of the National Institute of Economic Research. Negotiations have begun in earnest in December with the appointment of delegates by the parties. Subsequently – and particularly in negotiations with the LO – these have been deployed in smaller groups charged with the responsibility for considering special problems. If the parties have been unable to reach agreement, they have usually called in an impartial chairman. If they have still been unable to reach agreement, a mediation commission has been appointed under the Collective Agreements Act of 1928. Alternatively, the negotiations have moved directly to this stage without calling in an impartial chairman.

In the case of manual workers the procedures for industry level negotiations have been regulated to ensure that these presented the minimum of hold-ups once the central agreement has been signed. First, the negotiators at branch level have been aware of the basic content of the central agreement throughout the period of negotiations, so they were able to settle, in principle, the method of applying the various elements of the central agreements to their own industry before the actual figures were known. In this way, difficult problems and particular issues of application have been dealt with in conjunction with the negotiations between LO and SAF. Where these problems have proved intractable, representatives of LO and SAF have been brought in.

A second device to ensure quick results is the provision in the central agreement that the parties recommend their respective organizations to settle within the framework within a specific period of time – usually 2–3 weeks hence. Outstanding failures to agree after that deadline have then to be settled centrally by a small SAF–LO delegation. In practice, given the constitutional problems surrounding the autonomy of LO organizations, these small delegations have usually given an arbitrated decision, although there is no formal agreement for this.

A third device used in SAF–LO negotiations has been the so-called 'yardstick' or model clauses dealing with the application of low wage measures in particular. If the industry organizations have been unable to agree on how to distribute the low wage kitty elements, then these model clauses have automatically come into force.

In the final analysis a successful outcome depends largely on the SAF. To quote Victorin (1974: 173):

> SAF does not reach central agreements without making sure that they are generally acceptable to the member associations. As a consequence of this centralisation it is practically impossible for an LO organisation to avoid the co-ordination of a central agreement. The technique which is used by SAF is to keep the whole agreement on a provisional basis until agreement has been reached in the whole LO–SAF area. An LO association which delays and demands an agreement more favourable than the central agreement runs the risk therefore of having to face SAF on its own. Furthermore, it risks drawing the whole of the LO area into a conflict through sympathy measures which SAF can choose to take [against non-involved unionists].[17]

In the case of non-manual workers represented by PTK, SAF has been the employers' bargaining agent at the second as well as the first level of negotiations. That is to say, negotiations within the central cost framework have taken place between SAF and the individual trade unions. This is because these trade unions are occupational and not industrial in membership structure; they therefore cut across the boundaries of SAF's own member organizations.

The intention has been that these second-level or national agreements should be applied with the absolute minimum of change to the various industry organizations affiliated to SAF which have white-collar employees. Given the structure of bargaining, there has been no need to set deadlines for the completion of industry negotiations. There is, however, a body which performs an equivalent function to the small delegation in the case of manual workers. It is known as the Salaried Employers' Labour Market Board, and is made up of equal numbers of SAF delegates and delegates from the salaried union involved in the case.

Essentially, agreements between SAF and white-collar unions have provided for individual salary settlement, but with a degree of central control which has resulted from the use of a nationally agreed job

---

[17] As Victorin (1974: 180) himself points out, there has been no detailed study of the extent to which the SAF-LO agreement in particular is adhered to. His research suggests that there are breaches from time to time. He also offers (1974: 177) a plausible explanation for SAF's tolerance of these breaches:

> In interviews with negotiators one frequently hears that the major problem with industry negotiations is not in convincing the opposite party of the justice of extra increases but in obtaining SAF approval, or more bluntly, as one negotiator maintained, in adjusting the figures so that extra wage increases could not be immediately detectable. There are varying opinions about why SAF allows this to happen. In my opinion the main reason is that an inflexible attitude would put at risk the industrial peace (of Sweden) in the short term and in the long term could endanger the continuance of centralised bargaining. Employers' associations would be less willing to participate in a co-ordinated bargaining arrangement unless a certain freedom existed at industry level.

nomenclature for all salaried jobs, and accurate and sophisticated statistics from SAF 'partners' on what they were paying their salaried employees and their hours of work. The pay increases have been detailed as general percentage increases for *all* job categories, unlike the equivalent metalworking agreement for manual workers, where differing increases have been attached to the various wage groups or tariffs. The agreements have, however, contained clauses attempting to apply differing rates of pay increase for special categories of employees such as women in the lower salary groups and older employees at the limits of their job category. Such extra increases have often been given as kitties to be applied in workplace negotiations.

By way of summary, the complex structure involved in pay negotiations in Sweden can be illustrated in Table 4.1:

TABLE 4.1

Pay Negotiations in Sweden

	Manual		Non-Manual	
1.	SAF	LO	SAF .... PTK	
2.	SAF Member .... Employers' Organizations	LO Member Trade Unions	SAF .... White-collar Trade Unions	
3.	SAF 'Partners'	Factory Clubs	SAF 'Partners' .... Factory Clubs	

The motives for SAF's involvement in collective bargaining require some comment here, even if the explanation for its dominant position must be postponed until chapter 6. Two main motives may be identified. First, SAF has been anxious to avoid forms of government intervention which it believes are not in the best interests of employers. For example, SAF entered into the 'Basic Agreement' in 1938 largely out of a desire to avoid compulsory arbitration to deal with disputes of interest. Similarly, the moves towards multi-industry pay bargaining were in part prompted by the desire to avoid direct government involvement in pay determination. Thus SAF and LO met and agreed upon a national wage policy in 1940 which was to last for the duration of the Second World War in order to avoid the necessity for direct government control on wages.

Similarly, the move towards central bargaining over pay in the early 1950s was prompted by fears of political intervention. There was great concern among employers that the post-war boom and the accompanying full employment which had shifted the balance of power to the unions had been the result of definite measures on the part of the Social Democrat government as well as the prevailing economic situation abroad. There were fears the government would adopt LO proposals to allow employers and unions to bargain and then drain off any excess purchasing power by indirect taxation (Kugelberg, 1951). Government statements about the need to limit wage increases prior to the 1956–7 negotiations, coupled with veiled hints of sanctions in the form of new taxes and a law on compulsory saving, are also said to have been introduced to prod the parties to agreement.[18]

The second motive, already discussed in this chapter, is SAF's anxiety to maximize the bargaining power of employers. The co-ordination of the bargaining policy of its member organizations, which began systematically during the 1914–18 war with annual discussion of bargaining policy for the ensuing year, proved increasingly inadequate with the passage of time. In principle, SAF was opposed to centralized bargaining since it did not take into account the ability to pay of different industries. But it was largely a question of which was the lesser of two evils. Competition between the different national unions, it was argued, was resulting in larger and larger wage increases during the course of the annual negotiating session and considerable divergencies between industries which workers then sought to exploit to increase earnings in the workplace (Kugelberg, 1951).

Centralized pay bargaining was and is a means of buying uninterrupted production. The significance of exports to the Swedish economy makes SAF's trade-off of industrial peace against equalization of pay increases all the more rational, especially as SAF is in a position to escalate any conflict by the use of a lockout. Nor should the attraction of the general wage restraint SAF has obtained for its members by centralized bargaining be underestimated; it was not until 1969 that the central agreement gave a basic increase of more than 5 per cent for industrial workers or until 1971 that it provided for increases, in terms of the cost framework, in excess of the rise of productivity for the year.[19]

Italy

In Italy the role of CONFINDUSTRIA in collective bargaining has changed significantly in recent years. In the immediate post-Second World War

[18] It is important to note that, despite its deep roots in the trade union movement, LO's so-called 'solidarity' wage policy was not strong enough itself to bring about co-ordination among the trade unions. To quote Meidner (1973: 39): 'It was not until the end of the 1950s, nearly a decade after the lively debate within the trade union movement on the need for co-ordination, that co-ordination itself was accepted as the necessary precondition for the realisation of a solidaristic wages policy'. Even this acceptance does not mean that LO is empowered by its rules to negotiate multi-industry agreements with SAF. LO must on each occasion secure the agreement of its members' trade unions to enter into such negotiations.
[19] It remains to be seen how multi-industry bargaining in Sweden develops. The future of multi-industry pay bargaining, in particular, appears to be in some doubt. In 1983, for example, the metalworking employers' organization, SVF, withdrew from the arrangements for centralized bargaining to negotiate separately with the metalworkers' union – largely, it is reported, because of the growing dissatisfaction with the implications of LO's 'solidarity' wage policy and the tendency of governments to use the multi-industry negotiations as an instrument of incomes policy. Multi-industry pay bargaining resumed in 1986, but only in the wake of the assassination of the prime minister. For further details, see Lash (1985).

period multi-industry agreements between CONFINDUSTRIA and the then unified trade union confederation not only dealt with matters such as the 'internal commissions' and dismissals, but also set both the level and the structure of basic rates of pay. Earlier agreements on cost of living bonuses and piecework payments gave rise in October 1947 to the so-called 'wage pause' agreement stipulating basic rates of pay across the entire range of CONFINDUSTRIA membership. Basic rates were set for five groups of industries covering four categories of manual workers, three of white-collar, and two with special qualifications, together with sex, age and territorial differentials. Multi-industry negotiations also dealt with the renewal of the wage pause agreement in May 1949 and with some of the problems arising from the absorption of bonus payments. Between then and the so-called 'package' agreement of 1954, discussed below, there were to be no further changes in the basic rates of pay. The control which was exercised over the pay structure during this period, it has been suggested (Merli Brandini, 1971), was not even equalled in the Netherlands.

The first step in the process of decentralization was the 'package' agreement CONFINDUSTRIA signed with the trade union confederations, CISL and UIL in June 1954. As well as incorporating a number of different types of payment into the basic rates, the agreement recognized that henceforth negotiations at the national or category level should set the general level of basic rates in each industry.

A second step came with the events leading up to the metalworking negotiations in 1962–3. These were significant for the development of the structure of collective bargaining on two accounts: first, there was the split between CONFINDUSTRIA and INTERSIND leading to separate negotiations for the private and public sectors and, second, there was the formal recognition for the first time of the trade unions' right to deal with certain issues at the workplace. Increasingly the nature and extent of workplace bargaining became the major issue between CONFINDUSTRIA and the trade unions.

In some respects, however, these changes were not so dramatic as they first appeared. Of crucial importance was the fact that for another 17 years after the package agreement CONFINDUSTRIA was to remain the bargaining agent of the private sector metalworking employers. Given the size and significance of metalworking, CONFINDUSTRIA was able to use its involvement in these negotiations to maintain a measure of central control. To quote INTERSIND (1968: 18):

until 1962, metalworking constituted perhaps more a category 'at the centre of gravity than the "pilot"'. From 1962, it undoubtedly acquired, within the sphere of manufacturing industry, the function of the 'pilot' and the contract became the keystone of the greater part of the contracts in industry.

Only in 1971 did CONFINDUSTRIA finally relinquish its role as bargaining agent of the private sector metalworking employers. For it was in that year, following the upheaval of 1968–9 and the intense debate surrounding the Pirelli report[20] on the future of CONFINDUSTRIA, that FEDERMECCANICA was established to represent the metalworking employers directly.

Even so, CONFINDUSTRIA continues to play an important role in collective bargaining. Relations between CONFINDUSTRIA and FEDERMECCANICA officials are very close – the small secretariat of FEDERMECCANICA remains very reliant on its CONFINDUSTRIA counterparts – and the metalworking negotiations continue to be something of a pattern-setter or 'pilot'. CONFINDUSTRIA officials attend the negotiating meetings in each industry thereby ensuring a measure of co-ordination and continuity. In clothing and printing, CONFINDUSTRIA officials take a major part in the negotiations as well as being involved in the preparations leading up to them.

CONFINDUSTRIA also continues to be the employers' bargaining agent so far as the cost of living agreement is concerned. Briefly, the agreement provides for a sliding scale which relates bonus payments to an index of

[20] The special committee which produced the Pirelli report had been set up in March 1969 to prepare modifications to the statutes of CONFINDUSTRIA. The committee's report, which was published in February 1970, did this and more. It prefaced its proposals for changes in the statutes with a discussion which sought to clarify the role of employers in a modern industrial society. Italy, it was argued, was a pluralist society, conflicts of interest are inherent, responsible trade unions must be accepted and recognized, and employers must play an innovatory role.

The publication of the report led to intense debate among employers. For example, one of CONFINDUSTRIA's vice-presidents is quoted as seeing the problem in terms of integrating the two 'souls' of Italian employers: 'the Poujadist spirit which is still honoured in a great part of the employers' world and the progressive and innovatory spirit' (Ammassari, 1976: 139). So far as the role of CONFINDUSTRIA is concerned, representatives of some of the larger enterprises and the Agnelli Brothers of FIAT in particular, argued that CONFINDUSTRIA had become too involved in the day-to-day routine. In practice, it was performing many of the tasks which should be performed by the national category organizations. Instead, CONFINDUSTRIA should develop its representative role, particularly to government, and should concern itself more with the development of long-term policy. The second school of thought can perhaps be associated with the smaller members and many CONFINDUSTRIA officials. In 1973, for example, the president of the National Committee for Small Industrial Enterprises, having asked what the small industrialist wanted, replied:

> a strong unitary organisation which does not run away from its real responsibilities; an organisation which provides certain services and which has full contractual responsibility in both the political and labour sphere. Our position, on which we cannot turn back, is clear and precise. Why? Because the large industrialists defend themselves very well on their own while the small industrialists have no use for an organisation which can at most act as a screen in relations, for example, with the government bodies. What we need are services and contractual power.
>
> (quoted in Ammassari, 1976: 161).

The struggle for power became fairly intense, although the first view seems to have prevailed. The appointment, first, of Giovanne Agnelli and then Guido Carli to the presidency is one piece of evidence to confirm this. The withdrawal of CONFINDUSTRIA from its position as the bargaining agent of the metalworking employers and the formation of FEDERMECCANCIA in 1971 is a second.

retail prices. Adjustments in the bonus are made quarterly dependent upon movements in the index and payments made across-the-board throughout CONFINDUSTRIA's membership. The significance of this agreement in times of high levels of inflation is self-evident. The existence of the agreement has also provided employers with the opportunity to raise with the trade union confederations the wider issue of labour costs and the scope of workplace bargaining. Indeed, these issues figured prominently in the negotiations between CONFINDUSTRIA and the trade union confederations in 1977, 1983 and 1984.

Looking back, there seems little doubt that in the immediate post-war years there was general support for the principle of multi-industry negotiations even if the motives of the parties were different. The unitary CGIL was not opposed – far from it. Negotiations at this level offered a unique opportunity to take maximum opportunity of the political situation to seek the widest possible coverage of collective bargaining during the years of reconstruction and rapid inflation. Large numbers flocked into the trade union movement and it was through multi-industry negotiations that the trade union confederation, the CGIL, could justify its claims to be a mass organization by meeting the demands for equality of treatment in terms of wages. The practical realities were important too. The trade union movement was being re-established from the top downwards, and it is doubtful if the individual category trade unions were in any position to carry on meaningful collective bargaining themselves. Only with the change in the political climate – the departure of the communists from the government in May 1947, the victory of the Christian Democrats in the general election of April 1948, and the breakaway of UIL and CISL from CGIL – did trade union attitudes begin to change.

The employers' position is more complicated. The tradition of centralized bargaining inherited from the fascist period, which will be discussed in more detail in chapter 6, died hard among the officials of CONFINDUSTRIA and the territorial organizations. A strong preference for multi-industry negotiations was expressed by the territorial organizations which were very concerned by the prospect of giving the category associations the freedom to negotiate. A category organization in an industry with few female workers or few pieceworkers, it was argued, might be tempted to make concessions which could be embarrassing in industries with large numbers of these groups. There were also more subtle motives for preferring multi-industry negotiations. Costa, the first post-war president of CONFINDUSTRIA, it has been suggested, was particularly anxious to stabilize relations with the CGIL. This could be done most effectively by direct negotiations between CONFINDUSTRIA and the CGIL and by agreements which were automatic in their effect, like those dealing with the cost of living. There is little doubt that this motive also helps to explain the intensity of the negotiating activity in the years 1945–7. With the change in the political situation and the break-up of the unitary CGIL there was little incentive for employers to change. To quote Giugni (1957: 43):

> the high degree of centralised bargaining had constructed a protective fence around marginal enterprises and had granted efficient or monopolistic enterprises a large margin of freedom of action.

Much as some employers might have wished to maintain CON-FINDUSTRIA's central control, it proved difficult to sustain. Increasingly, the trade unions began to chafe under what they described as a wage freeze. Demands for greater freedom for the national or category negotiations began to be voiced by CGIL; while CISL began to promote the idea of workplace bargaining. Unlike Sweden, then, there was no longer any common ground. Rapid industrial expansion also made it more and more difficult to work with a pay structure which had been set several years before. In the absence of category negotiations this meant that many of the larger employers in industries which were expanding especially rapidly began to be drawn into workplace bargaining with the 'internal commissions'.

In Italy differences between the large and small employers were exaggerated by the *distacco*[21] or separation of the public enterprise employers from CONFINDUSTRIA following the Law of December 1956 setting up the Ministry of State Participation. Not only did the *distacco* remove these predominantly large employers from a position of influence within CONFINDUSTRIA, but it also led to a major rift between them and their counterparts in the private sector which the trade unions exploited to the full. Policies pursued by the employers with state participation, individually and through their newly-created employers' confederation, INTERSIND, went a long way towards undermining the position adopted by CONFINDUSTRIA. This was above all true of the negotiations in metalworking over the period 1961–8. In the absence of a private sector employers' organization in metalworking – CONFINDUSTRIA itself conducted the negotiations in this sector until 1973 – INTERSIND virtually came to play the role of a national employers' organization in metalworking and 'articulated bargaining' was the beginning of the end of CONFINDUSTRIA's policy of 'exclusive national negotiations'.[22]

[21] It seems that the role of the enterprises with state participation had been under active discussion for some years. Some wanted these enterprises to play a more active role in the process of industrial development. Others, perhaps more significantly, wanted them to play a more active role in the development of social policy. This is particularly true of leaders of CISL and the Left Christian Democrats. The changing political situation was also a factor: the long reign of De Gasperi from December 1945 to August 1953 had come to an end and with it the close relationship between the government and CONFINDUSTRIA. It has even been suggested that with the *distacco* some Christian Democrats were repaying CONFINDUSTRIA for their support of the Liberal Party in the recent election. For further details, see Collida *et al.* (1972: 88–90).

[22] Some of the developments in which it engaged, INTERSIND candidly admitted, were 'an expression of the function which the enterprises with state participation were destined to undertake, a function which is not to establish positions of privilege, but, by reason of a

France

On two occasions the French employers' confederation has been drawn into wide-ranging multi-industry negotiations, involving both government and trade unions. The first was at the Hôtel Matignon in 1936 during the height of the 'Popular Front' movement. As well as a number of economic concessions, the employers' confederation gave an undertaking that its members would in future negotiate collective agreements which they had consistently refused to do throughout the 1920s and early 1930s. The second occasion was in May 1968 at the Ministry of Social Affairs in the Rue de Grenelle. Again, the negotiations covered both economic and political issues. This time the employers' confederation committed its members not only to an increase in the statutory minimum wage and a phased increase in pay of 10 per cent across-the-board, but also to the acceptance of trade union 'sections' into establishments with more than 50 workers and further multi-industry negotiations.

On both these occasions the employers' confederation was forced to assume the role of bargaining agent. In the intervening period there had been significant opposition on the part of French employers to its doing so. In 1938, faced with the general hostility of employers to the Matignon agreement, Gignoux, the new president of the employers' confederation declared his organization was 'unwilling to obligate once more all of French management by its signature and to give the CGT, where now the communists were in the ascendancy, a new claim to the monopoly of labour representation' (quoted in Ehrmann, 1957: 37). As in metalworking, in the post-Second World War period the fear persisted that centralized negotiations would provide the CGT with a platform to 'politicize the social question' and would provide the trade unions in general with the opportunity to press issues such as a general increase in wages, reductions in working week, trade union rights in the workplace – all of which they were too weak to force through in branch negotiations. The CNPF continues to oppose such multi-industry negotiations. Even with the revision of statutes in 1969, which formally gave the CNPF the authority to engage in multi-industry negotiations, wages are specifically excluded.[23] Also proposals that the CNPF should seek to co-ordinate the pay bargaining of its member organizations have been firmly rebuffed.

---

wider evolution of general interests, to make itself the promoter of new types of relations, which can even be assimilated by the private sector – as in fact has happened – in so far as they do not contradict the demands of efficiency and economic management' (INTERSIND, 1968: 12). But there was a more or less coherent philosophy underpinning most of the innovations. There was a need, INTERSIND argued, for a ' "rationalization" of industrial relations' based on the recognition that conflicts of interest are 'an inherent movement in the dynamics of modern industrial society'. In this view 'the importance of a contractual system directed to channelling the conflicts according to rules which are not imposed is certainly destined to grow' (1968: 12–13).

23 Strictly speaking, it was only with the revision of its statutes in October 1969 that the CNPF acquired the authority to enter into multi-industry agreements. Under Article 2 of the

For all this, the opposition of the CNPF to multi-industry negotiations has not been total. The CNPF has been actively involved as a bargaining agent on social issues.[24] The first of such multi-industry agreements or *accords* was reached in 1947 and was concerned with the introduction of a scheme for supplementary retirement for senior white-collar workers. A second *accord* relating to supplementary retirement followed in 1957, and concerned wage earners not in existing systems. A third *accord* was signed in 1961 and was followed by an order of the Minister of Labour making membership of a supplementary scheme obligatory for all the activities grouped under the membership of the CNPF. The arrangements introduced by these various *accords* covered 7 million workers and are jointly administered and financed by contributions from employers and employees.

One of the justifications put forward for the negotiation of these *accords* was the need to have the largest possible membership of the schemes involved. In part, the same logic helps to explain the negotiation of the 1958 *accord* providing for a complementary insurance scheme against unemployment. Also financed by contributions from employers and employees, the jointly-run scheme provides in the event of unemployment for the payment of a special allowance for one year. The scheme was subsequently amended and extended by further *accords* and *avenants* as well as by government ordinances. The 1972 *accord*, for example, deals with the particular problem of workers over 60 who have difficulty in finding a job.

The pace of activity quickened following the events of May 1968. The 1969 *accord* dealt with the question of the security of employment. Essentially, it built on an earlier agreement covering the iron and steel industry. It provides for joint employment committees to be set up to monitor the employment situation generally in each industry and at the regional level, and to consider the steps to be taken in conjunction with the authorities. It also defines the procedure to be followed and the period of notice to be given to the works committees in the event of redundancies, and lays down scales of compensation for workers who are downgraded. The 1970 *accord* on training complemented that of

---

statutes it is expressly provided that:

> wages are a matter for undertakings and their *organisations professionnelles*. In other fields, the Conseil may in exceptional cases with the approval of the Permanent Assembly be empowered to discuss general agreements for all or practically all branches of economic activity. Those branches wishing to be excluded from the scope of any such agreement shall announce their decision before it is signed.

As in the case of Italy, this constitutional change did not simply reflect the upheavals of 1968–9. There had been a growing debate in the 1960s about the role which employers and the CNPF, in particular, should play in society. See, for example, the discussion in Brizay (1975: 136) and Lefranc (1976: 164).

[24] For more detailed information on the various multi-industry agreements, see Delamotte (1971: 330–40) and Reynaud (1975a: 286–90).

1969. Subsequently modified by *avenants* this accord deals with both the 'initial' training of youth workers and the 'further' training of adult workers. Other agreements followed: on staff status (1970), joint consultation with the senior white-collar workers (1974), and improved working conditions (1975).

It was government pressure which was the significant factor in bringing about the negotiation of many of these *accords*. Fears about the effects on employment following the opening of the French economy to greater competition on the formation of the EEC had been expressed as early as 1958. It was difficult to envisage the issues being tackled in an *ad hoc* fashion given the weakness of collective bargaining at branch level. As the pace of growth in the early sixties slackened, the fears intensified. The government was intimately involved in the negotiations which led up to the signature of the agreement in the iron and steel industry of Lorraine and which was to set the pattern for the later multi-industry *accord* on security of employment. Following the issue of ordinances in 1967 designed to promote an active employment policy, Prime Minister Pompidou wrote to the CNPF and the union confederations expressing his hope the parties would supplement the framework of the ordinances by collective bargaining. In particular, he urged them to carry out a joint examination of five questions, viz. the appointment of joint employment committees like those already in existence in the iron and steel industry; higher benefits for the unemployed; adequate notice of redundancies; the procedure to be followed in the event of mergers and concentration; and compensation for short-term unemployment.

Government pressure mounted with the election of Pompidou to the presidency in the Spring of 1969. Anxious to make progress following May 1968, the government preached the virtues of a policy of collective bargaining. In the private sector it offered the parties the opportunity to meet and negotiate agreements which could even be substitutes for the law. For example, the initiative of Pompidou in the case of staff status is very clear. If the subject had already been discussed in general terms, it was one of Pompidou's presidential election broadcasts in 1969 which brought it to the fore.

As in 1936, in the short run there was little employers could do but respond to the pressure from government. More positively, support for the negotiation of the *accords* came from those employers who were equally desirous of modernizing the economy and yet anxious to avoid the excessive state interference of the past.[25] Some hoped – vainly as it

[25] For a discussion of the employers' position on the negotiation of the multi-industry agreements, see Oechslin (1972), Brizay (1975), and Reynaud (1975b).

In particular, employers were unhappy with the organization and funding of the social security system in general. It was, they argued, largely based on the notion of charity and funded entirely out of public funds.

In the case of the various agreements with senior white-collar workers, it seems that the employers acted largely out of a desire to maintain the relatively privileged position of this group.

happened – that the negotiation of the *accords* might help to stimulate negotiations at branch level and, within specified guidelines, at workplace level; that the development of a contractual system would help to begin to institutionalize industrial conflict. UIMM perhaps had other motives. The negotiation of the *accords* between the CNPF and the trade union confederations meant that UIMM itself was by-passed and yet common patterns were set throughout the metalworking industry. In this way differences between regions and establishments were avoided without dismantling the system of local bargaining described in the previous section.

West Germany
Prima facie the role of the employers' confederation in West Germany is not dissimilar to that of the CBI. The BDA is the signatory of only one major multi-industry agreement with the DGB. The 1954 Margarethenhof agreement is a recommendation to their respective member organizations that they should either adopt the principles of conciliation set out in the agreement or draw up something similar. The agreement was the result of initial contacts between the leaders of the BDA and DGB made as early as 1949. They had met originally to discuss the then on-going legislation on co-determination, but eventually produced their recommendations out of a common desire, spelt out in the preamble, to avoid a system of conciliation and arbitration being thrust on them by the government. Some indication of the limited authority of the two confederations at this time is given by the fact that, although the form of agreement was adopted in many branches, a conciliation agreement was not introduced in metalworking until 1964 following the dispute in Baden-Württemberg.

Appearances, however, were deceptive. Against a background of growing demands for greater responsibility in collective bargaining on the part of Gesamtmetall, AC and other branch employers' organizations, the role of the BDA developed significantly. In particular, in November 1958 a so-called 'Co-ordination' Committee of the Executive Council was established. Its task was to formulate a unified wage and salary policy for BDA member organizations in the light of the national economic situation. Limits and targets were to be set and every effort made to ensure that BDA member organizations (and their member firms) obeyed them in the interests of employers as a whole (Erdmann, 1958 and 1966).

As a result of the successful outcome to the lockout involving the Gesamtmetall member organization in Baden-Württemberg in 1963, referred to earlier in this chapter, the role of the Co-ordination Committee was expanded and strengthened in 1965. A *Tabu-Katalog* was introduced in which the Co-ordination Committee sets down minimum or maximum standards which BDA members must not depart from. The *Tabu-Katalog* is not published and its contents are deliberately kept secret, but it is known that the basic working week and annual holidays are issues that appear.

An 'enabling instrument' was also introduced. The 'enabling instrument' is a set of rules and basic principles agreed by the representatives of BDA member organizations with the aim of improving co-ordination and solidarity. Some of these rules concern the relationship between the various member organizations and are designed, above all, to improve the chances of agreement on the range of minimum and maximum acceptable percentage wage increases for any given year. Others are recommendations for common rules to be applied within the member organizations of the BDA themselves, so that there is no weakness in the collective bargaining position on the employers' side. For example, there are recommendations for setting up both single-industry and multi-industry lockout and strike compensation funds as well as sanctions to be applied to regional organizations failing to comply with agreed policy. Within the regional organizations, these sanctions include the expulsion of individual employers not heeding the call to lock out something which happened during the national printing lockouts in 1976 when there were twelve expulsions from membership.

The co-ordination undertaken by the BDA has been given added legitimacy by subsequent developments in government intervention in pay bargaining. With the setting up of the so-called Council of Experts in 1963 and the Act for the Promotion of Stability and Growth in 1967, the federal government committed itself to the publication of guideline data for pay determination and to the tripartite consultative process which came to be known as 'concerted action'.[26] The guideline data are not compulsory, but under the Act the federal government has to ensure that the various parties are fully aware of their implications. Meetings involving representatives of the BDA, if not the DGB as well, have taken place regularly and so the parties are drawn into discussing pay, the level of investment and employment, and the value of the D-mark. In the full knowledge of the pay increase assumptions which the government will be making in determining its overall economic policy, the BDA is equipped with the information to persuade member organizations to seek to reflect these in their pay agreements. Here the part played by Gesamtmetall, described on pp. 88–9, is vitally important. Once a pattern of settlements has been established in metalworking, the other branches, where trade unions are much weaker, can be expected to fall into line.

Significantly, however, employers were opposed to the introduction of 'concerted action' on a statutory basis; they have also shown no signs of developing multi-industry bargaining as SAF did in Sweden. The explanation is that the ability of the BDA to co-ordinate the bargaining of its member organizations with some measure of success has secured many

[26] For further details on the background and on the various phases of 'concerted action', see Clark (1979) and Clark *et al.* (1980: 13–20).

of the advantages of centralized bargaining. It also avoided what employers perceived to be a major disadvantage of centralized bargaining: that the trade unions might use it to exercise much greater influence over economic policy. Trade union aspirations in this regard had occupied a prominent place in the programmes of the DGB since 1949; the programme agreed at Düsseldorf as recently as 1963, for example, made explicit reference to a 'framework plan' involving increased state control over the market economy. Against the background of the formation of the 'grand coalition' in 1966 and the coming to power for the first time of the Social Democrats, the opposition of employers to multi-industry bargaining seems hardly surprising.

Conclusion
Clearly, the role of the CBI is very different from that of employers' confederations in the other countries. The CBI is essentially a pressure group; its main task has been the representation of its members' interests to the government and the public at large. As well as undertaking this task, the employers' confederations in the other countries play a pivotal role in collective bargaining. They are either bargaining agents in their own right or, in the case of the BDA in West Germany, intimately involved in co-ordinating the bargaining of the branch organizations. By itself, the involvement of the employers' confederations does not explain the support which multi-employer bargaining enjoys in the other countries. But this involvement has made it easier for employers in these countries to achieve a consistency of approach on a wide range of issues. It has given employers a greater sense of common interest. It has made them more conscious of the advantages of employer solidarity.

The Significance of the Levels of Negotiations

However important the contrast in the role of the CBI and the other employers' confederations may be in the context of the present study, there are very considerable differences in the levels at which multi-employer bargaining takes place from one country to another that must call into question any simplistic interpretation of employers' behaviour. For example, in Britain, Italy and Sweden multi-employer bargaining within the branches takes place at the national level. In Britain and Italy it was the government that was primarily responsible for bringing about a shift from local to national negotiations – especially, so far as pay is concerned, in Britain; in Sweden it was the employers who were primarily responsible. In France multi-employer bargaining continues to take place at the local level in a number of industries and in particular in the metalworking industry; in West Germany it takes place at the regional or *Land* level in metalworking and chemicals. Furthermore, in neither country are these local and regional negotiations to be explained simply in terms of the preference of employers for negotiations which cover the local labour market. Indeed, in West Germany employers in the metal-working and chemical industries were reluctant to accept decentralized negotiations.

There is also little evidence of a consistent pattern so far as multi-industry bargaining through the agency of the employers' confederation is concerned. Certainly many employers in Italy favoured multi-industry bargaining in the immediate post-Second World War period. In Sweden too employers have come to accept and support multi-industry bargaining, albeit with less enthusiasm than is sometimes suggested. But employers in France resisted multi-industry bargaining for many years, despite the pressure of both governments and trade unions; they continue to resist multi-industry bargaining over pay. West German employers have also shown little enthusiasm for multi-industry bargaining.

How is sense to be made of this diversity? Employers have an essentially contingent approach to the level at which negotiations take place; their attitudes and policies towards these levels are conditioned first and foremost by what they perceive to be in their best interests in the particular circumstances. This is why they appear to adopt contradictory positions in relation to the same level of negotiations; why they change their positions; why in some cases they are prepared to put up with levels of negotiations which are not of their own choosing. They do so because multi-employer bargaining is primarily a political institution. The levels at which multi-employer bargaining takes place both reflect the power relationship that exists between employers and trade unions and are a major influence on it. From the evidence of this chapter, it should be clear that not only do employers use multi-employer bargaining to control the activities of the trade union *inside* the workplace, but they also seek to use the levels at which multi-employer bargaining takes place to control trade union activities *outside* the workplace as well.

Further support for this contingent or tactical explanation of employers' behaviour comes from the evidence of co-ordination of negotiations which are apparently decentralized. Indeed, much of the variety witnessed in bargaining levels disappears when this co-ordination is taken into account. In metalworking in France, for example, employers are able to secure many of the benefits of national negotiations without the drawback of presenting the trade unions with the opportunities which go with bargaining at this level. Similarly, employers in metalworking and chemicals in West Germany are able to secure some of the benefits of national negotiations while meeting trade union demands for greater decentralization. In some cases co-ordination takes place at a higher level as well. Of the employers' confederations only SAF is directly involved as the bargaining agent so far as pay is concerned. Yet there is considerable co-ordination of pay bargaining by the employers' confederations in both Italy and West Germany. Again, many of the advantages of centralized negotiations are secured without the drawbacks.

To understand what exactly are the differences in circumstances which have produced the varied and contrasting behaviour described in this chapter, it will be necessary to examine in some detail the origins and early development of multi-employer bargaining in each of the countries. Before doing so, however, it will be appropriate to consider the implications of differences in the contents and status of the agreements to which the negotiations described in this chapter give rise. For not only are the levels of multi-employer bargaining and the contents and status of multi-employer agreements intimately related in practice, but they also have common historical origins.

5

'Common Law' or 'Statute Law' Collective Bargaining?

Following Kahn-Freund (1954a: 1959), Flanders (1970b: 94–9) suggested that there were two major differences between Britain and other countries in the contents and status of the agreements that employers' organizations negotiate with trade unions. First, in Britain the relationship between employers' organizations and trade unions was based on procedural rules, whereas in other countries it was mainly built on a code of substantive rules in force for a specified period. Second, in Britain priority has been given to voluntary rather than compulsory collective bargaining; that is, the procedural rules were made by the parties themselves rather than being imposed by government and, along with any substantive rules negotiated, were deemed to be 'gentlemen's agreements binding in honour only rather than legally enforceable contracts. It was on the basis of these differences that Clegg (1979: 116–9), also following Kahn-Freund, distinguished between two models or types of collective bargaining: the 'common law' model, of which Britain was the most obvious example, and the 'statute law' model, to which most other countries are inclined. Accepting these distinctions, it remains to explore in more detail the main differences in the contents and status of multi-employer agreements between Britain and the other countries and to establish their significance in the context of the present study.

The Contents of Multi-Employer Agreements

Kahn-Freund (1959: 262–3) described the differences between Britain and other countries in the following terms:

> Here [in Britain] all the emphasis is on institutions such as joint industrial councils and the like, on the machinery, its constitution,

above all its procedure. The substantive rules about wages, hours and other conditions are not, as they are in many foreign countries, built up as a series of systematically arranged written contracts between employers and unions. They appear as occasional decisions emanating from permanent boards on which both sides are represented and sometimes they are informal understandings, 'trade practices' never reduced to writing. A very firm procedural framework for a very flexible corpus of substantive rules, rather than a code laid down for a fixed time – such is the institutional aspect of much collective bargaining in this country.

Procedural Contents

There is very little to add to Kahn-Freund's description so far as the procedural contents of the British multi-employer agreements are concerned, but there are differences between the five industries to be noted. First, joint industrial councils are to be found only in three of these industries. In engineering there is no standing joint committee. This is because the 'Provisions for Avoiding Disputes' introduced in 1898 gave trade unions *de facto* recognition and provided for joint meetings to take place as and when required.[1] Similarly, the introduction of bi-partite statutory wage-fixing in the clothing industry under the Wage Boards Act of 1909 obviated the need for a joint standing committee in this industry. Second, there are differences in the procedures for dealing with disputes. For example, in engineering a system of 'employer conciliation' prevailed for many years;[2] in the other industries there is joint conciliation; and for many years building had two procedures. Third, there are differences in the treatment accorded to workplace trade union representatives. Only in engineering[3] and building/civil engineering[4] is the role of the shop steward dealt with formally. In the other industries there are references to trade union workplace representatives – usually in connection with

[1] For a discussion of the reasons why a standing committee was not established in engineering, see Marsh (1965: 16).
[2] In theory, groups of employers were to hear the complaints brought by workers and their representatives against the employer immediately involved; they were also to judge the issue on its merits as a specific and isolated case; trade unions committed themselves not to take industrial action until the procedure had been exhausted. The procedure was terminated in 1971 and a revised version substituted in 1976. For further details see Marsh and McCarthy (1968) and Hyman (1972).
[3] Under the 'Provisions for Avoiding Disputes' grievances could be brought forward for discussion either by the worker individually, or by the group, or by the representative of the union. It was only in 1917 and 1919 that the role of the workplace representative, the shop steward, was formally written into the procedure agreement. The Shop Steward and Works' Committee Agreement of 1917, which with some amendments was accepted by the ASE in 1919, provided for the setting up of works' committees; gave the shop steward a formal role in the disputes procedure; afforded the shop steward the right to move from one shop to another in the establishment, providing he had the previous consent of the management.
[4] In building/civil engineering it was only in 1964 that National Working Rule 7 – Trade Union Recognition and Procedures – was incorporated into the multi-employer agreement.

provisions for handling disputes – but no clearly prescribed functions. Even so, these differences do not detract from the overall conclusion. Procedural contents are of primary importance in the British agreements. Significantly, too, they deal with relationships inside the workplace as well as those between the employers' organization and trade unions.

Of the other countries, Sweden comes closest to Britain in the attention given to procedural issues. The questions of recognition, negotiation and disputes in the five industries are governed by the multi-industry 'Basic Agreement' reached by SAF and LO in 1938.[5] Chapter 1 of the agreement provides for the setting up of a jointly-constituted Labour Market Council 'for the handling of certain questions specifically set out below'. Chapter 2 then sets out a number of general principles which are to govern the negotiation procedure between the parties. Article 1, for example, states that, 'should a dispute arise regarding working conditions or other relations between the two parties, action may not be taken as referred under Article 7 and 8 below (i.e. industrial action) before either party has sought through negotiations with the other party in the manner as prescribed below, to bring about a settlement of the issue under dispute. It is incumbent upon either party to enter into such negotiations upon the request of the other party. Articles 3–5 then detail the arrangements: negotiations shall in the first instance be conducted between the parties concerned at the workplace; if no agreement can be reached, it shall rest with the party wishing to pursue the issue to refer the matter to central negotiations, involving the national union and employers' organization. Time limits are also attached. Article 7 requires that the parties must not request a reference to the Labour Court nor an arbitrator on questions of interpretation or application of a collective agreement before they have duly fulfilled their obligation to negotiate in the matter.

Chapter 3 of the 'Basic Agreement' is devoted to the question of termination and lay-offs, chapter 4 to the limitation of strikes, lockouts and other direct actions and chapter 5 to the handling of conflicts threatening essential public services. Direct action may be resorted to 'provided its purpose is, by extending the scope of an original dispute in negotiating a collective contract, to assist either party to the dispute'. In this way, the SAF retained the right to resort to a sympathetic lockout in disputes over the negotiation of collective agreements.

The trade union presence in the workplace, which was acknowledged in the 'Basic Agreement' and earlier understandings, was further reinforced by the agreements reached between SAF and LO in 1942 and 1944

---

[5] Subsequently, the terms of the 'Basic Agreement' have been incorporated into the various national agreements. Thus section 1 of the agreement in metalworking says that the 'Basic Agreement' shall apply; and section 2 states specifically that chapter 2 of the 'Basic Agreement' shall apply in the event of any dispute.

dealing with safety and vocational training respectively; in each case provision was made for the appointment of specialist trade union stewards. The agreements reached between SAF and LO and SAF and TCO in 1946 on wages councils did not depart from the principle of single-channel representation either: they were to be applied in establishments only where at least 50 per cent of the workers belonged to bona fide trade union organizations and only union members were qualified to take part in the election of the workers' representatives. As chapter 4 pointed out, LO and PTK have recently sought to extend the rights of their members at the workplace by means of both collective agreements and legislation. This has meant considerable increases, some of which have been reflected in the multi-employer agreements, in the formal powers of safety stewards, works councils and 'factory clubs'.

Multi-employer agreements in France, Italy and West Germany are relatively silent on the question of trade union recognition and the procedure for multi-employer negotiations; in most cases they simply state the period of notice which is to be given to terminate the agreement and what is to happen in the event of no agreement being reached. The agreements are more detailed in their provisions for disputes. In France[6] and West Germany the provisions are more or less standard in the five industries. In France these provisions reflect the requirements of the law of 1950 and in West Germany the principles of the 1954 multi-industry conciliation agreement referred to in the previous chapter. In Italy there is much greater variety between the five industries. In some cases there are separate procedures or specific clauses for dealing with discipline, grading and issues arising from the operation of payment by results schemes.

So far as workplace representatives are concerned, most French multi-employer agreements simply refer to the various laws or restate them; in some cases, printing and chemicals being the notable examples, the agreements provide for slightly more advantageous conditions in respect of the number of 'delegates' or the time that is at their disposal.

In West Germany the most detailed multi-employer agreement is that in printing: it provides for the election of union 'trustmen' within the workplace outside working hours; the communication of the names of

[6] The situation in printing in France deserves special attention because it seems to be the exception that proves the rule. As early as 1895 the master printers and the main trade union, *Fédération du Livre*, had set up a joint standing committee, together with local arbitration committees, to settle disputes between them. This tradition of negotiating voluntary procedures by the parties themselves seems to have survived. Significantly, the national agreement is prefaced by a preamble which must be unique in France. Article 1 states that:

> The signatory organisations . . . established the present agreement with the first aim of maintaining and developing relations of good understanding and perfect honesty among all the members of the trade, and with the second aim, following the first, of leading to a harmonious development of the trade, a development which must be beneficial to all the members without exception.

The articles which follow reaffirm that the parties will honour the principles of conciliation and arbitration in the event of disputes.

elected 'trustmen' to the employer in writing; remedies for discrimination against 'trustmen'; and discussions between the signatory parties in the event of a proposal to dismiss a 'trustman'. In metalworking the agreement negotiated in 1969 by IG Metall and the member organizations of Gesamtmetall simply provided for the disclosure of the names of 'trustmen' to management, and non-discrimination on very general terms; in chemicals and clothing the agreements are very similar. In building/civil engineering there does not appear to be any provision for 'trustmen' in the agreements.

The Italian agreements have clauses dealing with the subject matter of the 'workers' charter': the right to workplace trade union representation, workplace meetings, referenda, paid leave of absence, the right to post notices, trade union dues and premises. Attempts by FEDERMECCANICA in metalworking in 1973 to seek agreement on the scope and competence of trade union workplace organization were firmly rejected by the metalworking unions on the grounds that such an agreement would be unduly restrictive. The employers in chemicals, it seems, were more successful. The trade unions, which were weaker than those in metalworking and still divided, wanted to secure a statement of their rights. The agreement explicitly bestows the rights specified under the 'workers' charter' on the factory council.

The development of 'articulated bargaining' in Italy has already been referred to in chapters 2 and 4. This represents perhaps the most systematic attempt in any of the countries to make provision for workplace negotiations in multi-employer agreements.[7] Much more than multi-tiered bargaining was involved; 'articulated bargaining' involved an attempt to relate and co-ordinate negotiations taking place at national, sector and enterprise levels. Although the structure of collective bargaining did not develop in the way envisaged, 'articulated bargaining' left two legacies that deserve comment. One is the *premessa* or preamble which the metalworking employers insist on retaining in the national category agreement. In essence, this more or less follows the wording of the original INTERSIND-ASAP *protocol* of 1962: the trade unions commit themselves 'not to promote and to intervene to avoid action or claims intending to modify, complete, alter what has been the object of agreement at the various levels'. The second is the provision in the metalworking and chemical agreements for a production premium.[8] Both the

---

[7] The only other attempt to introduce multi-tiered bargaining took place in Britain in the late 1960s; in both chemicals and national newspapers framework agreements were negotiated at the national level which attempted to define the scope and content of workplace productivity bargaining.

[8] The intention was that the production bonus should be linked in some objective way to the overall performance of the enterprise. In practice, it has become little more than a workplace supplement to be negotiated by the 'factory council' and the individual employer. However, it is not without significance. The fact that provision for its negotiation exists in the multi-employer agreement has tended to reinforce the supplementary nature of the workplace bargaining so far as pay is concerned and to concentrate this bargaining on a single payment.

amount and method of negotiating the premium are set out, together with the steps to be taken in the event of a dispute.

Substantive Contents

Flanders' and Kahn-Freund's account of the substantive contents of multi-employer agreements is correct as far as it goes. To appreciate the full significance of the differences between Britain and the other countries, however, it is necessary to take the matter further. For the purposes of analysis, the multi-employer agreements employers' organizations and trade unions negotiate can be considered along three dimensions so far as their substantive contents are concerned. First, these agreements, like single-employer agreements, can differ in the *scope* or *range* of their contents. In this case it is possible to think in terms of continuum. At one extreme, for example, the agreement may be comprehensive in its coverage; that is to say, it may cover all aspects of the employment relationship. At the other extreme, the agreement may be extremely limited with only one or two items covered.

Second, multi-employer agreements can differ in the *detail* of their coverage. For example, two agreements may have clauses dealing with payment by results. One may deal with the issue in very general terms or simply state that the worker paid by results should receive a minimum of, say, one third over and above the pay of the time worker. The second agreement may deal in great detail with both the procedure for fixing piecework times and the calculation of piecework prices.

The third dimension comprises the different type of rules in multi-employer agreements. There are four main types. First, there are the rules intended to be applied in the workplace without any alteration or supplementation. These rules might be referred to as *standard*. Second, there are the rules intended to be applied directly in the workplace, but as basic or *minimum provisions*; the implication is that it is open to the individual employer, either unilaterally or jointly with workers' representatives, to improve upon them. Thus, for example, the rates of pay in multi-employer agreements may be either *standard* or *minimum*. Third, there are the rules requiring further negotiation in the workplace. For example, except in the rare case of standard piecework prices, a multi-employer agreement will almost invariably give some latitude to the individual employer and workers' representatives in the implementation of payment by results schemes. This type of rule might be referred to as *incomplete*.[9] The fourth type is the rule of *principle*. For example, there may be a statement of the employers' right to manage or a commitment on the part of trade unions

---

[9] The term 'incomplete' follows usage in France which distinguishes between agreements which are *parfait* and those which are *imparfait*. *Parfait* agreements are those which do not allow for subsequent negotiation and adaptation at lower levels and *imparfait* agreements, such as the joint recommendation in 1970 on staff status, those that do. For further details, see UIMM (1968: 94).

and their members to improve productivity. Here there is an intention that something should happen in the workplace. Unlike the other types, however, the rule of principle is not specific in its application. Clearly, each of these types of rule limits the freedom of the enterprise and its members in their rule-making, but the extent to which it does is very different.

Scope and Detail.   It is on the first and second of the three dimensions – scope and detail – that the main differences between Britain and the other countries are to be identified. For example, although engineering is the only one of the five industries to have had an explicit statement of the employers' right to manage,[10] the coverage of other issues is extremely limited. Rates of pay for a small number of benchmark jobs, hours of work, overtime and shift premia, holidays and holiday pay, and special provisions for apprentices is the sum total of the contents. The coverage of the chemicals agreement is very similar. By comparison, agreements in building/civil engineering and printing are more comprehensive and, to quote one example, provide rates of pay, either directly or indirectly, for a far larger range of job titles. Even so, they certainly cannot be described as comprehensive or detailed.

In the other countries the only example of an explicit statement of the employers' right to manage is to be found in Sweden. As chapter 6 will explain in more detail, in 1905 SAF placed an obligation on its member organizations to insert the following clause in any collective agreement:

> The employer is entitled to direct and distribute the work of his enterprise, to engage and dismiss workers at his own discretion, and to employ organised or unorganised workers as he sees fit.

This was the famous 'Article 23', subsequently Clause 32, of the SAF constitution. Following the threat of a lockout, LO members were forced to

---

10 The 'Terms of Settlement, 1898' enunciated a general principle for the engineering industry: 'the Federated Employers, while disavowing any intention of interfering with the proper functions of trade unions, will admit no interference with the management of their business, and reserve to themselves the right to introduce into any Federated workshop, at the option of the employer concerned, any condition of labour under which any members of the Trade Unions here represented were working at the commencement of the dispute in any of the workshops of the Federated Employers'. The rights of workers were limited to bringing forward grievances which they might have under the 'Provisions for Avoiding Disputes'; while the matter was under discussion, they were required to work on current conditions, and not to stop work until the procedure had been exhausted.

Following the lockout in 1922, the principle of managerial prerogatives was reaffirmed in the so-called 'Management Functions Agreement, 1922' which brought together a number of the changes in the various procedures which have been made since 1898. The agreement opened with the broad statement, 'employers have the right to manage their establishments and the trade unions have the right to exercise their functions'. The clause remained in this form until 1971 when the trade unions gave notice to terminate the procedural arrangements. The reference to management rights finally disappeared only in the revised agreement in 1976.

acquiesce in the insertion of this clause into collective agreements as part of the 'December Compromise' of 1906. The full impact of the clause was watered down during the 1930s, especially in the light of the regulation of job security in chapter 3 of the 1938 'Basic Agreement'. Nonetheless, it remained of importance in relations between SAF and LO. The spate of legislation in the 1970s – on share ownership, board representation, working environment, security of employment, trade union representation, time off for training, and co-determination at work – bears witness to LO's recognition of the need to outflank SAF's insistence on the maintenance of managerial prerogatives. The second paragraph of Clause 32 currently reads:

> the employer has the right to engage workers who are members of any organisation whatsoever or who are not members of any organisation. Workers may secure a right to decide jointly (*medbestammanderatt*) on questions which involve the signing or termination of contracts of employment, the direction and allotment of work and the management of the enterprise in general only in accordance with the guidelines established by the Board and set out in the agreement (with LO and PTK) on democracy in working life.

Overall, the coverage of multi-employer agreements in Sweden and the other countries is far more comprehensive than in Britain. As well as the contents of the British agreements it embraces annual bonuses, cost of living bonuses, health and safety, individual and works bonuses, investment, job classification schemes, payment by results, pensions, redundancy, savings schemes, security of employment, service increments, short-time working, staff status, technological change, trade union representation in the workplace, training, working environment, and so on. Most of the agreements are also far more detailed than they are in Britain.

Not surprisingly, there are differences between the four countries. The coverage tends to be more comprehensive where the employers' confederation is a fairly active bargaining agent. Sweden and, to a lesser extent, France stand out. Against this, the national category agreements in Italy and the regional agreements in West Germany are more detailed in their coverage of specific contents. As in Britain, the agreements in building/civil engineering and printing are more comprehensive than in the other industries.

A better idea of the differences between Britain and the other countries can be gained by considering two issues central to pay determination: pay differentials and payment by results. As has been pointed out already, the coverage of agreements in Britain is very limited so far as pay differentials are concerned. For example, in chemicals there is one single rate each for non-craft workers and for craftsmen. In engineering there are two key rates, one for skilled fitters and one for labourers, plus a small number of differential rates for groups such as skilled maintenance workers, setters-up and markers-off; there are also references to such occupations as pattern-makers and millwrights who are to enjoy the same rate as skilled fitters. The coverage is more comprehensive in the other industries. Significantly, however, this is achieved by listing named occupations, as in printing, or by providing for a series of plus rates dependent upon the possession of different skills, which is the method used in building/civil engineering. Non-manual workers receive even less coverage. There are minimum salary scales in engineering (for clerical workers and for designers and draughtsmen) and in printing (for clerical workers and journalists); there are no multi-employer provisions for non-manual workers in the other industries.

By comparison, the treatment of pay differentials is extremely detailed in other countries' agreements. The arrangements are broadly similar. The national job classification scheme introduced in metalworking in France in 1975 will serve as an illustration. The scheme, which covers both manual and non-manual workers up to the level of senior white-collar workers, makes provision for five categories each with three so-called 'échelons'. Attaching to the 15 'échelons', there is a detailed list of the duties, responsibilities and tasks that would justify a particular job being allocated to it. The system does not, however, allocate specific named occupations to the 'échelons', but simply gives a named occupation or occupations as examples. Each 'échelon' also has a fixed coefficient to be used by the employer to determine pay relationships. In effect, then, the multi-employer agreement provides metalworking employers with a standard system of job evaluation, but one that is also flexible in its operation.

So far as payment by results is concerned, the coverage of the British agreements is very general. There may be provisions for a minimum earnings level for pieceworkers or for a minimum earnings level over and above that of the time workers. Overall, however, there is very little attention to the substantive aspects of payment by results schemes.

The provisions in the metalworking agreement for the North Rhine-Westphalia region dealing with payment by results provide a strong contrast. The agreement has separate clauses dealing with such matters as measurement, estimation, planned times, pre-determined times, manual recording, automatic recording and so on. The agreement is no less specific when it comes to the question of the calculation of basic piece rates. The wage table setting out the coefficients for time workers also refers to a table of 36 grades of work difficulty to be used in calculating basic piece rates by means of a points system ranging from 0 to 45. Each grade is correspondingly expressed in DM per hour. The operation of the points system and piece rate calculation is dealt with further in a separate agreement on work measurement. To supplement the terms of the regional agreement, individual employers are supplied with copies of 'pattern' agreements by the employers' organization as the basis of the agreement with the works council.

A combination of individual and group merit schemes is also common in the metalworking agreements in West Germany. For example, the agreement for the Bavarian region first introduced in 1975 establishes four performance criteria for payments: work quantity, work quality, work flexibility and approach to co-operation in the workplace. There is a five-point weighted scale of 0.28 for each of the first two criteria, 0.16 for the third and 0.12 for the fourth. For manual workers each point is worth 0.20 per cent of the hourly basic rate and for non-manual workers 0.15 per cent of salary. With a maximum of 100 points, the manual bonus can therefore amount to 20 per cent of the hourly basic rate and 15 per cent of the salary level; average performance is deemed to be 10 per cent and 7.5 per cent respectively. The agreement stipulates the procedure which is to be followed in arriving at the performance measurement. The performance measurement takes place annually and the results communicated in writing to the employee who then has the right to appeal to a joint committee and thence to the works council. It is also made very explicit that this procedure is the result of the negotiations at the regional level and that the works council has no fundamental right to determine its implementation in the workplace beyond the terms of the agreement.

Types of Rule.   There is little difference between Britain and the other countries in the type of rule in multi-employer agreements. Very few of the rules are of the *standard* type and these are common to the five countries: they deal with hours of work, overtime and shift premia, and holidays. As chapter 2 has already pointed out, the rates of pay are almost invariably intended to apply as basic minimum provisions. Indeed, of the agreements studied in the five industries in each of the countries, only one did not state that the rates of pay were minima or basic. Ironically, that agreement was in the building industry in Britain. Most other rules are of the *incomplete* or *principle* type.

Even so, it might be thought that the relationship between changes in rates of pay and earnings would be important. An increase in the rates of pay, for example, might benefit all workers, regardless of their earnings; or it might benefit only those workers whose earnings are between the old and the new rate of pay. Prima facie the fact that the rates of pay can provide 'floors' or 'safety-nets', to use the distinction drawn by Brown and Terry (1978), appears to be relevant in helping to explain the different significance of multi-employer bargaining in the five industries in Britain. In chemicals and engineering, it has become more or less explicit policy to regard the rates of pay as 'safety-nets'. In the other three industries the fact that the rates remain 'floors' appears to explain why they remain important even in cases where the size of the earnings gap is substantial: if the 'floor' moves, it can produce a significant increase in earnings. Thus in national newspapers workers can earn upwards of four times the rate of pay and yet still benefit significantly from increases in these rates.

Paradoxically, the situation in the other countries is more like that in chemicals and engineering in Britain: the rates of pay in the multi-employer agreements are essentially 'safety-nets' rather than 'floors'. Indeed, in West Germany the position would appear to be that the employer is not legally obliged to continue to make supplementary payments in the event of increases in the rates of pay (Ramm, 1965b: 205). Whether the employer treats the rates of pay as 'floors' or 'safety-nets' in practice depends on the situation in the workplace and, in particular, the pressure he experiences from his workforce to pass on increases to those already earning in excess of the rates. Certainly, it is not uncommon for employers to reduce workplace supplements in the light of changing circumstances. Nor is this practice restricted to the smaller enterprises.

It remains to consider why most rates of pay are minima rather than standard. There would be enormous practical difficulties in negotiating standard rates, especially when the level of negotiations moved upwards from regional to national level. The needs of large and small enterprises differ. A wide range of product markets is covered by enterprises in the same industry; and they can operate in very different labour market situations too. But there is also a need to take into account more fundamental objections. The negotiation of minimum rates serves a number of objectives: first, it maximizes the bargaining power of the employers; second, the rates negotiated place a floor under wage cutting as well as meeting trade union and government demands for the widest possible coverage; and, third, it makes it possible to exclude the trade union from the workplace. For the employers' organization to seek to negotiate standard rates of pay would, in most cases, be regarded as a major infringement of the employers' right to manage. This was a point stressed time and time again in interviews with employers' organization officials.

Provisions for standard working hours also deserve some comment. This is one of the rare examples of the standard type of rule mentioned above: the rule which is to be applied directly in the workplace without alteration or supplementation. Trade union pressure has been important in bringing this about and so too has legislation, especially in France, Italy and West Germany. From the employer's point of view, however, the negotiation of standard hours does not involve the same kind of constraints as standard rates of pay. The employer has the advantage of a yardstick: it is much more difficult to justify differences between grades in hours than in earnings. And yet, in principle, he remains free to vary the amount of work performed by overtime or short time in cases of special need. Clearly, this is not analogous in practice to paying standard rates and varying the numbers employed. This helps to explain why individual employers continue to regard hours as standard, even in cases where other provisions of these agreements have declined significantly in their importance. Engineering in Britain is a very good example.[11].

Procedural or Substantive Control?

It is possible to conceive of the procedural and substantive contents of multi-employer agreements as having two distinct functions: the one the regulation of conflict between the parties and the other the precise regulation of the employment relationship (Flanders, 1970b: 99). In an important sense, however, this distinction is arbitrary and misleading. For example, a willingness to meet and discuss differences of interest may well obviate the need for a comprehensive and detailed substantive agreement. Similarly, in dealing comprehensively with the substance of the employment relationship, an agreement may make a far greater contribution to regulating conflict between the parties than any procedure for handling disputes. Essentially, procedural and substantive rules offer different means of achieving the same result: that is, the institutionalization of conflict between the parties. From the employer's point of view, therefore, they can also be viewed as different means of controlling the relationship with trade unions.

From this perspective, the difference in emphasis in the agreements in Britain and the other countries is profoundly important for the issues raised in chapter 2. On the face of it, the multi-employer agreements in Britain, especially in engineering and chemicals, impose few limitations on the rule-making of the individual employer; the limited coverage and the lack of detail in the agreements mean that they do not prevent him from settling most matters in the workplace as he sees fit. Indeed, this was the logic of the managerial prerogative clause in the engineering agreement. But – and this is the point which must be emphasized – the price of this freedom is that the trade union and, perhaps more importantly, its members in the workplace also have few limitations imposed upon them. In general, the agreements give the employer few points of reference that can be defended as legitimate in the event of unilateral action by him being challenged by union members in the workplace; most issues have to be settled in a vacuum or in the light of previous decisions or against the background of custom and practice. Moreover, in the absence of detailed substantive agreements lasting for a fixed period, issues have to be dealt with as and when they arise rather than periodically and collectively with other employers. Other things being equal, then, the individual employer

---

[11] In 1979 there was a major dispute in the engineering industry over trade union demands for a reduction in the then 40-hour week which involved the largest number of strike days in that industry in one dispute since the 1926 General Strike. Altogether sixteen million days were lost due to the strike. For further details, see Rice (1980).

is given little protection from workplace claims and grievances. Also the disputes procedure may or may not be honoured by the trade union and its members in the event of a failure to agree. Even if it is, they are free to take industrial action against the individual employer as soon as its provisions are exhausted. As Clegg (1979: 117) points out,

> the procedure may experience considerable difficulty in resolving disputes over managerial rights unless the matter is specifically regulated by agreement. Once procedure has failed to resolve the issue, however, the union is free to take industrial action against a managerial decision.

In practice, a great deal depends on the relative power of the parties. In the 1920s and 1930s the 'common law' model allowed the individual employer a fair measure of autonomy. In the context of the full employment and buoyant product markets of the post-Second World War period, however, a policy of controlling the workplace through procedures was nowhere near so successful.

Paradoxical as it may seem, the more comprehensive and detailed multi-employer agreements in the other countries give the individual employer greater control. Three points can be made. First, the limitations agreements impose on the employer are not so extensive as might be imagined. As the previous section pointed out, few of the rules are standard; most establish minimum conditions only or allow considerable flexibility in their application. Second, and perhaps more importantly in the present context, the comprehensive and detailed coverage of the agreements imposes limitations on the activities of the trade union and its members in the workplace, and tends to exhaust the scope for further negotiations or ensure that these negotiations are largely administrative or supplementary. For example, it is one thing to negotiate over the position of a job in a detailed job classification system: it is quite another to negotiate an independent and separate rate for a job. Third, comprehensive and detailed multi-employer agreements that are fixed-term tend to concentrate workplace bargaining in the period following the negotiation of the multi-employer agreement; because of the status of the agreement, a topic discussed in the next section, it is difficult for the trade union or its members to take industrial action during the life of the agreement in support of claims and grievances. In brief, then, the comprehensive and detailed coverage of substantive issues in multi-employer agreements makes a major contribution to the neutralization of the workplace in the other countries.

The Status of Multi-Employer Agreements

There are also important differences between Britain and the other countries so far as the status of multi-employer agreements is concerned.

Clearly, the contents of multi-employer agreements are an important consideration in their status. Other things being equal, the more comprehensive and more detailed they are, the greater the authority they are likely to enjoy. But the contents are not the only consideration. The legal framework is important too. As the introduction to this chapter pointed out, multi-employer bargaining in Britain has been governed by the procedural rules employers and trade unions have made themselves rather than by rules laid down by the state. Until the 1971 Industrial Relations Act, developments in the legal framework in Britain had taken the form of the granting of immunities in respect of the activities of employers' organizations and, more particularly, trade unions; there were no positive legal rights of association or recognition for the purposes of making collective agreements (Department of Employment, 1981: 15). It is perhaps a reflection of the significance in which multi-employer bargaining was held that even with the attempt of the Industrial Relations Act to introduce a comprehensive legal framework of industrial relations, the right of the employers to belong to employers' organizations or to be represented by them for the purposes of collective bargaining was not legally recognized. Nor did the procedures for recognition appear to envisage an employers' organization as a unit of bargaining in the Industrial Relations Act and, indeed, in the Employment Protection Act of 1975.[12]

The position so far as the legal status of collective agreements is concerned is complicated. Strictly speaking, multi-employer agreements were debarred by statute from being enforced as legal contracts. Section 4 (4) of the Trade Union Act 1871 states that 'nothing in this Act shall enable any court to entertain any legal proceedings instituted with the object of directly enforcing or recovering damages for the breach of any agreement between one trade union and another. Since most employers'

---

[12] Significantly, too, by extending the periods of notice laid down under the 1963 Contracts of Employment Act, the Industrial Relations Act further undermined the ability of employers to engage in sympathetic lockouts.

So far as the legal status of the sympathetic lockout discussed in chapter 3 is concerned, there is no right to lockout in Britain any more than there is a right to strike. But the lockout is not regarded as unlawful in principle. Broadly speaking, in locking out his employees the employer would be deemed to be acting lawfully if he gave the appropriate period of notice, but unlawfully if he did not. In practice, however, the ability of British employers to engage in sympathetic lockouts has been severely restricted in recent years. Prior to the 1963 Contracts of Employment Act, the employer could more or less lock out at will. This is because in some industries the period of notice required in the case of manual workers could be as little as one hour. With the passage of the Contracts of Employment Act 1963, the Industrial Relations Act 1971, and the Employment Protection Act 1975, however, the period of notice the employer is required to give has been lengthened considerably. Consequently, the costs of indulging in a sympathetic lockout have increased significantly. In many cases they are likely to be prohibitive. Only where workers refuse to give an undertaking that they will work normally is the employer likely to be freed from the requirement to give notice or payment in lieu (for a detailed analysis of the law relating to lockouts in Britain see Hepple, 1980: 25–32.)

organizations were trade unions in the eyes of the law until 1971,[13] this meant that multi-employer agreements could not be enforced.[14] But, to quote the Donovan Commission (1968: 126), there was nothing to stop the parties from making their agreements indirectly enforceable or one or other of them seeking a declaration from the courts. That this did not happen, the Donovan Commission emphasized (1968: 126) 'is not . . . due to the law. It is due to the intention of the parties themselves. They do not intend to make a legally binding contract, and without both parties intending to be legally bound there can be no contract in the legal sense'.[15] Furthermore, the agreements employers' organizations and trade unions negotiated did not lend themselves to legal enforceability. 'To make them enforceable would in the first place require their re-drafting, a task which could only be undertaken by or with the assistance of professional lawyers' (Donovan, 1968: 127). In short, multi-employer agreements were 'gentlemen's agreements' to be binding in honour only.

Evidently, it is difficult to say whether or not things would have been different had multi-employer agreements and, in particular, disputes procedures been legally enforceable. That said, by the 1960s many employers had been persuaded by the growing number of unofficial strikes that the lack of legal status of these procedures was an important defect and ought to be remedied. For example, both the CBI (1965: 33) and the EEF (1965: 26) argued in their evidence to the Donovan Commission that procedural agreements should be made legally enforceable and trade unions should be required by law to guarantee the execution of the agreement by their members. Certainly the Donovan Commission itself did not take the matter lightly: the enforcement of collective agreements was given fairly exhaustive treatment in a separate chapter of its own. Added to which, the majority of the Commission rejected the proposals to make collective agreements legally enforceable not so much on grounds of principle but in view of the practical realities of collective bargaining in Britain.[16]

[13] The legal status of employers' organizations in Britain and the other countries has been discussed in chapter 3.

[14] The Industrial Relations Act 1971 provided that collective agreements would be intended to be legally enforceable unless the parties stated otherwise. The overwhelming majority of negotiators took the necessary steps to ensure that their agreements should not be regarded as legally enforceable; so-called TINA LEA clauses (this is not a legally enforceable agreement) became more or less universal. Under the Trade Union and Labour Relations Act of 1974, which repealed the 1971 Act, the position was reversed. That is to say, it is assumed that the parties do not intend their agreements to be legally enforceable unless they agree in writing to the contrary.

[15] It was primarily on the grounds that the parties did not intend to create legal relations that Ford's case against the AEU for breaking an agreement was decided in 1968. Significantly, too, the agreement in question was a single-employer agreement and so did not come within the restriction of section 4(4) of the 1871 Act. For further details of the Ford case, and a discussion of the legal status of collective agreements, see Lewis (1970 and 1979).

[16] The Donovan Commission (1968: 128–35) was particularly exercised by the problem of how any sanctions might be implemented in the event of a breach of a legally enforceable agreement.

The situation in the other countries is very different. The rights of the parties and the making of collective agreements are regulated by specific pieces of legislation in the case of France (1950, 1970 and 1982), Sweden (1928) and West Germany (1949 and 1952) and in the Italian constitution. In France, Sweden and West Germany the legal status of collective agreements is clear-cut: they are required to be in writing and are deemed to be contracts enforceable by and against those who are parties to them. In Italy there has been no specific legislation giving effect to the provisions of the 1948 Constitution. Even so, under Italian civil law collective agreements are regarded as legally enforceable contracts at least so far as the parties to the agreements are concerned (Giugni, 1965b: 94, 98).[17]

From the point of view of the present study, the legal status of collective agreements in the other countries is important in two respects. First, multi-employer agreements are deemed to be compulsory contracts in that they establish the rights and duties of the parties to one another; and, second,[18] they are deemed to be compulsory codes with the force of legal statutes. The combined effect, it can be argued, is to give multi-employer agreements a significance they have never had in Britain. Each of these aspects will be considered in more detail.

Multi-Employer Agreements as Compulsory Contracts
The contractual status of multi-employer agreements in the other countries imposes a number of obligations on the parties. In the context of the present study, however, one stands out above all the others. In its discussion of possible remedies for the large number of strikes in breach of the procedural provisions in multi-employer agreements in Britain, the Donovan Commission (1968: 124) put it thus:

> Of the obligations thus imposed upon the parties the most important is the 'peace' or 'no strike, no lock-out' obligation which means that the unions or employers or employers' associations parties to the agreement may not use industrial sanctions during the currency of the agreement, not at any rate with a view to changing to their advantage or to the advantage of their members the terms laid down in the agreement. If they violate this obligation, they may be liable to heavy damages, and injunctions or their equivalent may be issued to prevent them from taking such action or to compel them to stop it.

> The 'peace' obligation is imposed upon both sides, but it is more important in practice as a remedy to assist the employers than as a remedy to assist the unions; strikes everywhere are a more significant feature of industrial relations than lockout. This aspect of the

[17] See Guigni (1956a: 94–6) for some of the reasons why legislation was not introduced. See also chapter 6.
[18] For the basis of this dual effect of collective agreements, see Kahn-Freund (1954b: 55; 1977: 124–8).

legal enforcement of collective agreements is therefore of special importance to protect the interest of management in the continuous flow of production.

The precise implications of the contractual status of multi-employer agreements differ from country to country. At the risk of over-simplification, however, the four countries may be divided into two groups. The first comprises France and Italy. Here the 'peace obligation' implicit in multi-employer agreements is not unqualified and there are few, if any, legal sanctions to support it. In Sweden and West Germany, which make up the second group, the situation is very different. The 'peace obligation', which is imposed by statute, is more or less un-qualified so far as the employers' organizations and trade unions making the agreement are concerned. The operation of the 'peace obligation' is also supervised by labour courts which can and do award damages in the event of its being breached.

In France the legal framework provides for both contractual and statutory conciliation of disputes. If a trade union enters into an explicit agreement with employers not to take strike action during the period of an agreement or until the conciliation procedure has been exhausted, such provisions can and have been enforced by the courts (Brun, 1965: 195; Blanc-Jouvan, 1971: 48). The qualification is that such clauses are not deemed to constitute an excessive restriction of the right to strike enshrined in the constitution (Blanc-Jouvan, 1971: 48). In the absence of specific clauses dealing with the 'peace obligation', the statutory provisions (which, in any event, the parties are obliged to include in the multi-employer agreement if they wish to be extended to cover an industry) come into play. This means the parties must seek to conciliate the dispute, but the law does not require that conciliation precede a strike and the parties are not under an obligation to settle the dispute. In fact, there are many examples of strikes being held lawfully, even though not preceded by attempts at conciliation (Blanc-Jouvan, 1971: 49). In practice, then, the legal sanctions underpinning the 'peace obligation' largely depend on the wording of the agreement; if trade unions refuse to restrict the right to strike voluntarily – and it is very much the policy of the CGT so to refuse – the 'peace obligation', to all intents and purposes, has moral authority only.

In Italy the individual's right to strike, which is spelled out in the 1948 Constitution, has assumed even greater significance. This is because of the failure to introduce specific legislation dealing with collective bargaining. Under the civil law, the multi-employer agreement is deemed to be binding on both parties. But the individual, it is argued, cannot waive the constitutional right to strike nor can the trade union do so on the individual's behalf (Giugni, 1965c: 219). The 'no-strike' clauses which began to make their appearance in multi-employer agreements from 1960 onwards are therefore of very doubtful legal validity, although the debate among lawyers has been intense. Certainly, trade unions and their members have taken strike action in breach of such clauses; and it seems that employers have not thought it worth their while to seek redress in the courts in these circumstances. In the words of Giugni (1965c: 219) 'the value of these clauses has up to now been primarily of a moral and political nature'.

There is one other important point to make about France and Italy at this stage. In both countries the right to strike is set out in the constitution and is regarded as a fundamental political right, which is the property of the individual. This is profoundly important for the ability of the employer to engage in the sympathetic lockouts discussed in chapter 3. The lockout is not viewed as being the equivalent of the strike (Kirsch, 1980: 32–9; Pera, 1980: 39–43). In neither country is there a reference to the lockout in the constitution. The courts, if not treating lockouts by individual employers as illegal, have nonetheless tended to regard them as extreme measures to be taken only in exceptional circumstances: these include situations where *force majeure* is held to apply or those where there has evidently been a failure to work. Lockouts taken by employers in sympathy with other employers would almost certainly be deemed to be unlawful; the employer participating in such action would at the very least be liable for the reimbursement of loss of wages.

In Sweden the 'peace obligation' is imposed by section 4 of the Collective Agreements Act of 1928. During the period of the validity of a collective agreement, industrial action is prohibited in the following four circumstances:

1. On the grounds of a dispute about the validity, existence, or correct meaning of an agreement, or on the grounds of whether a particular action violates the agreement or the provisions of the Act. Thus the parties may not resort to direct action merely because they disagree about the provisions set out in the contract.
2. In order to bring about alterations in the terms of the agreement.
3. In order to enforce provisions intended to come into force after the contract has expired.
4. In order to assist others in cases where they are not themselves entitled to resort to direct action. This prohibits the giving of help to someone who as himself repudiated his obligations under a collective agreement or the Act (quoted in Johnston, 1962: 50).

The parties to a collective agreement must not give support to illegal industrial action to which a member has resorted. Second, the party to an agreement must 'endeavour to prevent its members from committing unlawful offensive actions' and, where they have occurred, 'endeavour to cause such members to cease committing such action'. The peace obligation, it should be noted, not only binds the trade union and its representatives but also individual trade union members. Furthermore, individual trade union members as well as the trade union are liable for damages in the event of the Labour Court establishing there has been industrial action in breach of the peace obligation. In the case of the trade union the damages are limitless.[19] The maximum amount of damages the individual trade union member can incur is 200 kroner. This sum has not been increased since the Act was first introduced in 1928; but at that time it was almost equal to the monthly earnings of an unskilled worker (Schmidt, 1971: 182).

Some impression of the impact of the compulsory effect of multi-employer agreements in Sweden can be gained by studying the events which had taken place in one of the establishments visited during the course of the research. In the year before the visit the 'wage drift agreement' negotiated in the autumn had been preceded by a week-long strike on the part of a number of workers which was clearly in breach of the peace obligation in the multi-employer agreement covering the industry. There seems little doubt that during the strike contact was maintained between the 'factory club' and the strike committee and that information was passed from one to the other. It is also clear that the works' club used the strike in its negotiations with the management. Significantly, however, factory club members did not feel able to join the strike and, indeed, felt obliged to demand a return to work in order to protect the union's interest. It also seems that the factory' club representatives were able to do little to help the unofficial strikers when the strike ended. Not all Swedish employers take advantage of the legal framework to seek damages from the Labour Court against trade union members who act in breach of the peace obligation. This particular management did. Each of the unofficial strikers was subsequently fined the statutory 200 kroner by the Labour Court.

There is one type of industrial dispute in Sweden in which the peace obligation can be overridden, which is significant for the discussion of the sympathetic lockout in chapters 2 and 3. The Collective Agreements Act 1928 gives wide scope for sympathetic action by both employers and trade unions (Johnston, 1962: 151–2). Indeed, it goes so far as to accept that the right to take sympathetic action takes precedence over the peace obligation implicit or explicit in collective agreements. Thus employers in one industry can support those in another with a sympathetic lockout even if they have no dispute with their own employees. Sympathetic action of this kind is likely to be regarded as illegal only if the party which is being supported is itself not entitled to take industrial action in the primary dispute.

In West Germany the peace obligation is also imposed by legislation. Under the Collective Agreements Act of 1949 (as amended in 1952) the parties to a collective agreement are required to maintain industrial peace

[19] For further details see Schmidt (1971: 180–4).

and take positive steps to ensure that their members do so. The peace obligation, it should be noted, is deemed to be implicit in collective agreements; it need not be expressed. Except where there is an unconditional peace obligation, however, the peace obligation applies only to the collective agreement dealing with the issues in question. For example, a collective agreement on wages does not stop a trade union from striking for longer vacations (Ramm, 1971: 90). As in Sweden, damages can be awarded in the event of one or other of the parties taking action in breach of the peace obligation, although there are no special provisions so far as individual trade union members are concerned.

In both Sweden and West Germany there are labour courts which have responsibility for overseeing the operation of the respective pieces of legislation. In Sweden there is a single labour court; in West Germany a hierarchy of labour courts at local, *Land* and federal level.[20] The case law these labour courts have developed in interpreting and enforcing the legislation has itself been profoundly important. For example, through its definition of the disputes and its interpretation of the contents of collective agreements, the labour court in Sweden has given wide-ranging meaning to the peace obligation and has consistently upheld the employers' right to manage (Johnston, 1962: 158; Schmidt, 1971: 202–13).[21]

If anything, the labour courts in West Germany, especially the Federal Labour Court, have been even more creative. Especially significant to the question of the peace obligation is the Federal Labour Court's development of the doctrine of 'social adequacy'. In effect, the court has come to the conclusion that any industrial action is illegal if it is of such a nature as to make it impossible to terminate by a collective agreement. In practice, this means that any unofficial industrial action is by definition illegal because only a trade union can reach a collective agreement in the eyes of the law. A stoppage has also come to be regarded as 'socially inadequate' if the aim it pursues can be attained by other lawful means, and if all chances of arriving at a peaceful settlement have not been exhausted (Ramm, 1965b: 203–9; 1971: 145–57).

The Federal Labour Court is also the source for the legality of the sympathetic lockout discussed in chapter 3. In West Germany the ability of employers to engage in sympathetic lockouts is not set out in the constitution or the relevant statutes. Indeed, in the constitution of the state of Hesse the lockout is expressly outlawed. In a famous judgment in 1955, however, the Federal Labour Court developed the doctrine of 'equality of weapons'. Taking a collective view, the court argued that the

[20] For further details of the Labour Courts in Sweden and West Germany, see Ramm (1965a, b and 1971) and Schmidt (1971: 198–227).
[21] In one sense the fact that the Swedish Labour Court has upheld the employer's right to manage is not too surprising in view of the management prerogative clause in multi-employer agreements. One effect of the 1928 Collective Agreements Act was to make this clause legally enforceable.

employer should be entitled to undertake sympathetic action in order to achieve 'parity of combat' with trade unions. The lockout was not to be subject to the rules ordinarily imposed in cases of individual dismissals. Unlike Sweden, however, the use of the lockout is restricted to the industry or region in which the primary dispute takes place. The doctrine of 'social adequacy' referred to above requires that industrial action be taken only when an outcome can be reached by a collective agreement. By definition, sympathetic lockouts or strikes are illegal if the dispute is one which cannot be settled by collective agreement. In effect, then, the sympathetic lockout is legal only if it is confined to the region which determines the geographical scope of application of an agreement to be made (for further details, see Goll, 1980: 22–5; Löwisch, 1980: 1–14; and Söllner, 1980: 14–22).

To conclude this discussion – and to illustrate the significance of the contractual status of multi-employer agreements for this study – it will be useful to return to Ford's decision in 1963 to join the metalworking employers' organization in North Rhine-Westphalia which was first raised in chapter 2. It will be remembered that Ford made this decision when faced with industrial action by IG Metall in support of demands for a company agreement. In the absence of any collective agreement governing its relationship with Ford, this was something IG Metall was perfectly entitled to do under the law. Once Ford joined the employers' organization, however, it immediately placed itself under the protection of the peace obligation of the regional metalworking agreement to which IG Metall was a party. Had IG Metall persisted with its industrial action, it would not only have laid itself open to the charge of infringing Ford's right of association, but would also have been vulnerable to action for damages for breaching the peace obligation in the multi-employer agreement. In the circumstances, then, it is perhaps not surprising that Ford joined the employers' organization.[22]

Multi-Employer Agreements as Compulsory Codes

Although collective agreements in Britain are not legally enforceable as between the parties, they do have legal effect through the incorporation of suitable terms into the individual contract of employment. This is known as the principle or theory of the 'implied term' (Kahn-Freund, 1965b: 28–9; 1977: 132–40). Strictly speaking, the principle does not apply to the collective agreement as such but to the custom or usage which it embodies. That is to say, in the absence of an express agreement between the employer and the employee, the courts would assume that the parties intended to incorporate into the individual contract of employment that which is customary in the industry or locality. In as much as collective agreements and, in particular, multi-employer agreements, are likely to be

[22] Schmidt (1971: 163) suggests that employers in Sweden have joined employers' organizations in similar circumstances.

an important source of what is customary, it is to these agreements that the courts have often had resort. The application of the principle is more or less automatic; it is not necessary for there to be an express reference to a collective agreement. But the application of the principle is not compulsory. The court may decide that the terms of a multi-employer agreement are unreasonable in the particular circumstances. More importantly, there is nothing in the law to stop the employer from reaching agreement with his employees on pay and conditions which are inferior or superior to those in the multi-employer agreement.

It has also been possible in Britain to extend the terms of multi-employer agreements to employers who are not members of the employers' organization. In recent years the provisions for doing so have been contained in Schedule 11 of the Employment Protection Act 1975, which was repealed by the Employment Act of 1980; before that similar provisions existed under the Terms and Conditions of Employment Act of 1959, the Conditions of Employment and National Arbitration Order 1950, Number 1305, and the Industrial Disputes Order 1951, Number 1376, Article 2.[23] Briefly, under these provisions it was open to an employers' organization or a trade union to claim an employer in the trade, industry or section covered by the agreement was failing to observe recognized terms and conditions. If the matter could not be conciliated, it went to the industrial court, which could issue an order making the recognized terms and conditions implied terms of the individual contract of employment. The effect of these provisions was therefore compulsory, but the provisions themselves were not automatic; they were essentially *ad hoc* in operation (Kahn-Freund, 1965b: 30–2; 1977: 131; Donovan Commission, 1968: 128). A general rule was not established either. Only the individual employer cited in the claim was affected.

The situation in the other countries is very different. The legal status accorded to collective agreements means that the terms and conditions in multi-employer agreements are mandatory so far as member employers of the signatory employers' organization are concerned (Kahn-Freund, 1965a: 11–12). That is to say, these terms have automatic and compulsory effect on the individual contracts of employment such employers enter into. In the words of the Collective Agreements Act of 1949 (as amended 1952) in West Germany, the terms 'regulate the content, the making and the termination of the employment relationship' (quoted in Ramm, 1965a: 87). In practice, this means that the employer who is a member of the signatory employers' organization cannot contract out of the terms of the multi-employer agreement to the detriment of the employee – although he can offer better terms – and any terms in the

---

[23] A similar principle was enshrined in the various Fair Wages resolutions which were rescinded in 1983. These resolutions – the first was passed in 1891 – required employers awarded government contracts to observe terms and conditions of employment not less favourable than those of collective agreements for the trade or industry.

individual contract of employment inferior to those of the multi-employer agreement are automatically void. The effect of the multi-employer agreement, then, is similar to that of an order made under the Wages Councils Act or Agricultural Wages Acts in Britain (Kahn-Freund, 1965a: 11).

In France and West Germany there are provisions making it possible to extend the automatic and compulsory effect of the terms of multi-employer agreements throughout an entire industry or branch. In France these provisions, which date back to 1936, enable the Minister of Labour, following consultations with the *Commission Supérieure des Conventions Collectives*, to extend the terms of the agreement provided it has been negotiated by a joint committee of the 'most representative organizations'; that it contains certain obligatory clauses, which will be discussed later in this section, and that it covers all the categories of a branch either in a single text or by a general text plus annexes. Under section 5 of the Collective Agreements Act of 1949 (as amended 1952) in West Germany either the Federal Minister of Labour or his counterpart in the *Land* may, on the request of one of the parties, issue a declaration of 'universal applicability'. In this case the employers covered by the agreement must employ 50 per cent of the workers coming within its scope if it were extended. The declaration must also be in the public interest, so that the 50 per cent can be waived if, for example, the wages paid by employers not bound by the agreement failed to meet minimum requirements of a decent standard of living. But neither of these conditions need to be present if the declaration appears to be required in order 'to remove a state of social distress' (Ramm, 1965a: 88–9). In effect, then, the agreements employers' organizations and trade unions negotiate can be approved and enforced as mandatory law on employers not members of employers' organizations.

It is clear that those who drafted the 1948 Constitution in Italy hoped to achieve a similar objective. Under Article 39, representative organizations of employers and employees are given the right to negotiate collective agreements with *erga omnes* effect; that is to say, they were to apply throughout an industry or branch. In the absence of enabling legislation giving effect to these aspirations, however, collective agreements have not been deemed to have *erga omnes* effect. But so important was the principle involved that an attempt was made in 1959 to achieve the extension of collective agreements without implementing Article 39. Law 741 of July 1959 made it possible for the Minister of Labour to issue decrees establishing minimum standards on an industry-by-industry basis in conformity with collective agreements negotiated before 3 October 1959. Although attempts to prolong this procedure were subsequently deemed to be unconstitutional, some 1,000 decrees were issued under this law containing minimum wages and conditions based on the multi-employer agreements then in force (Giugni, 1965a: 96–8).

The Italian courts have also used another avenue to secure the extension of at least the minimum wages clauses in collective agreements (Giugni, 1965a: 98–9). Article 36 of the 1948 Constitution establishes the right of workers to an 'adequate' wage. Basing their decisions on this article, the courts have proceeded to declare null and void the clauses of individual contracts which are 'inadequate' in comparison with those in the multi-employer agreements in the industries in question.

Sweden is the only one of the other countries in which no attempt has been made to introduce legislation to bring about the extension of the terms and conditions of multi-employer agreements. The high levels of organization, especially among employers, make this unnecessary. Even so, it is difficult for the rare employer who is not a member of an employers' organization to escape the effect of these terms and conditions. A trade union may invite such employers to sign a letter in which they declare their intention to comply with these terms and conditions; these so-called 'adhesion contracts' would then normally be regarded as legally binding (Schmidt, 1971: 169). Failing that, a claim can be made through the ordinary courts requiring the recalcitrant employer to comply with the terms and conditions of the multi-employer agreement and an award may be granted on the grounds of customary law (Schmidt, 1971: 172).

From the point of view of employers, the code or law-making function of multi-employer agreements is significant in two respects. First, if employers are going to be made the subject of the terms and conditions of multi-employer agreements, there is some incentive to belong to employers' organizations and to participate in the process of making the agreements. In other words, this is a factor which helps to explain the high levels of membership of employers' organizations. Second, the code-making function is not without advantages for employers. The obligations in the agreements which are given the force of law do not simply impinge on the employers; for example, workers can be obliged to work overtime at the request of the employer or to engage in shiftwork. Furthermore, in as much as the multi-employer agreement introduces minimum terms and conditions of employment throughout an entire industry or branch, it helps to prevent undercutting.

Important though these advantages are to employers, it is trade unions which are the major beneficiary of the code or law-making function of multi-employer agreements.[24] Indeed, it is difficult to escape the conclusion that it is largely because multi-employer agreements are compulsory codes that trade unions seem no more eager than employers to abandon multi-employer bargaining in the four countries. Multi-employer bargaining makes it difficult for trade unions and their

[24] For example, Kahn-Freund (1977: 129) writes, 'it is not a gross exaggeration to say that the contractual function of collective agreements is mainly for the benefit of management, and its normative effect mainly for the benefit of labour'.

members to challenge managerial prerogative in the workplace. Nonetheless, it does make it possible for the trade unions to participate in establishing a statutory floor of rights covering a wide range of substantive issues. This statutory floor can be used in well-organized establishments as the basis for further action by the members either independently or using the statutory machinery of workplace representation; it can be applied in the large number of small establishments where trade union membership is weak or non-existent; and, furthermore, in France and West Germany it can also be applied in establishments not even members of employers' organizations.[25] By negotiating comprehensive and detailed multi-employer agreements, then, the trade unions can compensate for their weakness in the workplace. They can also justify their claim – and this is especially important in France and Italy – to be 'mass' organizations primarily concerned with the interests of the working class as a whole rather than one section of it.

A structure of collective bargaining giving rise to agreements which can be made into compulsory codes also has considerable advantages from the point of view of governments. Much of the opposition which might be aroused by attempts to introduce direct statutory regulation is avoided by delegating the initial responsibility for drawing up the code to the parties themselves. It is, nonetheless, possible to put pressure on the parties to include subjects the government thinks should be covered. Along with trade union pressure, then, this helps to explain the emphasis given to substantive issues in multi-employer agreements.

To take one paradoxical example, much of the detail to be found in multi-employer agreements in Italy has its origins in the fascist period. The Charter of Labour of 1927 not only legalized the exclusive recognition of fascist employers' organizations and trade unions, but also required a number of subjects to be included in collective agreements: annual leave; pay; compensation in the event of death or discharge; retention of full rights in the event of a change of ownership; restriction on dismissal in the event of illness; and hygiene conditions. Subsequent rules and decrees made it necessary for collective agreements to make further and precise provision for discipline, probationary periods, wage and salary levels, and sickness benefits. Clauses relating to social security and welfare benefits followed; they included old age, disability, survivors' insurance; unemployment insurance; tuberculosis insurance; maternity insurance; and even family allowances.

---

[25] To quote an example, in the early 1970s the metalworking employers in Italy questioned the value of continuing to negotiate the national category agreements in their present form. The trade unions opposed any change on the grounds that the 'dual' system of multi-employer and workplace bargaining enabled them to win concessions from the larger employers which they could extend to smaller employers through the multi-employer agreements. The issue of investment is a good example. See discussion by Mortillaro and Fernex (1976).

Similarly, the Law of 11 February 1950 has dictated much of the detail of French multi-employer agreements. To qualify for extension, these agreements must not only be negotiated by the most representative organizations of employers and trade unions but also make provision for the following subjects: a guarantee of the freedom of individual employees to organize and to express opinions; compliance with applicable minimum wage payments; procedures and provisions for the hiring and discharging of employees, including term of notice for discharge; machinery for the election of 'delegates' and members of 'works committees'; paid holidays, and leave; clauses relating to revision, modification and revocation of all or parts of the agreement; a procedure for conciliation and settlement of collective disputes; apprenticeship provisions; special provisions for women and children (including equal pay for equal work).[26]

More generally, governments can use hints, suggestions and threats to get subjects included in multi-employer agreements. All the countries have to some degree been affected by these forms of government pressures. For example, in Sweden, the role of the government was not unimportant in securing the negotiation of the 'Basic Agreement' in 1938 between SAF and LO. In West Germany the 1954 'Margarethenhof agreement' similarly owed a great deal to government pressure. Perhaps France, however, offers the best example. Chapter 4 drew attention to the significant developments in multi-industry bargaining in the post-war period and in the post-1968 period in particular. A number of these agreements had their origins in government pressure. In particular, the ordinances of July 1967 promulgated by the Pompidou government led to the agreements on employment, short-time working, and training. The election of Pompidou to the presidency in the Spring of 1969 led directly to the agreement on staff status. In effect, the government invited the parties to meet and to negotiate collective agreements on social matters which were subsequently made into laws. Indeed, during this period it became extremely difficult to establish where collective bargaining ended and legal enactment began, so intertwined were the two.

Conclusions

The contents and status of the agreements employers' organizations negotiate with trade unions are fundamentally important in the context of the present study. The lack of substantive rules in British multi-employer

[26] The 'Auroux Laws' of 1981–3 also required a number of subjects to be covered in collective agreements. In particular, the law of 13 November 1982 sought to impose compulsory annual negotiations on 'real' wages and the organization and length of working hours at enterprise level. For further details, see Caire (1984), Delamotte (1985) and Eyraud and Tchobanian (1985).

agreements creates a vacuum in the workplace. In law, the employer is free to make the rules unilaterally, but the trade union and its members are also free to challenge the employer. The disputes procedure, supposed to provide the machinery to settle such issues peaceably, has the status of a 'gentlemen's agreement' only, and the employer is therefore extremely vulnerable to industrial action taken in support of claims and grievances. By contrast, the other countries' comprehensive and detailed coverage of substantive rules tends to exhaust the scope for further negotiations in the workplace or to ensure that these negotiations are largely administrative or supplementary, and that they are concentrated in the period immediately following the settlement of the multi-employer agreement. Multi-employer agreements are also legally enforceable contracts; both the rights and duties of the parties to each other and the substantive terms and conditions have the force of law. Notwithstanding the very considerable differences between them, the overall effect of their legal status is to give multi-employer agreements in these countries a significance they have never enjoyed in Britain; employers, trade unions and governments have a vested interest in their continued existence, even if the interest is not the same.

So far as the explanation for the differences is concerned, the relationship between the contents and status of the multi-employer agreements is clearly important. In Britain the absence of compulsory rules does not in itself explain the lack of substantive rules. But it does help to explain the emphasis given to procedural rules: in effect, the parties were obliged to draw up their own rules governing their relationship. In the other countries the relationship between the contents and status of agreements is stronger. First, the lack of procedural rules in such countries as France and West Germany reflects the detail of the legislation dealing with collective bargaining. Second, the fact that multi-employer agreements are compulsory codes in all four countries helps to explain the emphasis given to substantive rules.

It is tempting to conclude from this that the major differences identified in this chapter are largely to be explained in terms of the legal system. The justification for doing so is particularly strong in view of the parallel differences that appear to exist between the legal systems and collective bargaining systems in Britain and the other countries. As Kahn-Freund (1977: 54–6) has said of Britain:

> there is an extraordinary similarity between the spirit of the common law and the spirit of industrial relations in Britain. The common law is permeated by a deep distrust, by an almost obsessional fear of 'tidiness'. So is much of the British system of industrial relations. Both sides have a traditional desire of solving problems ad hoc, as they arise. So does the common law.

By the same token, it can be argued, there are striking similarities between the statute law and the 'contractual' method of collective bargaining: in both cases the emphasis is on rights and obligations explicitly spelt out.

Having said this, the temptation to conclude that the differences highlighted in this chapter are to be explained in terms of the legal system must be resisted. As Kahn-Freund (1977: 54) has also pointed out, there is no intrinsic reason why collective agreements should not be regarded as legally enforceable contracts under the common law; and Australia and the USA have a similar legal system to Britain but their legal frameworks of collective bargaining are both very different. Similarly, not all the countries where the statute law prevails regard collective agreements as legally enforceable contracts. Kahn-Freund (1977: 53) quotes Belgium as an example.

In making Britain the main focus of the comparison, there is the danger of forgetting the considerable differences in the legal framework of collective bargaining in the other four countries. To quote perhaps the most obvious, in Sweden and West Germany the legal framework allows employers to engage in sympathetic lockouts; in France and Italy, the sympathetic lockout is effectively illegal due to the constitutional status of the individual's right to strike. Again in Sweden and West Germany, the peace obligation implicit in collective agreements is more or less absolute; in France and Italy it is very much qualified by the individual's right to strike. In Italy the very status of collective agreements has come to be questioned. In these and other cases, then, it would seem that the legal framework of collective bargaining reflects influences other than the legal system. It is to these influences the study now turns.

6

Trade Unionism: Challenge and Response

Essentially, the differences identified in previous chapters represent variations on a common pattern of development : the resort to collective action by employers to deal with the challenge of trade unions and their acquiescence in multi-employer bargaining as the least unacceptable means of institutionalizing industrial conflict. As well as maximizing the employers' bargaining power, multi-employer bargaining made it possible to meet trade union demands for a wide geographical coverage of the substantive issues of collective bargaining. Indeed, it was the wide coverage to be achieved by a single act of recognition in each industry which prompted governments in four of the five countries (Sweden being the exception) to lend their support to the principle of multi-employer bargaining in the crisis years of the immediate post-First World War period. Multi-employer bargaining also made it possible to put a floor under wages competition; in some cases it helped employers to achieve a measure of market control. Finally, and above all, multi-employer bargaining made it possible to exclude the trade union from the workplace or, at the very least, to set limits to the role it could play there.

To understand the main differences between the five countries – and, in particular, the differences between Britain and the others – it is necessary to explore in some detail the origins of multi-employer bargaining. In particular, it is necessary to identify and explain the type of rule on which multi-employer bargaining developed, for this was to be profoundly important for subsequent developments. As the previous chapter explained, two main distinctions may be drawn so far as the type of rule is concerned. First, multi-employer bargaining could be based predominantly on either procedural or substantive rules. The word predominantly is used advisedly. There was little point in having procedural rules unless the object was to negotiate about some substantive issues; equally, it was impossible not to have some understanding about how substantive rules were to be made – even if there was only a tacit acceptance that the parties would meet again at the end of a given period. Second, the rules on which multi-employer bargaining developed could be either voluntary or compulsory. That is to say, the rules could be enforced by the parties themselves or they could be imposed by governments in the form of legislation. In the latter case, governments would seem to have had two main strategies available to them: they could either try to impose a common framework of procedural and substantive rules or they could simply require the parties to recognize one another and then give statutory effect to the rules the parties themselves made. Either way, the result was to make multi-employer agreements into legally enforceable contracts and codes.

In the beginning, it must be emphasized, it was not simply a question of Britain and the other countries following separate paths of development. In printing, building and parts of the clothing industry, the origins of multi-employer bargaining were remarkably similar from one country to another. Multi-employer bargaining developed on the basis of voluntary rules with a strong substantive bias; rates of pay or piecework prices and hours of work figured prominently.[1]

[1] In Britain printing employers came together to negotiate price lists and hours of work with groups of journeymen before the end of the eighteenth century. Similar developments took place in France during the July Monarchy. In Turin employers in the city had agreed to a price list with the printers as early as 1848. In Sweden one of the first recorded collective agreements was introduced in Stockholm printing houses in 1872 and, again, took the form of a price list. The first national collective agreement in Germany was signed in printing in 1874 in the form of guidelines for the negotiation of price lists at local level and for regional conciliation of disputes. The reasons given in 1934 by the French employers' confederation to explain why printing was exceptional in the extent to which pay and other conditions of employment were determined by collective bargaining in France also apply to the other countries.

> In printing, the regime of the collective agreement has constituted the general rule until these recent years for the following reasons: printing crafts have always constituted powerful and independent corporations where the conditions of work were different from those of other corporations; those involved have sought to maintain this traditional regime and to preserve it by texts conforming to the law of 25th March 1919.
>
> Furthermore, the labour force, because of its quality as well as its stability and remuneration, has a pre-dominant part in the work of printing – employers have a much greater interest than in other corporations in assuring themselves by contracts – however onerous for them – against the risks of conflict with their personnel. This question is above all of great importance for the daily press where misunderstandings with the personnel can cause heavy damages to the printers.
>
> Finally, and above all, the workers' organisations in printing have a particular strength: almost all workers must be qualified, and, by definition, they form part of the intellectual elite of the workers, they work in very closely united groups. This explains the unity and the numerical importance of organised workers in printing and their tendency to regulate in advance and in writing the difficulties which the execution of the contract of employment raises.
>
> Generally the collective agreements have been scrupulously observed by the two parties, but their renewal has often been difficult.
>
> (quoted in Conseil National Économique, 1934: 236).

It was in chemicals and metalworking that major differences emerged. This is above all true of metalworking which, due to its size and significance, had a determining influence on the overall pattern in each country. The details are as follows:

- In France there was no mutual recognition in metalworking prior to the First World War. Multi-employer bargaining emerged in the crisis years of 1918–19 with government support which was quickly followed up with legislation providing for compulsory rules. However, the simple legal framework introduced in 1919 proved inadequate to its task; more detailed legal frameworks were to follow in 1936, 1946 and 1950 including a comprehensive procedure for negotiations and a list of substantive issues to appear in agreements. There was also separate legislation in 1936, 1946 and 1968 dealing with the issue of workplace representation. In short, multi-employer bargaining had its origins in compulsory rules; multi-employer agreements were legally enforceable contracts and codes from the very beginning.

- In Germany there was also no mutual recognition in metalworking – or, to be more precise, in the key sectors of iron and steel production and heavy engineering – until 1918. Compared with France, however, the legal framework introduced in 1919 was far more comprehensive. As well as providing for the right to recognition and the legal enforceability of collective agreements, it also dealt with the questions of workplace representation and the extension of multi-employer agreements. It was this legal framework which was more or less resurrected following the Second World War. As in France, then, multi-employer bargaining had its origins in compulsory rules; multi-employer agreements were legally enforceable contracts and codes from the very beginning.

- Contrary to what might have been expected, in Italy multi-employer bargaining emerged on the basis of voluntary rules prior to the First World War in one or two of the main industrial centres of the north such as Turin in 1913. As in Sweden, the rules on which multi-employer bargaining were based were essentially substantive in type and took the form of *concordi di tariffa* or wage agreements. This uneasy compromise did not survive the First World War, however, despite the spread of national multi-employer bargaining under government pressure in the crisis years

---

For further details, see Howe and Waite (1948) and Musson (1954) on Britain, Sales (1967) on France, Stein (1969) on Germany, Bruno (quoted in Horowitz, 1963: 37–8) on Italy, and Hansson (1927: 4–5) on Sweden.

There is evidence to suggest that many of the developments that took place in printing also occurred in building and parts of the clothing industry, especially tailoring and hat-making.

For further details, see, for example, Price (1980), Lefranc (1976) and Werner (1968); for clothing, see Clegg *et al.* (1964: 133–8) and Horowitz (1963: 38).

of 1918 and 1919. It remained for Mussolini to re-impose mutual recognition. Under the Charter of Labour 1927 and subsequent legislation, detailed provision was made for both procedural and substantive rules, albeit the agreements were in effect administrative decrees drawn up by the employers. As in France and Germany, then, multi-employer agreements became legally enforceable contracts and codes. Significantly, however, the fascist framework of industrial relations, the one element of the corporate state to survive the royal decree of 23 November 1944, was not put on a statutory basis under the new Republic.

- In Sweden multi-employer bargaining emerged on the basis of voluntary rules agreed by the parties themselves. The key developments were the national engineering agreement 1905 and the imposition of the 'December Compromise' by SAF on LO in 1906. In contrast to the engineering industry in Britain, however, the rules were embodied in fixed-term agreements and covered such substantive matters as rates of pay and hours of work as well as procedures for handling disputes. Furthermore, whereas in Britain the rules remained voluntary, in Sweden they were made compulsory by the Collective Agreements Act of 1928.

- In Britain multi-employer bargaining emerged on the basis of voluntary rules agreed by the parties themselves. The two key developments in engineering and a number of other industries were, first, district bargaining over substantive issues and, second – and much more important for the longer term – the introduction of a national disputes procedure which in the engineering industry was imposed by employers after the major lockout of 1897–8. Significantly, government intervention during and immediately following the First World War, which was responsible for a very considerable expansion in multi-employer bargaining, did not change the status of the rules. In other words, multi-employer agreements remained 'gentlemen's agreements', binding in honour only.

These then are the key developments and dates so far as the origins of multi-employer bargaining in the five countries are concerned. The differences identified – both inter-industry and international – are largely to be explained in terms of the impact of industrialization. In printing, for example, the impact of industrialization was very similar from one country to another. There was a growth in the market and in the size of operations – leading to the split between masters and journeymen. But there were no significant changes in technology until the end of the nineteenth century. In such an industry, where establishments were relatively small, labour constituted an important share of total costs, and competition was intense, employers were confronted with the challenge of craft trade unions able to establish an effective control over the supply of labour. Much as they might find it distasteful, employers were more or less obliged to join forces and to come to some form of accommodation with trade unions. Added to this, multi-employer bargaining not only helped to institutionalize industrial conflict but also to regulate wage competition; – hence the emphasis on substantive rules.

By contrast, in metalworking the impact of industrialization was very different from one country to another. It was not so much differences in the industrializing elites that were important. There were significant differences in the timing, the pace, and the concentration of industrialization, all of which had a profound effect on the nature of the trade union challenge and of the employers' response. There were also significant differences in the structure and functions performed by the state in the five countries.

It is, then, with the origins of multi-employer bargaining in metalworking and their implications that the remainder of this chapter is primarily concerned. In particular, the aim is to explain why in France and Germany employers did not come to an accommodation with trade unions before the First World War and why multi-employer bargaining came to be based on compulsory rules imposed by government in the form of legislation; why in Italy some employers in the industrial centres in the north came to a short-lived accommodation with trade unions on the basis of voluntary rules primarily substantive in form, and why mutual recognition was reimposed by the fascist regime; why in Sweden employers in engineering reached an accommodation with trade unions in 1905 on the basis of voluntary rules primarily substantive in form, and why in 1928 they were in favour of the Liberal government making these rules compulsory; why, finally, in Britain employers in engineering came to an accommodation with trade unions on the basis of voluntary rules initially substantive in form and why, and with what effect, in 1898 they forced the trade unions to accept a set of procedural rules at national level.

France

The explanation for the absence of collective bargaining in the metalworking industries in France before the First World War would appear to be relatively straightforward. Some commentators (Clapham, 1968: 53) have argued that France did not experience an industrial revolution in the nineteenth century; others (Landes, 1972: 236) have argued that it did but that it was 'muffled'. In any event, for a variety of reasons – the early start of Britain, the revolutionary and Napoleonic wars, the self-perpetuating pattern of small-scale peasant ownership in agriculture – industrialization was not nearly so pervasive as in some of the other countries. Large employers did emerge, especially in iron and steel and heavy engineering. For example, as early as 1870 the Schneiders employed some 12,500 workers at their works in Le Creusot: that is, more than half the town's population (Fohlen, 1973: 60). Even so, the small family-owned business was dominant. In the main, French manufacturers put their energies into markets where they had a competitive advantage or a monopoly: that is to say, high quality consumer goods or those destined for the local market. Both relied on the handicraft type of manufacture in relatively small artisan workshops. According to Brogan (1949: 406), even as late as 1906 silk goods were the main export, closely followed by wine. An important corollary of this pattern of development was that there were few concentrations of employment to be found. Certainly there were few to match those that were to develop in Britain and Germany.

Business interests first emerged as a political force during the reign of Louis Philippe. Under the Republic after 1870 they and the landed nobility shared political power with the peasant proprietors and independent manufacturers and artisans. It was an extremely conservative alliance. In economic affairs the state was active in promoting the development of the railway system, but little else. Under the Republic it applied the traditional role of *garanti tutelaire* or 'guardian' to introduce wide-ranging protection culminating with the Méline Tariff of 1892. As Friedberg (1974: 120–1) has pointed out, tariffs made it possible for the effects of the market to be absorbed within a closed economy. The trade organizations[2] that grew up during the second half of the nineteenth century acted as an intermediary between the administration and the individual manufacturer; in this way they served to protect the discretionary power of the individual manufacturer – even to hide his very identity. Each manufacturer had the right to exercise his trade. Often the best-equipped and productive enterprise sold at prices that permitted the large number of small businesses a continued existence. It was against this background, then, that many of the attitudes that have come to be associated with the French *patron* – selfishness, independence and conservatism – were moulded.

The context in which the attitudes of the *patron* were moulded also had a profound effect on trade unions. The relatively slow development of industrialization and the lack of concentrations of employment meant that few groups except the printers and other craft groups were able to establish viable trade union organizations. To add to their problems, the repression that had marked the putting down of the Paris Commune in

---

[2] The early history of these trade organizations is described in Ehrmann (1957), Lambert (1969), Lefranc (1976), Priouret (1963). Most of these sources stress the relative weakness of the trade organizations. They also border on the psychological in their explanations for this, emphasizing the individualism which in some sense is held to constitute the very nature of the average French employer. See also Laroque (1938: 318). But one does not really need to go beyond the objective circumstances to explain the apparent lack of interest of employers in their trade organizations or, for reasons discussed in the text, why they were relatively slow to form employers' organizations.

1871 continued to be a feature of government policy even after the passage of the law of 1884 giving legal recognition to organizations of workers and employers for the first time. In the early years following the passage of the law it was the multi-industry groupings centred on the *bourses du travail* that seemed to offer the best hopes for trade unionism; local multi-industry organization was to continue to be important even after the emergence of national industrial unions in the 1890s. Even so, few workers could be persuaded to pay their subscriptions. As Guesde, the socialist leader unkindly remarked, 'Your unionism is very special. It is distinguished from unionism in other countries by the fact that it includes so few unionists (quoted in Lorwin, 1954: 42). Increasingly, the inability of the trade unions to win concessions, be they industrial or political, was rationalized and made into a virtue as the radical syndicalist ideology took hold. In 1906 the trade union confederation, the CGT, which had been formed ten years earlier, adopted the *Charte d'Amiens* committing its members to the general strike to bring down the existing order. Apparently, the trade union movement had set its face against any form of co-operation.

Nevertheless, there were significant developments in collective bargaining in France before 1914. Nor were the printing workers, who had negotiated a national conciliation and arbitration agreement as early as 1895, the only group involved. According to Stearns' research (1971: 88–92), by 1909 leading groups of leather workers were covered by collective agreements and by 1913 textile workers in at least twelve cities were similarly affected. Even significant groups of miners and construction workers, along with the metalworkers the main syndicalist groups, had come to terms with their employers. Indeed, most of the large coalfields were covered by collective agreements by 1902; by 1914 construction workers in at least 25 cities had agreements covering wages and conciliation. In short, of the major manufacturing industries in France at this time, only metalworking did not experience significant developments in collective bargaining before 1914.

The exceptionalism of the metalworking industries cannot be explained in terms of a lack of organization on the employers' side.[3] Most metalworking employers were organized in trade organizations well before the turn of the century; the iron masters had been organized since 1860. In 1900 these trade organizations had also established a specialist employers' organization, UIMM, covering virtually every sector of metalworking. The initial purpose in forming UIMM was to fight proposals for legislation and, in particular, the *décrets* Millerand establishing joint management–union committees to set wages and hours of work. But UIMM very quickly assumed a wider role. It established a number of strike insurance funds to compensate employers suffering from

[3] Sellier (1976: 37–9) would appear to think the lack of organization by employers was important.

industrial action; it also promoted the development of social security measures among its members. In 1907 it began to establish local organizations in the regions.[4]

The most plausible explanation for the lack of accommodation in the metalworking industries is that trade unions were too weak to force the employers to resort to collective bargaining. To understand why this was so, it is necessary to appreciate the very special features of the structure of the metalworking industries at this time. To begin with, it was extremely difficult for trade unions to bring pressure to bear on the large number of small employers. Unlike those in construction and printing, these employers tended to have a monopoly in the locality; they also manufactured a wide range of products. Then there was the particular problem posed by the presence of a small number of very large employers. These employers enjoyed the benefits of a highly protected market, which meant that they had little to fear from competition in the event of a strike, and most dominated their local labour markets. As happened at Le Creusot in 1899 and Longwy (where the de Wendels had their works) in 1905, this made it relatively easy for them to defeat attempts by the trade union to gain recognition. The positive strategies which the employers used were also important. For example, works police were employed to deal with the trade union at the Le Creusot works as well as a wide range of social welfare measures. Following the ending of the strike at Le Creusot in 1900, Schneider also introduced a joint management–labour committee to deal with claims and grievances. Other large employers formed company unions to perform the same functions.

It was only during the First World War that the first tentative steps towards the joint discussion of terms and conditions of employment were undertaken in some establishments manufacturing munitions, under the pressure of Albert Thomas, the Minister of Armaments and former socialist deputy. In 1918 and 1919 the pace quickened. Against the background of mounting agitation and the influx of large numbers into the trade unions, the Conservative government decided it must exploit the spirit of wartime co-operation which still in some measure existed. Two pieces of legislation were introduced in order to encourage the development of collective bargaining. The first, dated 25 March 1919, introduced a simple legal framework. Collective agreements were placed under the general heading of the law of contract, and the principle of the full freedom of association assured; collective agreements, which were to be written and recorded, were only to be valid as between the parties involved. The second, dated 23 April, provided for the introduction of the 8 hour day. Significantly, the law obliged the Ministry of Labour Inspectors to call together representatives of the parties involved to

[4] For the early history of UIMM, see Bezard-Falgaz (1922), François-Poncet (1927) and Villey (1923).

discuss the terms of the implementation of the 8 hour day; every effort was made to encourage a joint agreement.

Initially, the legislation had the desired effect. In industry after industry representatives of employers' organizations and of the industry federations of the CGT sat down together for the first time at national level.[5] But disillusionment was to set in quickly. The actions of the leaders of the metal federation were denounced as treason and class collaboration as the dissension between 'reformers' and 'revolutionaries' within the CGT reached fever pitch, leading to the setting up of the breakaway communist trade union confederation. Detailed discussions in the regions – some of which extended beyond the 8-hour day to wages and other terms and conditions of employment – also began to run into difficulties. For example, an agreement was reached covering the Paris region on 29 June 1919 only to be followed by a month-long strike involving 80,000 workers that ended without a settlement. In other regions agreements relating wages to the cost of living as well as dealing with the 8-hour day were denounced when prices began to fall. The defeat of the CGT by the government following the collapse of the General Strike in May 1920 only served to confirm the weakness of trade union organization.

The employers' sense of disillusionment with collective bargaining during this period was to be summed up in the following complaints made some years later to the inquiry undertaken by the Conseil National Économique (1934: 212):

1 In almost all centres collective agreements have been tried.
2 Almost nowhere has the experiment been successful.
3 The agreements were observed when they bring advantage to the workers; in the contrary case they are no longer observed.
4 The secretaries of the workers' organisations do not generally have sufficient authority to make sure that the agreements concluded are respected.
5 Nowhere do collective agreements appear to have contributed to the maintenance of the social peace, and the strikes have appreciably diminished since their disappearance.

In summary, of thirty regional collective agreements introduced since 1919 in the metalworking industry there remain today only five. The five agreements concern about 18,000 workers out of effectively a total of 1,350,000.

Significantly, Jouhaux, General Secretary of the CGT, did not question the employers' interpretation of these events in his communication to the

5 It was immediately following the First World War that the employers' confederation, the Confédération Générale de la Production (now the CNPF), was formed. As in Britain, the initiative came largely from the government which was anxious to have a representative spokesman for industry. Even so, UIMM, which before the war had blocked an attempt to establish an employers' confederation, continued to play a significant role in social affairs. For further details, see Duchemin (1940: 1–2) and Ehrmann (1957: 18–22).

Conseil National Économique. He admitted members of the CGT had shown some reluctance in the past to engage in collective bargaining. But this was no longer the case. It was the employers who had refused to move, after the immediate crisis was over.

In the circumstances this was not surprising. With the defeat of the CGT by the government in 1920, membership of the trade unions collapsed almost as quickly as it had grown. It was further weakened by the setting up of the predominantly catholic trade union confederation in 1921 and the communist breakaway in the following year. The paternalist policies of the larger employers and, in particular, their support for company unions continued to contribute to the trade unions' weakness. As Villey (1923: 245), a long-time official of UIMM, described in some detail,[6] employers' organizations also developed their own wage controls during this period. In short, the employers had no need of collective bargaining at this time.

There was to be little change in the state of affairs until the political and industrial upheaval of 1936. At the height of the 'Popular Front', the Blum government directly involved the CGPF as the employers' bargaining agent. A number of concessions were demanded from the employers' representatives at a meeting at the Hôtel Matignon, including a commitment to enter into collective agreements. Further impetus was given by the law of 24 June 1936 which set out to deal with a situation in which trade unions were weak and divided. There were two major amendments to the 1919 legislation: first, collective agreements were to be negotiated by mixed commissions comprising spokesmen of 'the representative organizations of employers and employees'; and, second, the Minister of Labour was given the power to extend the terms of the agreement, in full or part, to all firms of the kind referred to in the agreement. It was this legal framework established in 1936 that in effect was to be resurrected in 1950.[7]

[6] Briefly, the employers' organizations set minimum rates of pay in each locality, which individual employers used as the basis for calculating different job rates.
During the period of rapid inflation in 1919–20, the employers' organizations increased the rates in line with rising prices. In the following year, when prices fell, they sought to ensure that reductions in the rates did not exceed the amounts by which the price of foodstuffs 'officially' fell.
[7] There had been earlier legislation dealing with collective bargaining in post-Second World War France, the law of 23 December 1946. As under the 1936 law, collective agreements were to be negotiated by mixed commissions, either on the request of the organizations designated as 'most representative' or upon the invitation of the Minister of Labour or his representative. Unlike the 1936 law, however, the Minister's approval was required for all agreements. Moreover, wages and fringe benefits were excluded from collective bargaining and made the subject of administrative decree. Incidentally, it was these decrees, passed by the communist Minister of Labour, Parodi, that established the detailed framework of job classification referred to in chapter 5. But this was not all. Whereas the law of 1936 seemed to favour local multi-employer agreements, the law of 1946 attempted to promote national agreements on the grand scale. One and the same agreement was to cover all workers in an industry. The law also determined the sequence of negotiations; they were to take place at national, regional, local and then establishment level – and in that order. Perhaps it is hardly surprising that in the circumstances scarcely a dozen collective agreements were concluded in the three years following the passage of the

Germany

On the face of it, the pattern of industrialization in Germany would appear to have been favourable to the development of trade unions and collective bargaining. Industrialization in Germany was late and extremely rapid. The initial catalysts were the formation in 1834 of the customs-union, the Zollverein, and the development of the railway system; further impetus was given by the unification of Germany in 1871. In particular, the development of the railway system, as well as improving communications and enlarging the domestic market, led to considerable investment in the heavy industries of coal, iron and steel. In a second phase there was significant growth in chemicals and electrical engineering. Instead of the slow build-up of capital by a large number of individual entrepreneurs as in Britain, however, advanced forms of technology and organization were adopted from the beginning. Especially important in the promotion of large-scale developments were the joint stock companies; while a key role in providing the finance was played by the banks. By the turn of the century, the size of the average steel works had far outstripped that in Britain. In 1907 nearly half of those who worked in industry were employed in establishments with more than 1,000 employees (Kocka, 1978: 556). If Germany continued to exhibit some of the characteristics of a dual economy – agricultural interests remained dominant in the east and the south – key sectors such as the Ruhr saw the development of very considerable concentrations of employment.

It is true that the military autocracy that presided over industrialization, first in Prussia and then in the unified Germany, was hostile to trade unionism. It is also true that Bismarck's Anti-Socialist Law of 1879 effectively ended the initial flurry of trade union activity among craft workers in the 1860s. With the passage of the social security measures[8] in the 1880s, however, the government's approach began to soften. In 1890 the Anti-Socialist Law lapsed. Thereafter, there was a substantial growth of membership among the reconstructed industrial unions. According to Kendall (1975: 93–4), in 1890 trade union membership stood at a little over 250,000; it doubled in the period 1891–9 and again in the period 1899–1904. One million strong in 1904, trade union membership grew to two million in 1909 and three million by 1913. Figures quoted by Cassau (1927) suggested that by 1913 collective bargaining was also widespread: in building, woodworking, clothing, printing, food, drink and tobacco, even in some parts of metalworking.

law; only that covering the banks was of major significance. For further details, see Durand (1956) and Sturmthal (1951).

[8] The most significant measures were those dealing with health insurance in 1883, accident insurance in 1884 and old age and disability pensions in 1889. The cost of such measures was substantial for employers; many were prompted to seek to block or amend the details.

Only the employers in coal, iron and steel, heavy engineering, chemicals and textiles resisted trade union recognition. The very thought of collective bargaining was anathema to the leading industrialists involved. The following statement issued by their trade confederation, ZDI, illustrates the strength of their opposition:

> ZDI considers the conclusion of collective agreements between organisations of employers and of trade unions extremely dangerous for German industry and its continued development. The collective agreement deprives the individual employer of the necessary freedom to decide how to utilise his workers. It also brings the individual worker unavoidably under the control of the trade unions. ZDI is convinced that collective agreements constitute a serious restriction on the technical organisational programme of German industry; a fact confirmed by the experience of England and America (Braun, 1908, quoted in Hilferding, 1974: 493).

To understand what was happening, it is necessary to appreciate that German manufacturers were effectively divided into two main camps. Indeed, by 1895 they were represented by two different trade confederations: the Zentralverband Deutscher Industrieller (ZDI), which was formed in 1876, and the Bund der Industrieller (BI), which was formed in 1895. The employers represented differed in two major respects. First, there were their commercial policies. The ZDI represented the interests of manufacturers in heavy industry and textiles. It was these manufacturers who joined with the agrarian interests of East Prussia in pressing for the tariff law of 1878. It was also these employers who were instrumental in organizing the cartels with the powers to determine quotas, fix selling prices and co-ordinate technical development. The cartels were well entrenched before 1914; following a court decision of 1898, they were also able to enforce their agreements at law. By contrast, the members of BI were largely involved in the manufacture of consumer goods and were interested in freer trade policies. A second, and related, respect in which the members of the two organizations differed was their size. ZDI's membership included such large employers as Krupp, Siemens and Stinnes. For example, in 1913 Siemens employed a labour force of more than 25,000 (Lee, 1978: 475). The BI's members were mainly smaller employers.

From the point of view of collective bargaining, then, the position of members of the ZDI was very similar to that of the large metalworking employers in France. Their size meant they had considerable resources of their own to withstand trade union pressure even without the strike funds of their employers' organizations[9] that began to emerge from the 1890s

[9] Three main phases of activity can be identified so far as the formation of employers' organizations in Germany is concerned. The first followed the failure of Bismarck's Anti-Socialist Law of 1879 to stem the tide of social democracy and trade unionism. It was during

onwards. The domination of the labour market many enjoyed meant that they were able to exercise considerable control over their local communities. In the case of employers such as Krupp, for example, support for company unions or so-called 'plant societies' was underpinned by an all-embracing paternalism that sought to control the private as well as the working life of employees through pensions, profit-sharing, housing and so on. Above all, there were the implications of the cartels. It was not simply that the existence of the cartels meant that members of the ZDI, unlike many of those in the BI, did not see any attraction in collective bargaining in helping them to regulate the market. Much more importantly, the existence of the cartels meant that members of the ZDI, unlike those in the BI, had little to fear from competition in the event of a strike and so could take a far tougher line in dealing with trade unions.

As in France, it was only during the First World War that the employers were forced by the government to set up works committees in establishments with more than 150 workers and to participate in conciliation and arbitration boards with trade unions. Even so, most employers chafed under what they regarded as 'war-time socialism'. The employers' confederation, the Vereinigung der Deutschen Arbeitgeberverbände, was quite open in stating that it wanted a total return to pre-war conditions when the peace had been won.

From the employers' point of view, however, the situation was to get much worse before it got better. Against the background of the mounting tide of political and industrial unrest that followed the First World War, the employers found themselves obliged to reach an accommodation with the trade unions. In the words of the director of the iron and steel employers' organization:

> the situation was already clear to us in October. The question was how to save all German industry from the danger of socialisation which was to follow immediately upon the wake of the coming revolution. The only stronghold in sight then appeared to be the organised part of labour, the unions. In the midst of the general insecurity, in view of the rapidly waning powers of the government, there remained one way to save the industries – by making common cause with the workers' organisations, the trade unions.

> (quoted in Reindl, 1922: 258).

this period that ironmasters' organizations were established in Berlin in 1886 and Hamburg in 1887; these, in turn, were responsible for establishing a national metalworking employers' organization in 1890. The second phase followed the strike of textile workers at Krimmischau in 1904. In some respects this had a not dissimilar effect to the 1902 strike in Sweden discussed on p. 159. In particular, it led the ZDI and the BI to establish employers' confederations which subsequently sponsored the formation of a number of single-industry and multi-industry organizations at local level. It was only in 1913 that the two employers' confederations came together to form the Vereinigung der Deutschen Arbeitgeberverbände (VDA). The third phase took place in the years immediately following the First World War. Between 1919 and 1920 the number of employers' organizations in membership of the VDA virtually trebled from 575 to 1591. For further details, see Erdmann (1966), Hartwich (1967), Leckebusch (1966), Simon (1976), and Weber (1954).

As early as October 1918, discussions between representatives of the employers' organizations and trade unions began in the Ruhr. The Legien–Stinnes agreement, so-named after the respective union and employers' leaders, followed on 15 November. Essentially, the agreement provided for mutual recognition. The right of association for blue- and white-collar workers was conceded, and the employers pledged themselves to drop support for the company unions. Collective agreements were to be the means for regulating terms and conditions of employment and there were also to be joint conciliation bodies for dispute settlement. In every firm of more than 50 employees a works committee was to be established which, together with the employer, would ensure that the terms and conditions conformed to the collectively-agreed norms. Finally, a central joint economic committee was to be established at national level which would have the task of re-establishing industry and settling major disputes; the committee was also to be replicated at industrial and regional levels.

In the light of the known attitudes of employers in the heavy industries, it is perhaps hardly surprising that trade unions should have pressed for legislation to underpin the Legien–Stinnes agreement.[10] The legal framework of collective bargaining that followed in the new republic consisted of four principal elements. First, there was the legislation concerning the making and enforcing of collective agreements. The decree of 23 December 1918 established the legal status of collective agreements in Germany for the first time. It stated that only bona fide trade unions and employers and employers' organizations could enter into such an agreement. It established the principle of 'non-deviation' which stipulated that the parties must live up to the terms of the agreements. It also allowed the Minister of Labour to use his power to extend the scope of the agreement by special decree. Second, a system of tripartite conciliation and arbitration was introduced, the initial intention being to encourage collective bargaining. Third, works committees were to be elected in every establishment with more than 250 employees and to be invested with the rights of participation in certain areas of managerial decision-making. Fourth, a unified system of labour courts was gradually established within which trade unions were given a significant role. It was this legal framework which was more or less resurrected after the Second World War.[11]

[10] Significantly, in the light of post-Second World War developments, trade union dependence on the legal framework intensified in the 1920s. By the end of 1922 the danger of revolution which had induced the employers to seek the co-operation of the trade unions had passed. Increasingly, trade unions found themselves obliged to resort to the conciliation and arbitration clauses that were a major feature in most collective agreements. This practice was carried a stage further in 1923 with the passage of legislation designed to rationalize the mediation machinery. For further details, see Hartwich (1967) and Wunderlich (1940).

[11] In 1946 regulations were issued by the allies providing for the reinstatement of the labour courts, works councils and the conciliation and arbitration of disputes. Wages were

Italy

That there should have been collective bargaining in metalworking in Italy prior to 1914 might be thought surprising in the light of the discussion of the French and German experience. Industrialization came very late to Italy. Indeed, Gershenkon (1955) puts the first acceleration in growth as late as the period 1896–1908; even by the First World War manufacturing industry accounted for less than one quarter of total national product. In some respects the pattern of development was not dissimilar to that in France; small family-owned businesses emerged to cater for the local market. As in Germany, however, an advanced sector also grew up in a relatively short space of time. But it was not only on a very much reduced scale, but also concentrated geographically in the north in the so-called 'iron triangle' set by Milan, Genoa and Turin. Initially, the advanced sector was based on heavy industry and, in particular, on iron and steel, and shipbuilding. There was considerable state support in the form of public investment, contracts and tariff protection following the laws of 1878 and 1887. Indeed, such was the degree of protection enjoyed that, by 1914, the iron and steel industries were dominated by two interlocking trusts: Falk and Ansoldo. In a second phase, a broader base developed in engineering. For example, Agnelli began the process of making Turin into a major centre of the car industry with the formation of FIAT in 1898; Olivetti set up business in Ivrea in 1906. During the period 1905–11 the size of the labour force in metalworking in the province of Piedmont more than quadrupled from 12,000 to 53,000 (Baglioni, 1974: 255). Although the engineering industry was not as protected by tariffs as iron and steel, many of its sectors enjoyed government concessions and contracts.

It was the political context that made the difference in Italy. Throughout the 1890s the industrialists and southern landowners had used their control of the two-chamber parliament to secure government repression of the activities of the socialist party and the slowly emerging trade union organizations. By 1900, however, the policy was effectively bankrupt. In June 1900 the three opposition parties of the so-called *L'Estrema* increased their representation in the lower house to nearly 100. In July 1900 King Humbert was assassinated. The crisis brought a

the subject of a freeze that lasted until November 1948. Initially, the allies were hostile to the re-emergence of employers' organizations and the right of association was limited to single industries. It was only in May 1947 in the British and American zones that the first multi-industry employers' organization emerged. Subsequently, this organization evolved into the BDA in 1950.

Of the various measures passed to reintroduce the legal framework of the Weimar Republic, the one that deserves special comment is the Works Constitution Act of 1952. The trade unions sought to place the works councils under trade union control and to remove the peace obligation imposed on works councillors. But they were unable to repeat the success they had enjoyed in the previous year in causing the government to change its initial position on the co-determination legislation in the coal, iron and steel industries.

new monarch to the throne and a fresh approach. Under Giolitti, first as Minister of the Interior and then more or less continuously as Prime Minister until 1914, there was the so-called 'opening to the left': the attempt to draw the rapidly expanding working class and their represen-tatives into the political system. In industrial disputes the authorities were ordered not to intervene unless there was a threat to law and order. In wage disputes, in particular, employers were encouraged to come to terms with their employees.

Against the background of an expanding economy, the impact of these political changes was quite dramatic. There was a significant increase in the number of strikes from 383 in 1899 to 1042 a year later (Cabrini, 1905: 62 quoted in Horowitz, 1963: 60) with nearly three quarters of those in industry resulting in victory for the workers. There were also significant and related developments in trade union organization. Prior to 1900, if workers were organized at all, it was usually under the auspices of the multi-industry *camere di lavoro* modelled on the French *bourses du travail*. Only the printers and railway workers had been able to establish national unions. Throughout 1901 and 1902 most major groups of workers succeeded in following suit. By August 1902, there were no less than 27 national trade unions in existence including that of the metalworkers with a claimed membership of 50,000 (Cabrini, quoted in Horowitz, 1963: 62). With their efforts concentrated on specific industries, the national unions offered a firmer foundation for per-manent organization than did the *camere di lavoro* and they brought a greater emphasis on demands for improvements in wages and conditions.

Faced with the refusal of the government to take action against the trade unions after 1901, the immediate reaction of Italian employers was to form their own organizations for the purposes of defence. It was employers in Monza who set the trend. In 1902 they established the Federazione Industriali Monzese. The other main centre of activity in the early years was Turin where employers, among them Agnelli of FIAT, formed the Lega Industrialia Torinese[12] in 1906 following a strike in cotton textiles. Significantly, in the light of the present-day structure of employers' organizations in Italy discussed in chapter 3, the organizations were multi-industry in membership. The targets for their activities – and the immediate explanation for their multi-industry character – were the local *camere di lavoro*. The relatively small number of employers were too isolated within each industry to form single-industry local organizations to match the strength of the *camere di lavoro*. Nor was a national single-industry organization a feasible proposition at this stage because of the

---

12 In 1908 the scope of the activities of the *Lega* was extended to cover the whole of Piedmont with the formation of a multi-industry provincial employers' organization. Single-industry employers' organizations were also formed under the *Lega's* auspices. These included the car manufacturers who set up a separate organization in 1911 and a metalworking employers' organization that brought together 15 smaller organizations in 1913. For further details, see Baglioni (1974: 501–4).

very uneven development of industrialization. In this respect, then, the situation was not dissimilar to that in Sweden discussed later in this chapter.

The employers' new organizations achieved a fair measure of success through the use of the lockout and other forms of mutual support. It has been estimated that in the period 1906–7, of some 35 strikes in Turin, 21 had ended in complete or partial success for the workers; in the following year only two out of eleven ended in the workers' favour (Baglioni, 1974: 505). But with the government showing no signs of departing from a position of neutrality and, indeed, in some cases giving positive support to the demands of trade unions, the employers were forced to shift their ground. In this regard, the publications of the *Lega* and its associated organizations provide a fascinating insight into the thinking of the new entrepreneurs. Unlike employers in Milan,[13] they professed to accept that industrial conflict was a fact of life from which they could not escape. They were not, they claimed, opposed to trade unions as such or to their demands to maximize the economic situation of workers. Rather they were opposed to 'the irrational forms of workers' protest . . . the new feudalism of the visionaries and sectarians who substituted violence for the persuasion of arguments' (quoted in Baglioni, 1974: 511). As in Sweden, fixed-term wage agreements received qualified support. The reasoning was very similar to that of Swedish employers. Such agreements offered the prospect of a period of stability without seriously threatening the employer's ability to manage.[14] The FIAT-controlled *La Stampa* sought to explain the employers' acquiescence in an agreement with the metalworkers' union covering the car manufacturers in 1913 thus,

> having some time in hand before them, they [the employers] have the opportunity to prepare themselves and to conduct their enterprise not only in the case of competition, but also in such a way as to enable them to systematise new tasks. The labour force, for its part, considers itself in some way almost part of the factory, knowing full

[13] In fact, the metalworking employers in Milan had established an employers' organization modelled on the EEF in 1899. But it was relatively insignificant in terms of the number of members and its activities. Employers in the older industries in Milan, such as textiles, where the size of manufacturing units was relatively modest, were still very much in the ascendancy. They already had strong trade organizations and were more or less in control of the local political situation. They saw little need for the fighting organizations which their colleagues in Monza and Turin were developing. Indeed, they saw positive harm in these developments, on the grounds that they were likely to exacerbate rather than soothe class relations. Assolombarda, the subsequently powerful territorial employers' organization of the province, was not formed until 1910. For further details see Baglioni (1974: 460).

[14] One of the earliest examples of collective bargaining was the agreement reached between Itala, a car plant in Turin, and the metalworkers' union. It provided for union control of hiring, a grievance procedure and a workers' representative committee, old age pensions and housing, as well as a 'no-strike' clause guaranteed by a performance bond. (See Giugni, 1957: 427). This type of agreement did not find favour with the Lega. For further details, see Baglioni (1974: 537).

well that only from profits can it trim and perfect that state of work which allows the realisation of the benefit of high salaries.

(quoted in Castronovo, 1971: 66).

Unlike in France and Germany, then, there had been the tentative beginnings of collective bargaining in key sectors of the metalworking industry prior to the First World War. As chapter 4 has already explained, largely under government pressure both the scope and the coverage of collective bargaining expanded considerably in the period immediately following the First World War. Despite these developments, the tide of unrest mounted. Trade union membership soared. The Socialist Party firmly rejected the reformist position. A general strike leading to revolution was held to be imminent. In Turin the factory councils developed out of the works councils introduced by collective agreement in August 1919. In June of the same year substantial claims were presented to the metalworking employers in Milan. An occupation of the factories was followed by the declaration of a general lockout on 1 September. The immediate issue of a general wage increase in metalworking was settled following government intervention, but the attempt to set up a commission involving the re-established employers' confederation, CONFINDUSTRIA,[15] and the trade union confederation, CGL, in order to reach agreement on other issues ended in failure.

It was against this background that the larger employers, many of whom had expanded considerably as a result of their involvement in the war effort, began to turn to the fascists for support. Having secured a degree of respectability in the general election of May 1921, Mussolini went on to establish an independent fascist trade union organization, the Confederazione Nazional delle Corporazioni Sindicali. The CGL having played its last card with a call for a general strike in 1922, the way was open for the 'March on Rome' in October 1922 and the subsequent invitation from the king for Mussolini to form a government. In December 1923 a number of employers met at the Chiagi Palace and gave recognition to the fascist trade unions.

The period of the fascist regime was profoundly important for the subject matter of this study. First, the emerging structure of employers' organizations was reinforced. The basis of the fascist framework of industrial relations, the so-called Piatto Vidoni, gave exclusive recog-

---

[15] An early attempt had been made to set up an employers' confederation in 1910 by representatives of the Monza and Turin employers, but this did not survive the war. CONFINDUSTRIA was re-established in April 1919 at the height of the industrial unrest. In the absence of strong national organizations of employers, especially in metalworking, it quickly assumed a dominant position. Indeed, CONFINDUSTRIA officials were largely responsible for the rapid growth in the number of employers' organizations which took place during this period. By 1921 there were 76 organizations in membership of CONFINDUSTRIA; the employers' organization section had 64 members, more than half of which were multi-industry territorial organizations, and the trade organization section had 40 national organizations in membership. The source for these details of the early history of CONFINDUSTRIA is Zirano (1962).

nition to CONFINDUSTRIA to represent the interests of manufacturing employers. Law 536 on the legal discipline of collective labour relations was the first and most important of a series of laws and decrees that gave it far-reaching legal support. Until 1934 proposals for collective agreements in manufacturing had first to be ratified by CONFINDUSTRIA. Even after 1934, and the recognition accorded to groups of employers by industry, CONFINDUSTRIA continued to exercise a co-ordinating function. Financial control was also highly centralized. Individual employers paid a standard subscription to CONFINDUSTRIA to be distributed to member organizations according to need.

Fascism also consolidated the position of the multi-industry territorial employers' organizations. Under Law 536 these organizations were given exclusive recognition and the payment of dues was made obligatory. By contrast, the single-industry category organizations, most of which were defined as trade organizations, were relegated to the relatively minor role of encouraging production.

Even more significantly, to quote Neufeld (1961: 450), fascism 'revolutionized' collective bargaining. The scope of collective agreements increased considerably both in geographical coverage and contents, albeit they were more in the nature of administrative regulations – mostly drawn up by the Ministry of Corporations in accordance with employers' wishes – than the result of free collective bargaining. As chapter 4 explained, national multi-employer agreements, for which the employers' confederations were responsible until 1934, were concluded for the different categories, supplemented by provincial wage agreements based on differences in the cost of living. As chapter 5 explained, the procedural or normative aspects of these agreements were more or less dictated by the Charter of Labour of 21 April 1927, subsequent legislation and royal decrees. The Charter itself, for example, required a number of subjects to be included in collective agreements: annual leave, pay, compensation in the event of death or discharge (where there was no blame on the part of the individual); retention of full rights in the event of change in ownership; restrictions on dismissal in the event of illness, and hygiene conditions. By the Royal Decree of 16 May 1928 collective agreements had to make further and precise provision for discipline, probation, wage and salary levels and sickness benefits. Provision was also made for extensive social security and welfare measures, many of which were the subject of collective bargaining.

That the fascist regime should have introduced such a detailed framework is not too difficult to understand in the circumstances. As the speeches and writings of Alfredo Rocco, the Minister of Justice responsible for Law 536, suggest, it was accepted that the 'syndical phenomenon is an unsuppressible aspect of modern life' (quoted in Roberts, 1979: 245). A restoration of order within the context of a liberal state would not be sufficient to deal with the kind of revolutionary challenge that trade unions had presented during the two so-called 'red years' of 1919 and 1920. But neither would authoritarianism pure and simple. The masses had risen; the organizations they had created would not go away. The situation, argued Rocco, called for a totalitarian state that organized the mass society. In particular, it should try to exploit the intermediary organizations to mobilize society from above and to keep the workers permanently under control.

The fascist framework of collective bargaining was the one element to survive the Royal Decree of 23 November 1943 bringing the corporate state to an end. Significantly for the developments in collective bargaining discussed earlier in the study, however, and unlike France and Germany, there was no legislation giving statutory effect to the framework; and there was no legislation implementing the various articles of the 1948 constitution dealing with industrial relations. That this did not happen is largely to be explained in terms of the changing attitudes of the parties. In the immediate post-Second World War period demands by the unitary CGIL for statutory 'management councils' meant CONFINDUSTRIA was far from happy about any legislation in industrial relations. By the 1950s it was the trade unions, weak and now divided, who were opposed to legislation. In particular, they were afraid that any attempt to legislate for the right of association would inevitably lead to legal restriction of the right to strike. Then, when CGIL did an about-turn, demanding legislation dealing with the right to association and with the 'internal commissions', there was opposition from CISL.

Sweden

With the virtue of hindsight, it is not difficult to understand why Swedish employers came to an accommodation with trade unions at such a relatively early stage. As in Germany and Italy, industrialization was late and extremely rapid. Unlike these two countries, however, the employers that emerged were small in size as well as number. Indeed, few employed more than 1,000 workers by the turn of the century. Of major significance too was the fact that industrialization in Sweden was export-led; the protectionism that played such an important role in France, Germany and Italy was not a major consideration. Two main stages may be identified. The first, in the 1850s and 1860s, involved an expansion in demand for the raw materials with which Sweden was so well blessed. Iron and timber products, in particular, were in great demand due to industrial development and the building boom throughout the rest of Europe. The second stage, in the 1890s, saw the development of a substantial engineering industry. Here the catalyst was provided by the investment in and growth in demand for such highly specialized goods as the milk separator, turbines, internal combustion engines, electrical machinery, gas accumulators and ball bearings – most of which were Swedish inventions. According to Jölberg (1973: 444), by the end of the first decade of this century the engineering industry had outstripped the staple products industries so far as employment was concerned; by 1914 Sweden had overtaken many countries where industrialization had occurred much earlier.

In as much as the heavy involvement in competitive overseas trade demanded continuity of production, it proved to be particularly fertile ground for the growth of trade unionism among the mainly skilled workers involved. The first national unions, those of the printers and postmen, were set up in 1886; the iron and metalworkers' union was formed in 1888. According to Hansson (1927) by 1900 more than 32 national unions had been established; something of the order of 15 per cent to 20 per cent of the labour force was unionized. The central trade union confederation, LO, was formed in 1898.

The employers did put up a fight. Industrial action by trade unions was met with lockouts and closures. For example, there were particularly bitter disputes involving the sawmill owners at Sundesvall in 1879 and the mine owners at Norberg in 1891. But as Von Sydow (1931), managing director of SAF, was to explain many years later, trade unionism seemed to be too well-established in Sweden to be defeated outright. Even if the employers proved capable of winning a particular dispute, the unions took advantage of the next set of favourable economic circumstances to re-assert themselves.

But the economic context was not the only consideration. Employers were frustrated in their hope that the state would intervene with legislation to deal with the challenge of trade unions. On the face of it, they might have expected such intervention. Even after the reforms of 1867, the constitutional monarchy remained extremely conservative. The crown retained considerable powers; the upper chamber of the Riksdag was elected indirectly on an extremely restricted provincially-based suffrage, the lower chamber on a direct, but limited, suffrage until 1907. Even so, the industrialists who increasingly came to form a significant block in the upper chamber did not have things all their own way. The large number of independent farmers meant that the agricultural interest was far from united in its approach and there was a significant liberal presence in the lower chamber drawn from the towns. Furthermore, in the decade before the accommodation between employers and trade unions took place, demands for the extension of the suffrage united religious groups and the powerful temperance movement with the trade unions. The result was a delicate balance of political forces; there was a number of attempts to introduce legislation dealing with trade unions, but only the Akarp law of 1899 dealing with the freedom of the employer to strike-break was put into the statute book.

It is against this background that the path-breaking national agreement was negotiated by the newly-formed engineering employers' organization, SVF,[16] and the iron and metal workers' union in 1905 after a fairly lengthy period of industrial conflict. In one respect the accommodation reached was not dissimilar to that between the EEF and the ASE in Britain: the employers agreed to recognize the individual worker's right to associate in return for the trade union's recognition of the employer's right to employ whomsoever he wished. In a second respect, however, the agreement was very different. Mutual recognition was underpinned by a fixed-term agreement on such substantive issues as minimum rates of pay and hours of work.

Clearly the form of the agreement requires some comment in the light of the comparison to be made later with Britain. It is best explained as follows. Initially, the iron and metalworkers had aimed to establish their union on a craft basis. But the advanced state of technology used, coupled with the opposition of employers, made this impossible. Certainly there does not appear to be any evidence that the iron and metalworkers had been able to impose the kinds of craft controls that the ASE had achieved in Britain. In particular, they do not appear to have been able to impose the controls over the supply and use of labour that made it possible for the ASE to set rates of pay unilaterally by district. In the circumstances, then, the iron and metalworkers were anxious to establish minimum rates of pay for the various jobs their members performed. The employers exploited this demand. They agreed to negotiate minimum rates by age, experience and region, though not by material worked upon as the union demanded. In return, the employers insisted on a fixed period of agreement. In this way SVF sought to establish the principle that the collective agreement should be regarded as a contract during which employers should be free from not only industrial action but also further claims.

The second main development in Sweden referred to in the introduction to this chapter, the so-called 'December Compromise' involving the employers' confederation, SAF, and LO, came about more by chance than design. By 1905 some 40 per cent of SAF's membership was covered by collective agreements. But there was concern that concessions were being made by individual employers and employers' organizations on the issue of the closed shop. A circular was sent to all members requiring that the following clause be inserted into collective agreements:

> the employer is entitled to direct and distribute the work of his enterprise, to engage and dismiss workers of his own discretion, and to employ organised or unorganised workers as he sees fit.

[16] Although the foundry employers in Stockholm had signed a wage contract with the local representatives of the iron and metalworkers' union as early as 1890, the first formal organization of employers in the metalworking industry appears to have been established in Gothenburg in 1896. A key role was played by an Englishman, James Keiler. Attempts made to extend the organization to the country as a whole, however, were unsuccessful. It was after the 1902 strike in support of the suffrage that the national organization, SVF, was established. For the early developments of employers' organizations and collective bargaining in metalworking, see Stryman (1946). For brief details in English, Norgren (1941: 25–8, 34–6).

This clause was subsequently set out in the SAF constitution and became the famous paragraph 23 (subsequently 32).[17] Attempts by employers to include it in their collective agreements led to a number of problems with individual trade unions. In an attempt to resolve the issue, SAF went direct to LO with proposals for a discussion on the employers' right to manage. LO agreed to recognize the employers' right to manage, while SAF agreed to the right of association. When LO notified the terms of the so-called 'December Compromise' to its member unions, however, a number objected. SAF then threatened to lockout LO members unless the terms of the 'December Compromise' were accepted. LO backed down and the terms were tacitly accepted.

How is the important role played by SAF to be explained? The timing of its formation was dictated by the three-day strike of 1902 in support of an extension of the suffrage. The strike, instigated by LO and the Social Democratic Party but supported by other groups, was well organized and took the country by surprise. In total some 120,000 workers were involved: an impressive figure in view of the size of Sweden's industrial population at the time. The strike, reported by Von Sydow (quoted in Norgren, 1941: 15), 'opened the employers' eyes' and 'showed them how powerless they were *vis-à-vis* the unions'. Local trade unionism was one thing: a highly co-ordinated movement closely allied to the Social Democratic Party and prepared to indulge in industrial action for political ends was a very different proposition.[18]

But the relatively early formation of SAF cannot be explained simply in terms of the 1902 strike. Of fundamental importance was the industrial structure. It was not so much, as Ingham (1974: 42–8)[19] has argued, that high levels of concentration in Sweden facilitated collective action by

---

[17] The eventual 'compromise', which was ratified in January 1907 was in a form which could be included in collective agreements reached between members of SAF and LO. It read:

> in application of the terms of the agreement the employer has the right to direct and allocate the work, to engage and dismiss workers at his own discretion, and to employ workers regardless of whether they are organised.
> The right of association shall be left unrestricted on both sides.
> If the workers believe they have been discharged under circumstances which may be interpreted as an attack on the right of association, they may, before further steps are taken, through their organisation, call for an investigation.
>
> (quoted in Robbins, 1942: 79).

[18] As it happened, LO was not the highly centralized organization that it might have appeared. The original constitution of 1898 gave LO the powers to fulfil two basic tasks: first, to act as a central agency for the collection and dissemination of information; and, second, to provide an insurance fund on which the member trade unions could draw in the event of a lockout. In fact, it was the repeated threat of lockouts by SVF and SAF which led LO to intervene in the negotiations of its member trade unions. See, for example, the discussion in Casparsson (1966: 27–33), Johnston (1962: 31–3) and Westerstähl (1945: 63–5).

The links between LO and the Social Democrat Party were also less close than they had been. On the formation of LO in 1898, for example, it was a condition of membership that trade unions were affiliated to the party. This condition was rescinded two years later.

[19] See also the discussion in Jackson and Sisson (1976).

employers on a multi-industry basis. The essential point is that, as in Italy, employers in Sweden found it extremely difficult to establish viable single-industry organizations at this stage of industrial development. This is especially so in the case of many employers outside of the engineering industry. Significantly, it was these employers – men such as Almstrom, a porcelain manufacturer – who formed SAF and not the employers in engineering. Indeed, the engineering employers did not affiliate to SAF until 1919. Significantly, too, SAF did not have a monopoly of multi-industry representation in its early years. Employers in Halsingborg and, more importantly, Malmö had established their own multi-industry organizations before the formation of SAF. It was only with the affiliation of these organizations in 1906 and 1907 respectively that SAF could claim to have truly national coverage.

As Hallendorff (1927: 22–5), the historian of SAF, points out, the experience of their Danish counterparts also had a profound impact on the thinking of Swedish employers. In particular, this experience appeared to confirm the logic of a strong employers' confederation in the circumstances facing Swedish employers. As early as 1885, the Copenhagen metal trades employers had conducted a five-month lockout aimed at forestalling trade union organization among their workers. Subsequently, there had been considerable development of employers' organizations and multi-employer bargaining. In 1896 the Danish employers' confederation was formed. Following a strike of carpenters in Copenhagen and a number of provincial cities, the employers used the threat of a lockout to impose on the Danish LO a list of demands that included: (1) LO acceptance of full responsibility for the observance of collective agreements by its affiliates; (2) explicit recognition of the employers' sole responsibility for managing the enterprise and employing labour; (3) a guarantee of non-union status for foremen; and (4) a uniform expiration date of 1 January for all collective agreements.[20]

The third development in Sweden requiring some comment is the confirmation of the legal status of collective agreements with the passage of the Collective Agreements Act and Labour Court Act of 1928. Clearly, the passage of this legislation, which took place against a background of growing concern about the extent of industrial conflict in Sweden in the 1920s, assumes some importance in the light of the continuing support given to voluntarism in Britain. Given the significance of fixed-term substantive agreements in Sweden, however, the only surprising thing is that collective agreements had not been accorded legal status much earlier. Indeed, if SAF had had its way, they would have been as early as 1909 after LO's defeat in the general strike of that year. Initially, SAF had sought LO's agreement to a contractual system of collective bargaining as

---

[20] Hallendorff (1927: 22) suggested that the organization of employers in Denmark was probably earlier because industry was not so geographically dispersed or differentiated as in Sweden. See also Galenson (1969: 69–73).

part of its surrender terms.[21] When that failed, SAF had sought to secure its objectives by legislative means. Here too it was frustrated; the farmers' representatives in the Riksdag were afraid to give legal support to the lockout that the legislation entailed for fear that the equivalent right of trade unions to take sympathetic action might encourage agricultural workers to seek the support of their better organized colleagues in manufacturing.

In view of their substantial involvement in competitive overseas trade mentioned earlier, it is not surprising that a fully-fledged contractual system of collective bargaining was especially prized by Swedish employers. First, it meant that the employers' right to manage, which SAF had insisted should appear in every collective agreement since 1906, was given statutory force. Second, and relatedly, legal enforceability reinforced the peace obligation that Swedish employers, like their Danish counterparts, had sought to establish as the essential *quid pro quo* for their willingness to negotiate over the substantive terms and conditions of employment.

SAF was far from enthusiastic about having legislation dealing with disputes of interest, however, fearing that it would lead to compulsory arbitration and to interference with the employers' right to manage. Indeed, it was largely under pressure from SAF that sympathetic action was exempted from the peace obligation under the terms of the Collective Agreements Act; SAF did not want the sympathetic lockout, its main weapon in upholding managerial prerogative, to be subject to legal constraint. But such was the climate of opinion that even the Social Democrat government which was returned in 1932 found itself under mounting pressure to introduce legislation to deal with disputes of interest. In fact, in 1935 only the last-minute attempt by the opposition to include stiffer measures made it possible for the Social Democrats to vote against a bill that they themselves had introduced. It was against this background that SAF and LO seized the opportunity provided by the publication of the report of the Nothin Commission in 1935, to begin the discussions that eventually led to the negotiation of the 'Basic Agreement' of 1938.[22]

[21] The fact that SAF allowed workers to return to work on condition that they withdrew from trade union membership meant that LO itself was able to avoid signing the employer surrender terms. For further details of those developments, see Westerståhl (1945).
  The legal status of collective agreements had been tested in the courts before 1928. Almost the only case of note, however, had arisen out of the 1909 conflict. In 1915 the Supreme Court decided that the agreement which had been reached was binding on the parties, and that a trade union could sue and be sued for damages under the common law. The six-year delay in the Supreme Court's decision was itself a reason why both employers and the trade unions avoided the courts during this period. The 1928 Act, it seems, considerably speeded up the time in which such cases could be resolved. For further details and for the differing views of SAF and LO on legislation, see Johnston (1962: 120–1, 141–7).
[22] The Basic Agreement of 1938 and the other multi-industry agreements which followed are often referred to as the 'Saltsjöbaden Agreements' after the seaside resort outside Stockholm where the discussions between SAF and LO took place. For a more detailed

Britain

The protagonists in metalworking in Britain were very different from those in the other countries. The emergence of a large number of medium-sized employers, many of them concentrated around London, in the Midlands, in Lancashire, in the West Riding of Yorkshire, on the Tyne and the Clyde, was gradual. This is not simply because Britain was the first country to industrialize. The process of industrialization was relatively autonomous and market-based, with the role of the state being important only indirectly – in the maintenance of law and order, in the winning and the defence of the empire, and in regulating commercial and imperial relations. In contrast to Germany and Italy, where a number of employers organized their activities behind tariff walls on a large scale from the very beginning, in Britain small family-owned businesses grew by exploiting their competitive advantage. Relationships between business were largely based on market transactions. Finance was internally generated or came from local money markets: the state and the banks were rarely involved even in financing the development of the railways. To add to the complexity of the structure of employment, the range of products manufactured was extremely diverse. A variety of technologies was employed. Indeed, many employers, especially in the metalworking industries, relied on subcontracting well into the second half of the nineteenth century.

The diversity of employers was reflected in and reinforced by the trade unions that grew up to challenge them.[23] This is especially so in the engineering and shipbuilding industries. The relatively protracted nature of industrialization, coupled with the continued need for skilled craftsmen due to the demand for non-standard goods in export markets, made it possible for craft unions to establish themselves before the coming of the second wave of trade union membership among semi- and unskilled workers and before most of their members had received the vote. There was a large number of such unions, though two were to become dominant: the Amalgamated Society of Engineers (ASE) in engineering narrowly-defined, and the United Society of Boilermakers and Iron Shipbuilders in shipbuilding. Significantly, the craft unions did not depend upon formal recognition by the employers. The methods they employed to protect and promote their members' interests were essentially threefold. First, there was the enforcement of craft rules governing the performance and payment for specific types of work. Second, there was

discussion of the background and events leading up to the negotiation of the agreements see Johnston (1962: 169–74) and Sunesson (1974). For the views of a managing director of SAF, see Kugelberg (1953).

[23] Uniquely in the five countries, employers in engineering and shipbuilding in Britain were to establish separate employers' organizations. The fact that the key groups of workers in the two industries were already organized in different craft unions seems hardly a coincidence. For the background in the split, see Wigham (1973: 27–8).

the control of the supply of labour through the enforcement of the 'union shop', the apprenticeship system and a ratio of apprentices to journeymen. Both these methods depended on the ability of craftsmen in the workplace to uphold craft rules. The third – the provision of friendly society benefits, and especially out-of-work benefit – was initially organized by the local union, but, increasingly from the middle of the nineteenth century onwards, came to be centralized in the national union with strict rules on payment of benefit to enable it to protect funds. An added advantage of this arrangement was that leaders of the national union were able to exploit their apparent lack of involvement in industrial action to win parliamentary and public approval for the removal of restrictions on trade union activities.

It is against this background that the accommodation referred to in the introduction to this chapter took place. The first stage, local negotiations on substantive issues between employers and the district committees of craft unions such as the ASE, cannot be dated exactly, though there are examples as early as the 1860s in engineering. They were also a fairly *ad hoc* and often intermittent affair. In one respect these local negotiations developed fairly naturally out of the attempt of the district committees of the ASE to maintain their unilateral regulation of the main conditions of employment. Periodically the district committees would send employers a circular listing the main conditions under which their members would work, especially when they decided to make some change in those conditions; if individual employers objected, they would quickly find themselves without workers. As one shipbuilding employer, for example, complained to the Royal Commission on the Organization and Rules of Trade Unions in 1868:

> formerly I the master, used to fix the price . . . lately . . . I was obliged to submit to a way of engaging men at the price they themselves in their unions regulated that they would take. I must take those men or leave them alone, because if I did not take those men no other men were allowed to come to my yard to take those places (quoted in Clegg *et al.*, 1964: 6).

It was a tactic which more or less obliged employers to come together to deal with the union. They might not have liked negotiating changes in pay or hours of work. But joint regulation was preferable to unilateral regulation by the union. As for the union, joint regulation meant that the employers were forced to recognize what it might have had difficulty in imposing on all of them; it was also administratively convenient.

It is also reasonable to suggest that the general climate of industrial relations was important in the development of joint regulation in engineering. By 1867, when the Royal Commission on the Organization and Rules of Trade Unions and Other Associations began its deliberations, there had been significant developments in collective bargaining in a number of other industries. In particular, following an intensive period of industrial conflict, the North of England ironmasters had established a conciliation board which *de facto* involved trade union representatives.[24] As Clegg and his colleagues observe (1964: 22), 'major changes on wages were settled either on the basis of a selling-price sliding-scale or by negotiation, with arbitration as the last resort. . . .' The Royal Commission or, rather, a significant minority of its members, commented very favourably on the work of these and other similar boards. They also commended the growing practice of having a code of working rules agreed between employers and workers.[25]

The second stage in the process of accommodation between employers and trade unions in engineering, the 'Terms of Settlement, 1898', was altogether a more dramatic affair. In 1896 employers from the North East, Clydeside, Barrow and Belfast had joined together to form the Employers' Federation of Engineering Associations. In 1897 the Federation responded to strike action by members of the ASE in support of the 8-hour day with a lockout. The lockout gained surprising momentum. The Federation's membership grew by leaps and bounds to stand at over 700 at the height of the dispute. After more than six months of the conflict, the ASE was forced to sue for peace. The 'Terms of Settlement, 1898' were the price the employers demanded for calling off the lockout; the ASE not only had to accept a wide-ranging statement of the employers' right to manage, but also a detailed national procedure known as the 'Provisions for Avoiding Disputes'.

The struggle between employer and craftsman over the control of work at the heart of the dispute had never been very far from the surface. As Zeitlin (1983: 27–30) has argued, what gave the issue an immediacy in the 1890s was the threat to the stability of the division of labour that had prevailed since the 1850s. The threat came from two related sources:

[24] Space does not permit more detailed treatment of the other sectors of the metalworking industry. It is perhaps sufficient to note here that the ironmasters of the Midlands and South Wales had a long history of quarterly meetings dating back to the 1780s. The main purpose of these meetings was to fix the prices to which wages were automatically linked. Unlike printing employers, then, the ironmasters did not need the help of trade unions to regulate the market. It was the ability of trade unions to disrupt the unilateral price– and wage–fixing that led employers to reach some accommodation with them. By the 1860s, the trade unions had achieved the necessary strength to do this. For example, in 1864–5 30,000 workers struck for 21 weeks against wage reductions in North Staffordshire. It was the desire of the North of England ironmasters to avoid these and other bitter disputes that led them to involve the trade unions in the operation of the sliding scales. Other ironmasters followed suit as did employers in the newly-emerging steel processes. The relative success of the local arbitration and conciliation boards that were responsible for the operation of the sliding scales must be counted a major factor in explaining why a national organization of iron and steel employers did not emerge until 1922. For further details, see Clegg *et al.* (1964: 21–3) and Pugh (1951).

[25] For further details of such developments see Amulree (1929: 82–7), and Sharp (1950: 287).

competition and new technology. The competition from Germany and the USA, which increasingly began to threaten Britain's domination of world markets, led employers to try to reduce their labour costs. This meant the introduction of piecework, the intensification of direct supervision, and the employment of non-apprenticed workers in the production process. The new technology took the form of a range of machine tools including turret and capstan lathes, milling and grinding machines, and gauges which had originally been developed in the USA to meet the growing demand for mass production goods. Not only did the new technology make it possible for British manufacturers to begin to mass-produce goods such as the bicycle, but also to improve quality and performance on less standardized work.

It was one thing, however, for employers to insist that the union recognize their right to manage: it was quite a different matter to make it a reality. This is why the 'Provisions for Avoiding Disputes' were so important. The immediate target of the employers' attack in 1897–8 was the district committees of the ASE. These committees, which enjoyed a considerable measure of autonomy from the national union, had been entrusted with the prime responsibility for enforcing and, in some instances, defining the craft practices the employers found so irritating. Their tactics were also extremely difficult to combat even when employers organized themselves locally. Now, as Wigham (1973: 63) puts it, under the 'Terms of Settlement, 1898' the district committees were to be placed in 'a straitjacket of national control'. If they attempted to oppose the exercise of management prerogative with their own unilateral controls, they and the national union would be threatened with a lockout by the employers. If they or their members were unable to reach agreement on any local issue with employers, the dispute had to go through a procedure ending with a national conference. Even negotiations over changes in wages were to be subject to the same procedure. Significantly, too, there was to be no stoppage of work until the procedure had been exhausted. In this way, then, the employers sought to remove the immediate issue from the workplace and the district where the employers were most vulnerable. Equally important, the officials of the national union were to be directly involved in ensuring this happened.[26]

The 'Provisions for Avoiding Disputes' would appear to have met the employers' specific needs. Even so, it is necessary to appreciate why the employers did not resort to a national fixed-term substantive agreement in order to control the activities of the union. It was not so much that the engineering industry was extremely heterogeneous. As chapter 5 has pointed out, this was not to stop the employers in other countries in similar circumstances from negotiating a framework of minimum terms and conditions in similar circumstances. Much more important was the

[26] Details of the lockout of 1897–8 and the 'Terms of Settlement, 1898' are contained in Wigham (1973: 29–62, 285–9).

fact that district and workplace negotiations had already given rise to a very considerable and complex body of practices and rules. This led senior employers' representatives, such as Colonel Dyer, to argue that only matters of general principle were capable of being dealt with at national level; wages and conditions were a matter for local consideration.

Attitudes to wages and conditions were also important. As the Webbs (1920: 338–41) point out, the strength of 'capitalist' economic principles was such that it had become accepted that, even where they did take place, negotiations over wages were to be concerned not with minima but with rises and falls in line with market conditions. This was as true of district negotiations in the engineering industry as it was in coal and iron, where sliding scales linking wages to the selling price of the product were in operation. Clearly, such a view was hardly conducive to seeing the collective agreement dealing with wages and conditions as a contract for a fixed term.

In any event, the 'Terms of Settlement, 1898' were to be profoundly important for the subsequent development of collective bargaining. The employers' insistence that settlements reached under the 'Provisions for Avoiding Disputes' were to be restricted to the specific district or group of workers and were not to have wider application meant, in practice, that it was virtually impossible to develop comprehensive multi-employer agreements so far as substantive issues were concerned. Similarly, by insisting that they should be able to deal directly with individual workers or groups of workers – largely in an attempt to keep trade union officials at arm's length – employers not only set a seal of legitimacy on workplace bargaining and guaranteed that it would be largely autonomous of the trade unions and the employers' organization; they also made it more likely that workplace bargaining would be informal and fragmented. Significantly, too, given the engineering union's exclusive coverage of maintenance fitters throughout British industry, and the growth of the general unions with large numbers of their members in engineering, many of the features of industrial relations in engineering were to find their way into other industries.

More generally, the relative success of the arrangements that employers and trade unions in engineering had arrived at themselves meant that the ranks of those who favoured 'voluntarism' as opposed to compulsion in collective bargaining matters were considerably reinforced.[27] Opposition to legal compulsion – or, to put it more positively,

[27] Reference has already been made to the views of the Royal Commission on the Organization and Rules of Trade Unions and Other Associations of 1867. The Royal Commission on Labour, which sat between 1891–4, came to a similar conclusion. The majority declared firmly against the variety of proposals for compulsory arbitration and legal intervention and in favour of voluntary arrangements. In the words of Sharp (1950: 291) 'the Commissioners felt that less faith should be put in legal sanction in those matters so that more might thereby be expected from the moral sanction'. The passage of the Conciliation Act of 1896 confirmed the trend. The leading arbitrator and concili-

support for the view that arrangements voluntarily entered into were preferable to those imposed by the law – was especially important immediately following the First World War. As in France, Germany and Italy discussed above, government intervention during this period was directly responsible for the widespread development of employers' organizations and multi-employer bargaining. In particular, government support for the recommendations of the Whitley Committee[28] of 1917–18 was to lead to the setting up of Joint Industrial Councils in many industries with little or no organization among employers let alone collective bargaining. Chemicals is an example.[29] In contrast to France and Germany, however, the government did not introduce a legal framework for collective bargaining. In other words, multi-employer agreements remained 'gentlemen's agreements': they did not become legally-enforceable contracts and codes.

Even so, in the light of the position adopted by their Swedish counterparts, it might be asked why employers, in particular, did not press for

---

ator of the day, Askwith, sought to incorporate provisions for standing conciliation machinery in any settlement of a dispute in which he took part. The National Industrial Conference of 1911–12 also came down firmly in favour of voluntary arrangements. For further details, see Amulree (1929: 102–10), Charles (1973: 37–56), Sharp (1950 291–6).

[28] The Whitley Committee was set up in October 1916 at the height of industrial unrest to make suggestions for securing a permanent improvement in relations between employers and workers. Its reports – there were five in total – were published in 1917–18 and provided for a comprehensive system of negotiation and consultation through a hierarchy of national, district, and works' councils. A detailed list of subjects for consideration by the two parties covering a wide range of employment and conditions was also drawn up. It was envisaged that the arrangements should be entirely voluntary, but the Committee's recommendations were adopted by the government and steps taken to persuade employers and trade unions to introduce them through the Ministry of Labour. The effect of the Whitley Committee's recommendations varied widely from industry to industry. In the four years following the publication of the Committee's reports, some 74 Joint Industrial Councils were set up mainly in less well-organized industries. In some industries in which collective bargaining was more or less well established, including iron and steel, engineering and shipbuilding, the Whitley recommendations had less impact. Few industries even in the first group, it needs to be emphasized, followed the Whitley recommendations to the full; for example, most did not introduce works councils. For further details, see Charles (1973: 131–60).

The engineering employers in particular were opposed to the idea of works councils though in 1920 they agreed to works committees. Smith, the Secretary of the EEF who was a member of the Whitley Committee, was rebuked by some of his members for having agreed to put his signature to such recommendations. For further details, see Wigham (1973: 102).

[29] Under the pressure of war-time conditions, chemical employers had increasingly negotiated wage rates locally, taking disagreements to the government's Committee of Production. Dissatisfied with these arrangements, the firm of Brunner Mond canvassed a number of the employers with a view to establishing a national employers' organization. As a consequence the 'Wages Committee of Chemical Manufacturers' was set up in 1917 to perform a similar function to that of some of the local informal groups of employers. It was this committee that in October 1917 was asked by the Ministry of Labour to provide the employers' side of a future Joint Industrial Chemical Council. The formation of the Chemical & Allied Employers' Association followed in 1918 (for further details, see Robinson, 1976).

collective agreements to be made legally enforceable.[30] As has been pointed out already, the arrangements that had been introduced in engineering – and, indeed, other industries – were hardly conducive to the development of a contractual or 'statute law' model system. But this was not the only consideration. Even though they were voluntary, these arrangements proved more than adequate to deal with the problems posed in the immediate post-First World War period. This was especially so in the case of the engineering industry. For example, faced with attempts by district committees of the ASE to press particular issues with industrial action, such as a reduction of the working week on the Clyde in 1919, the employers successfully insisted the national union withhold its support. The ability of the employers to engage in lockouts also proved a potent weapon. Its threat was enough to cause sheetmetalworkers and electricians to call off industrial action in 1919 and 1920 respectively. In 1922 its application was used to impose on the ASE, along with every other union with members in the engineering industry, a restatement and amplification of the employers' right to manage. In these circumstances there appeared to be no good reason for employers to disturb the status quo, especially as growing unemployment further contributed to the weakness of the unions' bargaining power. Indeed, even many of the proposals for trade union legislation canvassed following the general strike of 1926 were opposed by engineering employers on the grounds that they might also apply to employers' organizations.

A similar line of argument helps to explain why a powerful employers' confederation did not emerge in Britain. The idea of setting up an employers' confederation was discussed briefly following the 1897–8 engineering dispute, leading to the setting up of the Employers' Parliamentary Committee (later Council), and again in 1912–13. But there was no general support. Employers in industries such as engineering, shipbuilding, printing and building were already well organized in industry organizations; they saw little need for an employers' confederation. It was government intervention during and at the end of the First World War that changed this situation. Even then, there was no great enthusiasm for the project. Indeed, it was to prevent the newly-established trade confederation, the Federation of British Industries,[31] from establishing itself as the

[30] In fact, during 1918 and 1919 a number of Joint Industrial Councils did express themselves in favour of making their agreements legally enforceable. At a conference of representatives from 45 Joint Industrial Councils and Interim Industrial Reconstruction Committees in January 1920 a resolution was passed calling for legislation to make agreements legally enforceable. The Industrial Courts Bill, which was intended to make it possible for the parties to give legal effect to their agreements, actually passed its second reading by a large majority in May 1924, and was only dropped when the Labour government fell. A number of similar bills were brought before Parliament in the 1930s without success. For further details, see Lewis (1970 and 1979) and Sharp (1950: 333–4).

[31] The Federation of British Industries and the National Union of Manufacturers, which was more concerned with the interests of the smaller firms, had been formed in 1916. Under pressure from the Engineering Employers' Federation, the Federation of British Industries was obliged to agree that it would not 'concern itself with, or interfere with any question

spokesman of British employers that the EEF finally took the initiative by inviting other employers' organizations to join with it in forming an employers' confederation. Only 45 years later did the three organizations, the British Employers' Confederation, the Federation of British Industries and the National Association of British Manufacturers, amalgamate to form the Confederation of British Industry in 1965. Here too government initiatives were important.

Summary

The differences between the five countries identified in previous chapters are largely to be seen as variations on a common pattern: the resort to collective action by employers in order to deal with the challenge of trade unions and their acquiescence in multi-employer bargaining as the least unacceptable means of institutionalizing industrial conflict. The key to explaining the differences lies in the impact of industrialization in the metalworking industries which had a determining influence due to their size and significance. Two main distinctions may be drawn between the countries. First, France, Germany and, to a lesser extent, Italy may be distinguished from Britain and Sweden. In France and Germany, where employers were not subject to market pressures and the larger employers dominated their labour markets, there was no mutual accommodation prior to the First World War as in Britain and Sweden. Multi-employer bargaining developed on the basis of compulsory rules introduced in the crisis years of 1918–19. In Italy, though there was some development of multi-employer bargaining on the basis of voluntary rules before the First World War, the main influence was provided by the compulsory rules of the fascist legal framework. Second, Britain may be distinguished from Sweden. In both countries employers resorted to collective bargaining on the basis of voluntary rules in order to achieve peace and stability. In Britain, however, with local bargaining on pay and conditions involving the district committees of the craft-based ASE well established, the means to secure these ends was a national procedure. In Sweden, where there was little or no history of local bargaining with members of the skilled, but non-craft iron and metalworkers' union, a national agreement on pay and conditions for a fixed term (entailing periodic negotiations on renewal) secured the employers' objectives. In each case the origins of multi-employer bargaining were profoundly important for subsequent events. In

affecting working arrangements or rates of pay except at the request of the Employers' Association or Federation established to deal with such matters'. Even so, the relationship between the FBI and the EEF was far from easy. The timing of the formation of the National Confederation of Employers' Organisations (subsequently the British Employers' Confederation) was dictated by the calling of the National Industrial Conference in 1919 and the formation of the International Labour Organisation: both required the nomination of representative employers. For further details, see Wigham (1973: 103–4).

particular, they help to explain why employers in Sweden, unlike those in Britain, were favourably disposed to making collective agreements legally enforceable; legal enforceability reinforced the peace obligation they had sought to establish as the essential *quid pro quo* for their willingness to negotiate over wages and the other conditions of employment. In Britain, on the other hand, where there was no tradition of negotiating fixed-term substantive agreements, employers saw no great virtue in legal enforceability. Indeed, engineering employers opposed legislation dealing with collective bargaining in the 1920s for fear that it would be to their disadvantage.

7

The USA and Japan: Special Cases?

Inevitably, the discussion in previous chapters invites questions about the behaviour of employers in the USA and Japan. In particular, if their counterparts in Western Europe have been so anxious to exclude trade unions from the workplace, why have employers in large-scale manufacturing industry insisted on dealing with them at this level? Clearly, it is not, as some commentators (Ross, 1962: 334; Kassalow, 1969: 136) have argued in the case of the USA, that employers in these countries are opposed in principle to collective action.[1] Not only does multi-employer bargaining take place in both countries: in the USA[2] in clothing,

[1] The 'individualism' of American employers is a recurrent theme in attempts to explain single-employer bargaining in the USA. For example, Ross (1962: 334) suggests that the 'prescriptive monopoly of trade union–management relationships in Western Europe enjoyed by employers' organizations reflects the strength of the cartel principle in European economic life, just as the relative unimportance of employers' associations in the United States reflects a deep-rooted individualism'.

By contrast, it was Bendix (1956: 167) who pointed to the apparent contradiction between 'individualism' and the resort to collective action on the part of United States employers to achieve the 'open shop'. He also perceptively observed that there was not really a contradiction: collective action was the means to maintain the employers' much-vaunted authority within the plant.

It is also important to remember that the 1860s and 1880s had already witnessed collective action on the part of US employers. For example the collapse of the 'Knights of Labor' in the late 1880s was due in no small measure to the aggressive campaign waged by employers' organizations. For further details, see Commons *et al.* (1966: 26–30, 55, 360–2, 414–17). See also Bonnett (1922: 21–2).

[2] The Bureau of Labor Statistics of the US Department of Labor publishes details of the numbers of workers covered by major collective agreements (that is, agreements covering more than 1000 workers). On the basis of these details, it would appear that in 1975, some 80 per cent of workers in large-scale manufacturing were covered by single-employer and 20 per cent by multi-employer agreements. In clothing, construction and printing approximately 90 per cent of workers were covered by multi-employer agreements. This pattern appears to have been more or less constant since the Second World War. For further details, see Kochan (1980: 94–7) and Derber (1984: 84–9).

construction and printing, and in Japan[3] in shipping and private railways as well as sectors of printing and textiles. There is also very considerable co-ordination by employers of the single-employer bargaining in large-scale manufacturing industry. In the USA this often takes the form of 'coalition' bargaining, where employers present a more or less common front to the trade unions, or 'pattern' bargaining, where the settlement of one employer is adopted by the others.[4] In Japan co-ordination takes place on a larger scale; first, NIKKEIREN,[5] the employers' confederation, is itself intimately involved in co-ordinating the approach of employers during the annual *Shunto* or 'Spring wage offensive' mounted by the trade union federations; and, second, the settlement in the private iron and steel sector, which involves the big five employers simultaneously offering uniform pay increases (the 'one shot offer'), subsequently forms the basis of the 'going rate' throughout private manufacturing.

As in the case of the Western European countries, to begin to understand the present-day structure of collective bargaining, it is necessary to explore in detail the origins of collective bargaining. In particular, it is

---

The developments in construction, printing and some of the other handicraft industries in the USA were very similar to those in Europe: organization and multi-employer bargaining were well established in many cities by the turn of the century. For construction and printing, see Bonnett (1922); for clothing, see Levine (1924), Seidman (1942) and Slichter (1941: 504–28).

Compared with the UK, multi-employer bargaining in these industries, especially in clothing and construction, appears to be far more effective from both the employers' and the trade unions' point of view. Two related factors can be suggested in explanation: first, multi-employer bargaining has remained essentially local in its scope; and, second, trade unions have been able to maintain their control of the supply of labour.

3 In textiles and private railways, bargaining is conducted by representatives of several employers and their enterprise unions meeting at the same time and place. In coal and synthetic chemicals representatives of the industrial federations attend the negotiations at enterprise level. This is known as 'diagonal' or 'radial' bargaining. Multi-employer bargaining in printing is usually area-based. For further details, see Shirai (1973: 297–306) and Levine (1984: 346–52).

4 'Pattern' bargaining is particularly common in the automobile industry. The United Automobile Workers choose a 'target' employer from one of the big three (Chrysler, Ford, or General Motors). Intensive negotiations take place with that employer and often a strike is called if an agreement is not reached before the expiry of the contract. Meanwhile, negotiations will be opened with the other employers, but the outcome in the 'target' employer will be awaited before a settlement is reached. For a discussion of 'coalition' and 'pattern' bargaining, see Kochan (1980: 96–7, 113–21).

5 NIKKEIREN was established in 1948 to represent the interests of employers in labour matters. NIKKEIREN is composed of branch and regional and prefectoral employers' organizations in roughly equal numbers. KEIDANREN is the trade confederation.

On the face of it, the role of NIKKEIREN is similar to that of the CBI. In practice, however, it appears to have been far more influential. For example, it was largely due to NIKKEIREN's efforts to change the principles of pay bargaining which led SOHYO to develop the tactics which have come to be associated with the *Shunto* or 'Spring Offensive'.

NIKKEIREN's public response to *Shunto* has been to produce an annual economic analysis and general 'guidelines' for maximum wage increases. For further details, see Okamoto (1973: 173–8) and Levine (1984: 342–5).

necessary to take into account that in both countries collective bargaining developed on the basis of compulsory rules introduced by governments at a time of great economic and social crisis – in the period 1933–7 in the USA[6] and 1945–7 in Japan; that the legislation introduced in Japan and, in particular, the Trade Union Law of 1945, was closely modelled on that introduced into the USA a decade earlier; and, perhaps most significantly, that although the 1935 National Labor Relations (Wagner) Act in the USA and the 1945 Trade Union Law in Japan do not prohibit multi-employer bargaining, they do not come down positively in favour of this type of structure as the relevant legislation does in a number of the Western European countries. Instead, they leave the National Labor Relations Board in the USA and the Labour Relations Committees in Japan to 'decide . . . the unit appropriate for the purposes of collective bargaining . . . (whether employer unit, craft unit, plant unit, or subdivision thereof') (National Labor Relations Act, 1935).

It will be argued here that, as in the case of the Western European countries, this state of affairs is largely to be explained in terms of the impact of industrialization in the manufacturing industries. In both countries relatively large individual employers emerged in these industries at an early date in the process of industrialization. In the USA, having initially come to terms with trade unions mostly on a multi-employer basis, these employers inflicted a major defeat on trade unions with the success of the 'open shop' campaign that was fought at the turn of the century. In Japan the large employers to all intents and purposes prevented the emergence of independent trade unions altogether. In both the USA and Japan these large employers used 'welfarism', 'internal job ladders' and 'employee representation plans', or company unions, to keep the external trade unions at bay. In these circumstances employers and governments did not come under strong pressure to introduce multi-employer bargaining. Moreover, single-employer bargaining meant employers could continue to deal directly with their own employees, albeit they were now organized in independent trade unions, rather than the external organizations they had struggled so long to avoid. Paradoxical as it may seem, then, it is single-employer bargaining that serves

---

[6] Strictly speaking, the 'New Deal' legislation began as a 'by-product of the attempt to promote economic recovery' (Ulman, 1961a: 399); section 7(a) of the National Recovery Act of 1933, which gave employees the right to organize and to bargain collectively (though not necessarily in independent trade unions) was intended primarily as an instrument for redistributing income in favour of wages as a means of stimulating consumer spending. The Act gave rise to an intensive organizing drive on the part of the trade unions which was matched by an extremely hostile response from the employers. Fearing the impact of industrial conflict and the Depression, the administration then sought to intervene with the introduction of tri-partite boards. It was only when this initiative failed – and the Democrats had made sweeping gains in the 1934 congressional elections – that the National Labor Relations Act (the Wagner Act) was introduced in 1935, enforcing the right of the employees to be represented by independent trade unions. Even then it was to take a decision of the Supreme Court in 1937 to make the Act operational.

to limit the activities of trade unions in the USA and Japan. The remainder of this chapter enlarges on these conclusions.

The USA

The large employer was already a dominant feature of the US economy by the turn of the century. If commentators differ in the emphasis that they give, there would nonetheless appear to be broad agreement about the reasons for this development. The growth in the population due to large-scale immigration and the opening up of the country by the railroads set the context; the enormous national markets and acute shortages of labour that followed encouraged investment in capital-using innovations that large-scale operations could exploit. The investment was made possible by the availability of the great accumulation of capital that took place following the Civil War and the development of a sophisticated banking and finance sector that channelled funds from investor to entrepreneur. As Chandler (1978: 71) has argued, developments within the emerging corporations were also important; improvements in organizational design and in the quality of management brought about by the development of the multi-unit enterprise themselves made a significant contribution to further expansion. Finally, there was the merger movement. Intensive competition between rival large-scale enterprises or between such enterprises and smaller firms led to attempts to avoid excessive price-cutting through the formation of trusts and cartels: a process that was taken further with the consolidation of competing enterprises following the passage of the Sherman Anti-Trust Act of 1890. Between 1897 and 1903 over 2,800 enterprises were involved in mergers, of which nearly half took place in 1899 (Ratner *et al.*, 1979: 290).

The merger movement was especially important in shaping the structure of the large employers. Some of the earliest developments took the form of the 'horizontal' combination, as in the petroleum industry, of a number of enterprises operating at the same level or stage in the production process. Crucially for the developments discussed below, this was also to be the pattern in the metal-producing sector with the formation of the US Steel Corporation or 'Big Steel' by Carnegie in 1901. In other sectors combination took a 'vertical' direction. For example, in the engineering industry the inadequacies of the distribution and marketing systems led enterprises in office machinery (Remington Typewriter and National Cash Register), agricultural machinery (McCormick Harvester, John Deere and J.I. Case), and heavy machinery (Otis Elevator, Western Electric, Westinghouse, Edison, General Electric, Babcock and Wilcox, and Worthington Pump) to assume these functions directly. Similarly, fears about the supply of materials and parts often led such enterprises to integrate backwards with the creation of purchasing organizations and the take-over of the component manufacturers. In Chandler's (1978: 109) judgement, these industries were 'almost from their very beginnings, oligopolistic or monopolistic. They never were competitive in the traditional sense.'

The emergence of the large oligopolistic or monopolistic enterprise was double-edged in its implications for the development of collective bargaining. Initially, 'trustification' in particular appeared to be favourable. Perhaps the best example is the stove industry. In 1891 the National Association of Stove Manufacturers negotiated with the moulders' union what has often been described as the first national collective agreement. According to Commons and his associates (1961: 480), the stove industry was unique in that the largest manufacturers had come to control the market, the product had become completely standardized, payment was by piecework and machinery had not yet replaced the moulder's skill. Years of bitter struggle between the Stove Founders' National Defence Association and the moulders' union only served to reinforce the logic of multi-employer bargaining to institutionalize industrial conflict.

The pace of negotiating activity quickened towards the end of the decade. The period 1898 to 1904 witnessed what has been described as the 'remarkable spread of trade agreements' (Commons *et al.*, 1961: 524). The Spanish-American and Boer Wars brought prosperous times to manufacturing industry. With the shortage of skilled labour, the bargaining power of trade unions increased; the membership of the American Federation of Labor (AFL) grew from 265,000 to 1,700,000 in the period 1896 to 1904. The example of the stove manufacturers was followed by the National Founders' Association representing employers in the general foundries, by the National Erectors' Association, and by the National Metal Trades Association which had been formed in 1899.[7] According to the First Industrial Commission of 1898 (quoted in Chamberlain and Kuhn, 1965: 35), other examples of national multi-employer agreements included those in iron and steel, tinplate, bituminous coal, longshoring, pottery and glass, as well as that in

---

[7] Montgomery (1980: 49–57) provides an account of the circumstances leading up to the negotiation and subsequent repudiation of the so-called 'Murray Hill Agreement' by the National Metal Trades Association. The agreement emerged out of claims submitted by the lodges of the International Association of Machinists in Chicago. Significantly, it was the employers who suggested a national agreement largely to avoid dealing with the local union and conceding demands for a union shop. The agreement, which reduced the basic working week and set up a grievance board, but left wages to local settlement, quickly ran into trouble. By May of the following year, many lodges were demanding pay increases to compensate for the reduction in the working week; employers also complained of restrictions on their employment and use of labour. The call for a national strike in May 1901 was met with firm resistance by the now 'belligerent' employers' organization. The union was successful in Chicago but was crushed elsewhere. In terms of a comparison of developments in Britain and the USA it is interesting to note that, whereas the Amalgamated Society of Engineers in Britain had some 78,450 members in 1897, the International Association of Machinists had scarcely 15,000.

printing. US employers, it seems, were following a path somewhat similar to that of their British counterparts.

But the so-called 'honeymoon period of capital and labour' did not last very long. So far as 'trustification' was concerned, the stove industry was to be the exception to test the rule. For as Commons (1961: 526) and his associates recognized, in general terms the coming of the trusts bestowed great power on the individual employer:

> As soon as the trust became the sole employer of labor in an industry, the relations between capital and labor were thrown almost invariably into the state of affairs which had preceded any organisation of labor whatsoever. By abolishing competition among employers for labor and by giving the employer unlimited power to hold out against a strike, 'trustification' destroyed every bargaining advantage which labour ever enjoyed.

Even where amalgamation and consolidation stopped short of bringing about a monopoly, the bargaining power of the large corporations was considerably enhanced. The existence of the trusts made it difficult for the trade unions to organize by industry, because co-operation between employers was made much easier and their control over individual establishments increased.

Perhaps the best example is the United States Steel Corporation. One of its constituents, the Carnegie Company, had already fought a bitter dispute with the skilled union iron and steel workers at Homestead over the introduction of mass production technology in 1892. Following the consolidation of the largest steel companies to form the United States Steel Corporation in 1901, there followed yet another bitter dispute which led to the exclusion of the union from all of the Corporation's plants.[8]

---

[8] A number of writers have commented on the contrast between the behaviour of US employers in iron and steel and that of their British counterparts described in the previous chapter. The following is based on the review by Edwards (1981: 125–9). Clearly the growth of the trusts in steel was important: it gave employers the power to defeat the union. But it does not explain the will to do so. Critically important in that respect was the competitive situation which continued and which made it essential to cut the costs associated with craft practices. For even with the formation of US Steel in 1901, complete domination of the market was not achieved. Not only did the formation of US Steel fail to stabilize the market; during the first 20 years of its existence, it actually lost some of its share of the market.

Later in the same study, Edwards (1981: 242–6) goes on to seek to explain more generally the apparently 'exceptional' hostility of US employers to trade unions. Given the absence of feudalism, he suggests that this can perhaps best be explained in terms of the problem of US employers in creating and maintaining their own legitimacy. 'If employers had to create loyalty, they could not afford any threat to the process; workers had to be tied direct to the employer and to no one else' (244). The new entrepreneurs also had to establish their legitimacy against challenge from other directions – 'from the commercial classes and other groups, notably farmers, who were opposed to the "corporate ideal"' (244).

The difficulty with this interpretation is that it does not really stand up to the test of the experience of employers in the other countries. Arguably, the problems which employers

The United States Steel Corporation's decisive defeat of the iron and steel workers had a catalytic effect. Frustrated in their hopes that collective bargaining would bring peace and stability, a special convention of the National Metal Trades Association in June 1901 declared void the agreement signed with the International Association of Machinists in the previous year. In 1904 the National Founders' Association terminated its agreements with the moulders' union. The National Erectors' Association terminated its agreements with trade unions in 1906. In other industries employers' organizations, some of them newly formed and representing small and independent employers, took advantage of Supreme Court decisions upholding the applicability of the Sherman Anti-Trust Act to industrial disputes to seek injunctions against trade unions. In particular, the National Association of Manufacturers, originally founded in 1895 to deal with tariffs and the protection of foreign trade, was transformed. In effect, it now became an employers' confederation at the centre of the employers' fight against trade unionism and for the demand for the 'open shop'.

The achievement of the 'open shop' by most of the large employers in manufacturing industry during the early years of the century was profoundly important for the subject matter of this study. Their expulsion from large-scale manufacturing establishments meant the trade unions of the AFL did not expand their base, remaining the preserve of highly-skilled, highly-paid craft workers employed mostly in the smaller establishments. According to Wolman's (1936: 92, 96, 118, 121) estimates, the craft unions of the AFL accounted for something like three-quarters of the total union membership throughout the first two decades of the century: a proportion that had increased to more than 80 per cent by 1929. But it was not just that the craft unions of the AFL were cut off from the growing numbers of semi- and unskilled workers in manufacturing industry that was important. The AFL's insistence on maintaining a policy of exclusive jurisdiction, whereby one national union was given sole recruiting rights in each trade or industry, added to the difficulties of semi- and unskilled workers in establishing independent unions of their own. The overall effect was to postpone the emergence of anything approaching the 'mass' movement of Britain and Western Europe – whether in the form of a combination of craft and general

had in creating and maintaining their own legitimacy were far greater in countries such as Italy. Not only were employers such as Agnelli unable to draw on the discipline of the craftsman (as US employers were able to do), there also was the hostility from the church as well as commercial and farming groups. Paradoxically, it would seem more plausible to argue that, if US employers did experience particular problems in creating and maintaining their own legitimacy, these arose largely out of their defeat of the craft unions. For in one sense the defeat of the craft unions can be seen as a pyrrhic victory. It was not simply that those unions continued to pose a threat from outside the workplace. To repeat the point made by Lazonick (1983: 115–17), employers had to find something to replace the discipline associated with the craft unions.

unionism as in Britain or industrial unionism as in Western Europe – until *after* the passage of the 'New Deal' legislation promoting collective bargaining.

In the 1930s the AFL leadership gave a further twist to the policy of exclusive jurisdiction that was to have an important bearing on the nature of the legislation itself. In an attempt to resolve the increasingly bitter division between the advocates of craft and industrial unionism within its ranks, in 1933 the AFL began to establish plant-wide federal unions. Such federal unions, it was envisaged, would provide a temporary unit of organization, especially for semi- and unskilled workers, prior to their re-allocation between the various national unions. In the circumstances it is not perhaps surprising those politicians anxious to promote collective bargaining should have adopted a similar approach in putting the emphasis on exclusive jurisdiction at the plant level rather than on multi-employer bargaining at the national level as in Britain and Western Europe. Equally, it is not surprising that, with the breakaway of the supporters of industrial unionism to form the Committee of Industrial Organizations (CIO) in 1935, the National Labor Relations Board had to tread very carefully in determining the question of bargaining units, especially in industries where AFL and CIO unions were in competition. Indeed, by 1940 the AFL was urging that the Wagner Act itself should be repealed because of the problems involved.[9]

Perhaps of even greater importance in determining the levels at which collective bargaining was to take place, however, were the personnel policies pursued by the large employers in the wake of the 'open shop' campaign. As Lazonick has perceptively observed (1983: 115–17), the employers may have successfully expelled the craft unions from their workplaces, but they still had to find ways and means of motivating people to work: mass production technology and close supervision provided no long-term answer to absenteeism, turnover and, in some cases, sabotage in the larger establishments. A variety of policies were pursued. In some cases – Ford is an example – above-average rates of pay were introduced. In Ford, United States Steel and many other enterprises, management introduced internal job ladders, partly because of the requirements of the technology but also with a view to holding out the prospect of promotion from within for those who demonstrated suitable behaviour. In most cases such policies were underpinned with extensive 'fringe benefit' programmes designed to influence attitudes of workers in their private as well as their working lives.[10]

As their counterparts in France and Germany had done several years earlier, the larger employers also introduced company unions or 'employee representation plans' as they were more commonly called. The

9 For a succinct review of these developments, see Ulman (1961b: 398–400).
10 For the various developments in personnel management in this period, see Braverman (1974), Edwards (1979), Lazonick (1983). For the development in employee representation plans, see Mills and Montgomery (1945: 870–90).

introduction of such plans was especially widespread following the setting-up of the National Labor Board in 1917; this Board, which was set up by President Wilson to be responsible for the final settlement of disputes could require employers to negotiate with representatives of their own employees, though not necessarily with trade union representatives. In the 1920s the movement embraced more than one million workers. In the 1930s it grew even more extensive. This was especially so during the period of the 1933 National Recovery Act giving workers the right to organize and to bargain collectively, though not necessarily through independent trade unions. Indeed, it has been estimated that the number of workers organized in company unions doubled from 1.25 to 2.5 million during the period that Act was in force (Chamberlain and Kuhn, 1965: 43).

In these circumstances the preference of employers for single-employer rather than multi-employer bargaining is easily understandable. First many employers had developed detailed systems of internal job regulation in the 1920s and early 1930s specific to the individual workplace. To have attempted to unscramble these arrangements in the interests of a multi-employer agreement would not only have been extremely difficult; there was also the danger that the trade unions would have sought to level up pay and other conditions of employment from one employer to another. Second, the employers had fought a vigorous campaign against the recognition of the external trade unions over many years. To accede to their requests for bargaining rights for entire industries was hardly an attractive proposition. For some, it was logical to hope that the trade union would not win a majority for recognition on an employer-by-employer basis. Even for those who calculated that the trade union would win such a majority, single-employer bargaining was preferable. In effect, in most cases the basic unit of the trade union was to be the company branch. In practice, then, single-employer bargaining meant that the employer would continue to deal with his own employees, even if they were now organized in the external trade union. Third, the main advantage of multi-employer bargaining – the exclusion of trade unionism from the workplace – was hardly feasible in the USA: *de facto* the employer had already accepted that many aspects of internal job regulation should only be introduced or changed with the acceptance of the workforce. Moreover, some of the other apparent advantages of multi-employer bargaining, such as the co-ordination of employers' responses to trade union pay demands, could quite easily be achieved by 'coalition' or 'pattern' bargaining.

Japan

The large employer emerged by a very different route in Japan from the USA. The initiative for industrialization came from those responsible for the so-called 'aristocratic revolution' in 1868 which ushered in the Meij restoration. Anxious to meet the growing economic and military threat from the West – the Japanese economy had been thrown open to international trade and competition by a series of commercial treaties negotiated in the period 1858–66 under the Tokugawa regime – their initial attempts to encourage private investment met with little success. Most merchants were too conservative in attitude and the immense sums of money required proved prohibitive. Although handicraft manufacture was diverse and well-developed – and there was considerable mining of both metals and coal – industry was essentially household-based. Many craftsmen were employed directly by the nobility; in industries such as printing the traditional master–apprentice relationship survived. The new rulers therefore had to take matters into their own hands. The arsenals, foundries, shipyards and mines set up and run by the various regional administrations were brought under firm central control. Others were established along with strategic chemical, cement and glass plants. In a relatively short space of time modern manufacturing industries emerged side-by-side with the handicraft industries described above.

The passage of the Regulations on the Transfer of Factories in 1888 marked a second phase in the development of industrialization. Concerned by the lack of profitability of some of the enterprises and anxious to concentrate resources, the government gradually began to transfer many of these state-controlled enterprises into private hands. The first transfers were in non-strategic industries like cotton spinning, glass, and cement. Then the government began to hand over some of its mining and shipbuilding enterprises. Among the latter were the Nagasaki Shipyards first leased and then sold to Iwasaki Yatero who was the founder of the firm of Mitsubishi. Incidentally, he had already benefited from the gift of the military transport used in the Formosa exhibition of 1874 and from government subsidies enabling him to build up a considerable merchant fleet. Not that the transfer of state-controlled enterprises, mostly at very cheap prices, meant a total break with the state. A Department of Agriculture and Commerce was set up in 1881 as the vehicle for continuing state patronage. The government also maintained firm control over the munitions industries.

This policy laid the foundation for the domination of the Japanese economy by a financial oligarchy. By the Second World War 22 Zaibatsu, as they became to be known, can be identified. Four, each of which remained a family enterprise in some degree, were outstanding: Mitsui, Mitsubishi, Sumitomo, and Yasuda. With the support of the government, these families acquired an interlocking control over banking, on the one hand, and industry and commerce, on the other. Other Zaibatsu were important in limited activities: Furukawa in copper and electric power; Kawasaki in shipbuilding, locomotives, and steel products; Okura and Kuhara in mining and engineering; Shibusawa in banking and engineering; and Asano in cement and steel. Some Zaibatsu were of later origin; Nissan, for example, came to prominence as a result of its involvement in the war in Manchuria in the 1930s. Setting aside their control over banking and insurance, it has been suggested that even if the seventeen leading Zaibatsu are defined so as to include only companies in which they had 25 per cent or more of the stock, their aggregate paid-up capital was of the order of 18 per cent of the paid-up capital of all Japanese joint stock companies in 1935 (Lockwood, 1964: 214–15). By this date, the control of the Zaibatsu had spread from the modern sectors of heavy industry to include an increasing share of small-scale commerce and manufacture.

As Bisson (1945a, b) has argued, throughout the 1930s and the years of the war, the relationship between government officials, the military, and the Zaibatsu became increasingly intertwined. The power of the Zaibatsu increased with the support of the other two groups. For example, the Depression of 1930–1 gave a marked impetus to the formation of cartels which were legally recognized by the Major Industries Control Law and Industrial Association Law of 1931. In 1941 the Major Industries Association Ordinance was passed establishing Industrial Control Associations. This meant that the cartels were formed into associations vested with official powers over materials, labour and capital supply. The Zaibatsu leaders who headed the Control Associations were given official backing to rationalize their industries and hence increase their control over the smaller enterprises. It has been estimated that in the years 1941–5 the big four doubled their position in the economy, increasing their share of total corporate and partnership capital from 12 per cent to 24 per cent (Hadley, 1970: 41).

The pattern of industrialization also had a profound effect on the structure of the labour market. In the textile industries, which continued to be one of the largest employers down to the Second World War, employers were confronted with the basic problem of recruiting and retaining labour in their largely city-based operations. The employers' solution was to hire girls on contract for specified periods and to house them in dormitories under very tight controls. In the heavy manufacturing industries extreme shortages of workers with the requisite skills to work on the technology imported from overseas meant that employers had no alternative but to provide the skills internally at considerable cost. Here several methods were introduced to retain the skilled workers once they had been trained; first, status distinctions were drawn between regular workers, who were guaranteed some permanency of employment, and those taken on casually; second, many regular workers were given status as monthly salaried employees; and, third, contracts were introduced whereby workers signed on for long periods (Dore, 1973: 383–90; Sumiya, 1973: 42–7). The effect of these developments was to lay the foundations for a dual labour market and, in particular, marked differences in the treatment of workers between large and small enterprises. They also led to significant differences from one large enterprise to another in as much as job structures and training programmes tended to be very specific to the workplace.

Trade unions found it extremely difficult to establish themselves in these circumstances.[11] First, they had to contend with the problems presented by a dual labour market comprising a large number of small employers and a small number of large employers. Second, they had to contend with Zaibatsu leaders careful to maintain a common front[12] and with close ties with the government. For example, the Public Police Peace Act of 1900, primarily aimed at political opponents of the new regime, served to emasculate trade union activity: associations could be prohibited, assemblies banned and police officers could attend meetings where they were allowed to take place. The passage of the Act effectively put an end to the brief flurry of trade union activity – which included attempts to form printers' and metalworkers' unions – following the Sino-Japanese War of 1904–5. Government repression of opposition groups and political parties was to be a continuing feature until 1945.

As with the large employers in the USA, the personnel management practices adopted by the Zaibatsu were also profoundly important. Paternalism in its many manifestations had deep roots and continued to be very much a reality in the handicraft sector. But it was in the larger enterprises that the full potential of the approach came to be realized.

---

[11] At the end of the First World War, trade union membership was of the order of 100,000; by 1924–5, in a slightly more favourable climate, it had risen to 225,000; and by 1936 was 420,000. Collective agreements were also a rarity. Between 1919 and 1928 only 17 instances have been reported; by March 1936 this number had increased to 121, although four fifths of those covered were seamen and others employed in marine transport.

The early trade unions were largely confined to skilled workers and put most of their emphasis on the provision of friendly society benefits. They were unable to gain any measure of control over the supply of labour.

It was out of the re-emergence of such societies that the trade union confederation, SODOMEI, was finally to emerge in 1921. Within four years SODOMEI had split in two, and then in 1927 into three, as the socialists, communists and syndicalists fought for power in what was by now a largely political organization. For further details, see Levine (1958: 59–66) and Sumiya (1973: 32–46).

[12] Despite the domination of the economy by Zaibatsu, employers' organizations were formed as in the other countries. When Japan joined the International Labour Organization there were already a large number in existence. Single-industry organizations covered cotton textiles, match manufacturers, paper manufacture, shipbuilding, railroad employers, sugar manufacturers and electrical employers. However, the trade union challenge was very rarely a major factor in bringing about the formation of these organizations; or not directly so. Wage fixing was one activity in which a number of them was involved. Agreements not to poach labour were also common. This is especially true of the textile employers who had come together before the end of the century in order to deal with the problems of poaching by reaching agreements on spheres of influence so far as recruitment was concerned. A major factor behind the increase in the number of employers' organizations in the 1920s – and the formation of an employers' confederation known as Zensanren in 1931 – was the prospect of factory legislation and the legal recognition of trade unions. Opposition to such proposals finally led the government to give up the idea in 1930. For further details, see Taira (1970: 128–41) and Levine (1984: 319–22).

Encouraged by the example of US employers in the 1920s, many of the practices that had their origins in the employers' difficulties in recruiting and developing a labour force increasingly came to be used as instruments of social control designed to tie workers to the enterprise and to avoid the spread of independent trade unionism. Guarantees of long-term employment and wage-for-age-scales were especially important. Again, based on the US example, there was a widespread development among some of the larger enterprises of works councils and company unions. For example, one estimate suggests that in the 1920s about a half of all trade union members were organized in such enterprise unions (Sumiya, 1973: 46).

Here too the activities of the Zaibatsu received active support from the government. As early as 1919 Kyochokai or the Harmonization Society had been set up with government backing in order to identify the causes of industrial unrest and to seek methods of dealing with them. Subsequently, Kyochakai gave active support to the introduction of works councils and company unions. Later, in 1938, Kyochakai also sponsored Sampo or the Industrial Patriotic Movement. In effect, Sampo was a nationwide organization of company unions which has been compared to the Arbeitsfront in Germany (Iwao, 1966: 229). Prefectoral governors were subsequently required to set up Sampo in their territories and also to act as the president of the local organization of Sampo. The ideology of the movement emphasized the traditional virtues. Its slogan was 'Jigyo ikka' or 'Enterprise, Family'. In 1940–1 Sampo had some 19,000 organizations affiliated to it with a total membership of three million workers.

That enterprise trade unionism and single-employer bargaining emerged in the post-Second World War period is not too difficult to explain in the circumstances. To begin with, there was no tradition of 'horizontal' unionism. Moreover, as in West Germany, the extreme dislocation of the immediate post-war period meant that the workplace inevitably became the focus of activity. In particular, against the background of rampant inflation and extreme shortages, this meant in Japan a struggle to maintain the long-standing guarantees of employment for the permanent employees. Significantly, too, both manual and non-manual workers were involved as they had been in the Sampo organizations. Indeed, junior and middle managers played an extremely active role in the emerging enterprise unions. Finally, the experience of the US-dominated 'SCAP'[13] administration officials was largely that of single-employer bargaining – which is why the Trade Union Law of December 1945, the

---

[13] 'SCAP' refers to the title bestowed on MacArthur (Supreme Commander for the Allied Powers for the Occupation and Control of Japan). It nonetheless quickly became the name by which the occupation administration was referred to. Strictly speaking, the 11-nation Far Eastern Commission was to be involved, but SCAP was almost entirely under US influence.

Labour Relations Adjustment Act of September 1946, and the Labour Standards Law of September 1947 were closely modelled on the US legislation.

Even so, it is not inconceivable that stronger forms of 'horizontal' trade unionism and multi-employer bargaining might have developed. Indeed, as Levine (1984: 341) has pointed out, multi-employer bargaining did develop in the immediate post-war period in a number of the controlled industries, including coal and iron and steel. Here the decisions taken by the 'SCAP' administration were crucial. Attitudes initially favourable to trade unionism quickly began to change.[14] There was growing opposition to what the administration perceived to be the developing political interests and militant tendencies of the trade union movement as a whole. The first indication of this was MacArthur's public statement of 20 May 1946 in which he cautioned against 'the growing tendency towards mass violence and physical processes of intimidation'. This was generally taken to refer to public demonstrations which had become increasingly common, culminating in a May Day demonstration. A second indication of the growing opposition was MacArthur's prohibition of the general strike called for 1 February 1947. The trade union movement was further weakened by a limitation imposed on the bargaining rights of government employees in July 1948 and by the so-called 'red purge' that followed the deflationary budget-cutting policies of 1949. The trade union movement outside the enterprise was left weak and divided.[15]

The 'SCAP' administration's approach to the employers was also profoundly important. The 'Initial Post Surrender Policy for Japan' (quoted in Livingston *et al.*, 1976: 78–82) of September 1945 provided for the dissolution of the Zaibatsu. But this never happened. Zaibatsu leaders had already managed to put their operations into temporary receivership so that the government should pay for the damages sustained by allied bombing. They then proposed their own disbandment in the form of the Yasuda 'plan'. The Yasuda 'plan' was accepted and other anti-monopoly regulations introduced. But there were no far-reaching changes. It was extremely difficult to get to grips with the interlocking nature of Zaibatsu ownership and control, especially as MacArthur had decided to work through the existing government bureaucracy. As time went on, the Zaibatsu also found perhaps unexpected allies among US

[14] For a discussion of the development of the 'SCAP' administration's attitudes and policies to trade unions, see Farley (1947: 131–4; 1950: 44–50; 144–53, 189–206, 227–39).

[15] Initially, two trade union centres had been established: SODOMEI, which was allied to the Socialist Party and SANBETSU, which was communist in orientation. Attempts were made to establish a liaison council in 1947, but met with little success. The internal strife was to continue into the 1950s leading to further splits and regroupings. By the 1970s no less than four trade union centres had emerged: SOHYO, which has its strength in the public sector and is identified with the Socialist Party; DOMEI, which is stronger in the private sector and has close links with the Democratic Socialist party; and CHURITSU ROREN and SHINSAMBETSU, both of which are composed of trade unions originally affiliated to SANBETSU. For further details, see Kawada (1973: 241–3, 254–61) and Levine (1958: 69–88).

business leaders who saw some of the measures being proposed as establishing damaging precedents. Finally, the USA was becoming concerned about China and Russia. By 1947 the so called 'reverse course' was in operation. Japan was to become a partner; its economy to be encouraged.

The failure to break up Zaibatsu control of the economy effectively clinched the issue of the structure of collective bargaining. Like their counterparts in the USA, the large employers were strongly opposed to multi-employer bargaining and for very similar reasons. First, there were very considerable differences in pay and the other conditions of employment from employer to employer which would have been costly to remove; second, multi-employer bargaining was seen as offering major tactical advantages to the external trade unions (and, in the case of Japan, the platform from which to push for more effective industrial unionism); and, third, the main advantage of multi-employer bargaining – the exclusion of trade unionism from the workplace – was no longer attainable. Significantly, the *Shunto* or 'Spring offensive' which the trade union federation, SOHYO, has mounted every year since 1955 does not appear to have altered the employers' position.[16] Indeed, it can be argued that it makes it possible for employers to enjoy one of the benefits of multi-employer bargaining, namely the placing of a floor under wages competition, without the drawback of being confronted by strong national trade unions.[17]

Summary

The preference of employers in manufacturing in the USA and in Japan for single-employer bargaining is not to be explained in terms of an opposition in principle to collective action. Far from it. Employers in both countries have been as willing to co-operate with one another to deal with the trade union challenge as they have in Western Europe. By the time they were forced by government intervention to recognize trade unions in the 1930s (USA) and late 1940s (Japan), however, employers had already exerted a profound influence on trade unions. The size of

[16] For example, there was considerable employer opposition towards the end of the 1950s to attempts by the industrial federations of metal miners and chemical workers to hold centralized multi-employer negotiations. The matter was referred for adjudication to the Central Labour Relations Committee which decided in favour of the trade unions. Subsequently, however, the ruling of the Tokyo District Court was that the bargaining rights of the industrial federations had not been established (see Mitsufuji and Hagisawa 1972: 306)
[17] Significantly, too, the 'Spring offensive' is primarily concerned with the 'basic' wage in each enterprise, which is calculated by dividing the total wage bill by the number of employees. The individual employer retains considerable flexibility in coming to decisions about his internal pay structure. For further details of the pay systems and internal structures in the large Japanese enterprise, see Funahashi (1973).

their undertakings, which had been a major consideration in their ability to defeat the early challenge of trade unions (USA) or to prevent its emergence (Japan), nonetheless made it necessary for employers to seek to institutionalize industrial conflict so far as their own employees were concerned. The main instruments used were 'welfarism', 'internal job ladders' and the 'employee representation plan' or company union. Against this background, single-employer bargaining appeared to be the lesser of two evils. In particular, single-employer bargaining meant that they were able to deal with their own employees (even if they are now organized in 'independent' trade unions) rather than the external trade unions which they had struggled for so long to avoid. Paradoxical as it may seem, then, it is single-employer bargaining which serves to neutralize the workplace.

A Review of the Findings

Although it is inappropriate to repeat in full the argument of the study, which has already been outlined in chapter 1, there are a number of conclusions that deserve emphasis. The first, and perhaps fundamental, point to make is that for the most part the recognition of trade unions in the seven countries included in the study has not occurred in a piecemeal and *ad hoc* fashion with individual employers weighing up the advantages and disadvantages of such a decision and the structure of collective bargaining is not the result of employers or, for that matter, trade unions or governments making a rational choice from a number of possible options. Instead, as chapters 6 and 7 demonstrated, both recognition and the structure of collective bargaining are deeply rooted in an historical compromise which reflects the impact of industrialization, in particular in the metalworking industries.

In Britain and Western Europe multi-employer bargaining emerged as the predominant pattern largely because employers in the metalworking industries were confronted with the challenge of national unions organized along occupational or industrial lines. Furthermore, in Britain the national procedural agreement in the engineering industry, the 'Provisions for Avoiding Disputes' of 1898, implicitly recognized that craft trade unions, such as the Amalgamated Society of Engineers, had already established a firm foundation in the workplace and that the district committees of such unions had the power to impose their own regulations. In Sweden the national substantive agreement reached in engineering in 1905 reflected the relative weakness of employers at local level and the apparent centralization of the trade union movement. In France, Germany and Italy, where the crisis in the years immediately following the First World War was on a much larger scale, the government was involved as well as employers and trade unions, and the compromise was underwritten by compulsory rules; in France and Germany both the government and trade unions were anxious lest the large metal-working employers, who hitherto had been able to resist trade unionism with little difficulty, would revert to their previous position once the immediate crisis was over; and in Italy the government was looking for ways and means of containing the revolutionary challenge presented by trade unions during the 'red years' of 1919 and 1920.

Only in the USA and Japan did single-employer bargaining emerge as the predominant pattern in the metalworking industries. By the time legislation was introduced requiring employers to recognize trade unions in the 1930s and 1940s respectively, the relatively large individual employers that had emerged at an early date in industrialization in both countries had already exerted a profound influence on the trade union movement. In the circumstances, employers and governments did not come under strong pressure to introduce multi-employer bargaining and most employers opted for dealing with trade unions at enterprise or establishment level – largely out of the desire to maintain their internal systems of job regulation and, especially in Japan, to deny the trade unions the platform from which to push for more effective national unionism.

As chapters 2 and 5 argued, employers in Western Europe other than Britain continue to prefer multi-employer bargaining to single-employer bargaining not just because, as many previous studies have argued, it makes for economies of scale in terms of time, effort and staff to negotiate an agreement covering an entire industry or because (in some industries) it helps to regulate the market. The system of multi-employer bargaining, being based on substantive and compulsory rules, is primarily valued by employers in these countries because it helps to neutralize the workplace from trade union activity. Contrary to the impression that has sometimes been given, few of the rules in the multi-employer agreements are standard; most establish minimum conditions only or leave considerable flexibility to the employer in their implementation. More significantly in the present context, the detailed coverage of the substantive rules tends to limit the scope for further negotiations in the workplace or to ensure that any workplace bargaining that does take place is largely administrative or supplementary.

As chapter 4 explained, the use of multi-employer bargaining to minimize the impact of trade unions also helps to explain the levels at which such bargaining takes place in these countries. In France local multi-employer bargaining at the level of the *département* in metalworking is largely to be explained in terms of the employers' desire to deny the trade unions, particularly the CGT, the national platform from which to launch a major campaign. In Sweden the move from industry to multi-industry bargaining in the post-Second World War period is largely to be explained in terms of the employers' attempt to combat trade union leap-frogging in national negotiations. In Italy in the same period it was the employers who were largely responsible for maintaining the highly centralized structure of multi-employer bargaining. In very different circumstances West German and French employers have resisted multi-industry bargaining for fear that this would be to the trade unions' advantage.

In emphasizing the significance of the origins and early development of multi-employer bargaining, the study has been able to offer an explanation for the decline of multi-employer bargaining in Britain that is fully consistent with the support that it continues to enjoy in the other Western European countries. Whereas previous studies have suggested that multi-employer bargaining in Britain declined because it failed to settle actual pay and conditions in the workplace, the present study has argued that it did so because of its failure to neutralize the workplace from trade union activity. In contrast with the other countries, multi-employer bargaining in Britain developed on the basis of procedural as opposed to substantive rules and these rules took the form of 'gentlemen's agreements' rather than legally-enforceable contracts. The relatively sparse coverage of substantive issues gave the employer in Britain few points of legitimate defence in the event of his unilateral action being challenged. The voluntary nature of the rules also meant that the employer found it difficult to enforce the peace obligation that was the key feature of the disputes procedure. To give matters a further twist, the more British employers dealt with issues in a piecemeal and informal way in their workplaces, the more difficult it became to develop common policies through their employers' organizations and to maintain the solidarity of their counterparts in the other countries.

If the struggle over the structure of collective bargaining has not been so obvious in Britain as in some of the Western European countries, it is because collective bargaining is so decentralized and informal. Unlike their counterparts in these other countries, British employers have never been seriously threatened as a group or class; the trade union challenge has been and remains essentially fragmented and the levels at which multi-employer bargaining takes place have never really been a major issue. Certainly the nature and extent of workplace bargaining have presented major problems at different times, notably during and immediately following the First World War and during the 1960s and 1970s, but here the informality of collective bargaining is significant. The incursions shop stewards made into management decision-making during these periods tended to take place gradually and almost imperceptibly as did the subsequent 'roll-back' of their advance.

In coming to these conclusions, as well as rejecting a simplistic economic explanation of employers' behaviour, the study has also suggested that there is a need to reappraise some conventional industrial relations thinking. To begin with, in stressing that the main motive for employers engaging in collective bargaining was the desire to maintain managerial control rather than to achieve market regulation, the study has emphasized that collective bargaining involves mutual recognition. In agreeing to make *some* issues subject to joint regulation, employers were implicitly requiring that trade unions should recognize the employer's right to make the *other* rules unilaterally. Certainly it did not mean that employers were committed to joint regulation as a matter of general principle or that they were any less anxious to minimize the impact of trade unions.

This helps to explain why legislation politicians hoped would promote collective bargaining has often had a very different effect and why, perhaps more importantly in the context of the present study, in some countries employers have come to give strong support to a structure of collective bargaining for which they may have had little responsibility in the first instance. In brief, the structure of collective bargaining is best seen from the employer's point of view as a system of control that defines the nature and extent of trade union involvement in the rule-making process. Employers have exploited any potential that the structure of collective bargaining allows to maximize their advantage and they have done so in the light of specific opportunities and circumstances available to them.

Another implication is that the well-attested association between the size of undertakings and trade union recognition is not as straightforward as it may at first appear. In particular, it is not necessarily true that the large employer is likely to offer less resistance to trade unions on the grounds that the negotiation and administration of jointly agreed employment rules are seen as making a contribution to managerial control. The evidence suggests that the larger employers in the USA and Japan – and, indeed, in France, Germany and Italy – were especially opposed to dealing with trade unions; that the large employer was unlikely to recognize independent trade unions unless obliged to do so by legislation; and that, even where the large employer was obliged to do so, he is likely to seek to create or re-create, if at all possible, a form of company or enterprise unionism – be it through single-employer bargaining as in the USA and Japan or under the guise of employee-based works council institutions as in France and West Germany.

A third point concerns the nature and extent of the employers' influence on the structure of collective bargaining. Clearly employers are an important influence on the structure of collective bargaining, especially in upholding those elements that maximize their advantage and minimize the impact of trade unions. But it is a moot point whether, as Clegg (1976: 118) has suggested, they are the most important influence in any of the countries. Certainly employers are not free to pick and choose the structure of collective bargaining; and even where it might be said that employers took the initiative, as in Britain and Sweden, the structure of collective bargaining very much reflected the nature of the trade union challenge. Moreover, just as many aspects of trade union behaviour can be explained only by reference to the structure of collective bargaining, the same goes for many aspects of employers' behaviour, including, to quote perhaps the most obvious example, the power and authority bestowed on employers' organizations.

At first sight, these conclusions might appear rather negative, given the way theory in industrial relations appeared to be developing (see, for example, Bain and Clegg, 1974; and Clegg, 1979: 447–56). Yet there is much in the study that is positive. To begin with, it has, hopefully, confirmed the analytical value of focusing on *who* regulates *what* and *how* in industrial relations. If the significance of collective bargaining has been questioned, at least from the point of view of the employer, the study has demonstrated that the structure of collective bargaining is profoundly important in influencing the behaviour of employers and trade unions alike. If the notion of one of the parties determining the structure of collective bargaining has been rejected, the study has shown how the structure of collective bargaining is deeply rooted in an historical compromise. Furthermore, the study has made some progress in establishing how different collective bargaining structures and, indeed, different personnel management practices have emerged, given differences in the timing and pace of industrialization, the level of technology, the size of undertakings and the nature and extent of competition.

For the policy-maker the message of the study is clear, but not optimistic. Rooted as it is in an historical compromise, the key features of the structure of collective bargaining, together with the attitudes and habits that go with them, are not easily changed except at times of great crisis. This is above all true of collective bargaining in the workplace, where the nature and extent of trade union involvement in the making and the administering of employment rules raises the most sensitive of issues. Witness the lack of success of attempts to extend the scope of collective bargaining in the workplace in several of the West European countries; while in Britain many of the aspects of workplace bargaining which the Donovan Commission criticized in 1968, including the tendency for earnings to rise faster than prices and productivity, continue to be identified as 'problems' 20 years later. Certainly the evidence suggests that exhortation is unlikely to be sufficient. Legislation, too, is likely to have little effect – or, indeed, a very different effect from the one intended – unless it is drafted with the utmost care and attention to the significance the parties attach to the structure of collective bargaining. All of which points to the need for policy-makers to develop a far greater understanding of collective bargaining than they have so far.

APPENDIX: WHO ARE THE EMPLOYERS?

The main task in this appendix is to identify the employers who are the subject of the study. More often than not employers are regarded as individuals: the Agnellis, Fords, Krupps, Monds, Schneiders, Wallenbergs, and so on. Strictly speaking, however, an employer is not an individual but a registered corporation which is regarded as a legal person: in the words of Wedderburn (1971: 41), an employer is 'a fiction endowed with personality by the law'. Behind the legal person in the case of the registered corporation stand the shareholders who own it and the managers who manage it. The shareholders may be individuals or financial institutions: that is, insurance companies, pension funds, banks, unit and investment trusts. The managers are the group of people who, by virtue of the authority vested in them by the board of directors, is legally empowered to represent the shareholders' interests and, in some countries, exclusively their interests. These managers may or may not be shareholders.

The first section gives details of the number and size of employers in the five industries in each of the countries. The second section discusses the ownership and control of the employers. For reasons which will be clear from chapter 1, the main focus of the comparison is on Britain.

The Number and Size of Employers

For the purposes of the present study, the two most important defining characteristics of employers are *enterprise* and *establishment*. The precise definition differs from country to country, but broadly speaking the enterprise is to be equated with the registered corporation and may involve a single establishment, or a group of establishments forming a registered corporation, or a group of registered corporations. The establishment is to be equated with the individual unit of employment or workplace: it may be an enterprise in its own right or it may come under the control of an enterprise or one of the subsidiary corporations of an enterprise.

Enterprises

For reasons which need not be discussed in detail here, statistics relating to enterprise are fraught with difficulties of interpretation.[1] The most comprehensive attempt at an international comparison is that of Prais (1981) which relies on data for the 1960s and early 1970s: the very period

---

[1] The main problem involves the definition of 'enterprise'. British and US censuses define 'enterprise' to include subsidiary corporations in which the parent owns a majority of the shares. In other countries each subsidiary corporation may be treated as a separate entity. For further details, see Prais (1981: 138, 158–9, 220–40).

during which major doubts were first raised about the will and ability of employers in Britain to maintain the system of multi-employer bargaining. Tables A.1 and A.2, which are largely based on his findings, give some idea of the number and size of large and small enterprises respectively in each of the countries.

A number of conclusions can be drawn. First, it must be clear that both the very large and the very small enterprise were a common feature in all seven countries. In terms of the number of enterprises it was the small enterprise that predominated. In terms of the numbers employed, however, it was the large enterprise that stood out. Second, it is equally clear that there was a general tendency for industries which were dominated by large enterprises in one country to have relatively large enterprises in the others. The reverse was also true. Of the large enterprises named by Prais, the overwhelming majority was in the metalworking and chemical industries. By contrast, none were in the construction and printing industries.

Third, in terms of the significance of large enterprises, Table A.1 shows that Britain stood second only to the USA. For example, in comparison with France and West Germany, Britain had two and half times as many large enterprises, and in comparison to Italy five times as many. Even if the *keiretsu* or 'linked groups' such as Mitsubishi, Mitsui and Sumitomo are taken into account, Britain had more large enterprises than Japan. In terms of the numbers employed in the large enterprises, Table A.1 massively understates the importance of the large enterprise relative to manufacturing in Japan because it does not include the overall employment of the *keiretsu*. Even so, this is probably not enough to dislodge Britain from second place. Certainly, the proportion or concentration of manufacturing employment in the large enterprises in Britain was very much greater than in the other European countries.

Fourthly, Table A.2 suggests that the differences between the countries in the number and relative importance of small enterprises were far greater than in the case of the large enterprises. Britain not only had the lowest number of small enterprises but also smaller numbers employed in them than the other countries. For example, Britain had only about a quarter the number of small enterprises of France and West Germany and only a tenth of the number of Italy. The small enterprise was even less important in Britain than in the USA. At the other extreme, Japan stood out. There were nearly twice the number of small enterprises as in Italy, which had the second largest number, even though the proportion of total manufacturing employment was less than in the other countries.

Establishments

The enterprises described above are made up of *establishments* or workplaces. Although not without its limitations,[2] information on

[2] For example, to quote Prais (1981: 138–9), 'if similar products are produced in geographically adjacent buildings under common ownership, they may appear on a single

TABLE A.1
Manufacturing Enterprises^a Employing Over 40,000, 1972

	Size of Country (Millions)		Large Enterprises^b (Millions)		Importance of Large Enterprises relative to:^{c} (Indices, UK = 100)	
	Population	Manufacturing Employment	Number	Employment	Population	Manufacturing Employment
UK	55.8	7.78	30	2.67	100	100
US	208.8	18.93	89	8.05	81	124
France	51.7	5.93	12	1.15	46	56
West Germany	61.7	10.53	12	1.59	54	44
Italy	54.4	5.83	6	0.64	24	32
Sweden	8.1	1.05	3	0.18	46	50
Japan	107.0	13.8	(11)^d	(0.85)^d	—	—

Sources: population – United Nations Statistical Office, *Monthly Bulletin of Statistics*; employment – International Labour Office, *Yearbook of Labour Statistics* (quoted in Prais, 1981: 156).

^{a} Excluding iron and steel.

^{b} Prais' list (1981: 221-3) is based on the company accounts for 1972 of manufacturing enterprises which appear in the reviews of large enterprises published by such sources as *Fortune*, *The Times*, *Forbes*, *Les Dossiers de l'Entreprise*. As well as enterprises primarily engaged in steel, it excludes the subsidiaries of multinational enterprises; for example, Ford is treated as if it were a US company and does not therefore appear in the West German and UK entries. In so far as it was possible, the number of employees represents the world-wide employment of the enterprises listed.

^{c} Ratios of employment in large enterprises to national population and to manufacturing employment converted to indices.

^{d} The source for the manufacturing enterprises in Japan, details of which do not appear in Prais' list, with more than 40,000 employees in 1972 is *Fortune*'s (1973: 202-9) list of the top 300 industrial enterprises outside the USA, ranked by sales. The figures are for individual enterprises only. They do not take into account the overall

TABLE A.2
Manufacturing Establishments[a] Employing Under Ten Persons,
United Kingdom Compared with Other Countries, 1963

	Small Establishments[b]		
	Number (000s)	Per 1,000 Manufacturing Employees	Proportion of Total Manufacturing Employment (%)
UK	27	4	2.1
US	121	6	2.4
France	186	31	10.8
West Germany	157	15	6.2
Italy	145	42	18.5
Sweden	6	na	5.4
Japan[c]	433	na	16.6

Sources: United Kingdom: *Census of Production* 1963; United States: *Census of Manufactures* 1963; EEC – *Industriezensus* 1963 (quoted in Prais, 1981: 160); Japan: *Small and Medium Enterprises Agency* 1976 (quoted in Sasaki, 1981: 22); Sweden: *Industri*, 1963. Details of Japan and Sweden do not appear in Prais' table.

[a] Excludes certain branches of manufacturing bordering on service trades.

[b] Defined for the United Kingdom as one with 1-10 employees, for elsewhere as one with 1–9 employees. British figures therefore slightly overstated in comparison.

[c] Figures are for 1966.

establishments is more readily available on a comparative basis than information on enterprises. Table A.3 draws on the work of Prais (1981: 148) to compare Britain with the USA; Tables A.4 and A.5, which compare Britain to the other countries, largely draw on the work of George and Ward (1975).

Again, a number of points can be made. First of all, as in the case of enterprises, there was a general tendency for industries which were characterized by relatively large establishments in one country to have relatively large establishments in the others as well. The reverse was also true. Thus, for example, vehicle establishments tended to employ workers in their thousands. Establishments in clothing and printing, on the other hand, tended to be much smaller. It was also the case that the degree of concentration of employment in the five industries was of

return according to the census rules of one country, but on separate returns according to the rules of another. . . . The initial unit of enumeration may also affect the ultimate treatment: thus in Britain the establishment is the basic census unit and totals for the enterprise are built up from the constituent establishments; whereas in other countries the basic unit is the legal entity and its total is apportioned to the constituent establishments as far as possible.'

TABLE A.3
Establishment Size by Industry:[a] United Kingdom (1968)
and United States (1967)

			Proportion of Employment in:			
	Florence-median[b] (No. of Employees)		*Small Plants*[c] (Percentages)		*Large Plants*[d] (Percentages)	
	UK	US	UK	US	UK	US
Chemicals and allied industries	740	540	8	12	19	20
Metal manufacture	1180	1480	6	5	34	40
Engineering and electrical goods	710	750	10	11	16	24
Shipbuilding and marine engineering	2600	1380	6	8	51	46
Vehicles	3000	6000[e]	3	2	55	68
Metal goods (not elsewhere specified)	220	230	23	19	2	8
Clothing and footwear	180	200	21	17	1[e]	1
Paper, printing, publishing	290	240	19	20	7	6[e]
Total manufacturing	480	420	12	14	17	20

Sources: Britain: *Censuses of Production*; United States: *Censuses of Manufactures* (quoted in Prais, 1981: 148).
[a] United States industries reclassified for comparability with the United Kingdom.
[b] Half of all employees in plants below that size, and half above.
[c] Under 50 employees (and including all unsatisfactory returns for the United Kingdom).
[d] 2500 employees and over.
[e] Approximate.

the same order of magnitude in each of the countries. That is to say, the larger estabiishments in vehicles accounted for a far higher proportion of the labour force in that industry than do their counterparts in clothing and printing.

Secondly, the above-average size of enterprises in Britain noted above does not appear to be reflected to the same degree in the size of establishments. Compared to the USA, establishments in Britain were larger in chemicals and shipbuilding, but significantly smaller in vehicles. Compared to West Germany, establishments were smaller in key sectors of the metalworking industries such as metals production, vehicles and electronics; they were also smaller in chemicals. In France too, vehicle establishments appeared to be larger than those in Britain; while establishments in metals production were broadly comparable.

TABLE A.4
Average Size of Twenty Largest Establishments by Industry:
Britain, West Germany, France, Italy, Sweden, and Japan, 1963

| Industry | Average Establishment Size (000s) | | | | | |
	Britain	W. Germany	France	Italy	Sweden	Japan
Clothing	1.40	1.11	0.75	0.93	0.4	0.43
Metalworking						
Iron and Steel	6.18	9.90	5.90	2.95	1.8	2.0
Automobiles	8.97	13.55	9.11	14.41	1.14	2.6
Aircraft	6.33	1.23	1.65	0.59	—	—
Electronics	3.78	5.92	1.54	0.80	0.73	—
Shipbuilding	4.75	3.24	3.28	1.85	0.87	4.47
Printing and Publishing	2.58	1.78	1.78	0.83	0.43	—

Sources: Britain: *Census of Manufacture* 1963; West Germany, France and Italy: EEC: *Industriezensus* 1963 (quoted in George and Ward, 1975: 456); Japan: *Census of Manufactures* 1965 (quoted in Bain, 1966: 177–9); Sweden: *Industri* 1963.

TABLE A.5
Four-Establishment Concentration Ratios:
Britain, France and West Germany

Industry	Britain	West Germany	France
Chemicals	13	33	11
Clothing	3	1	1
Metalworking			
Automobiles	16	18	38
Aircraft	18	42	20
Electronics	11	13	11
Printing and Publishing	5	5	5

Source: Britain: *Census of Production* 1963; West Germany and France EEC: *Industriezensus* 1963 (quoted in George and Ward, 1975: 46).

The third point is closely related. The degree of employment concentration noted in the case of the enterprises in Britain was not reflected to the same degree in the case of establishments. Compared to the USA, for example, although the proportion of employment in small establishments was less in Britain, the proportion in the larger establishments was broadly similar. Compared to West Germany, there is less concentration in the larger establishments in the metalworking industries and in chemicals. Compared to France, there was less concentration in vehicles. In other words, it would appear that the size and concentration of the large enterprises in Britain was not explained by the size and concentration of establishments: the British enterprises had more establishments under their control.

Ownership and Control

The existence of the large multi-establishment enterprise inevitably begs questions about their ownership and control. Drawing on a wide range of studies, Scott (1979: ch. 3) confirms that there has been a shift away from private and majority ownership by individuals or families in most countries. But this shift has not been as great as has been implied in the pioneering study of Berle and Means (1932). For example, in 1975 almost half of the top 250 enterprises in Britain were majority-owned or minority-controlled (Scott, 1979: 67). In 1937 between 44 and 49 per cent of the top 108 manufacturing and mining enterprises in the USA were family-controlled; by 1965 the corresponding figure was still 36 per cent. In some of the other countries the shift has been even less. For example, in Sweden 15 families and two corporations had majority ownership in 200 large industrial enterprises employing almost half of those working in the private sector; the Wallenberg family alone controlled 70 enterprises, including Electrolux, Scania, Saab, Swedish Match, Alfa-Laval, and SKF (Tomasson 1970, quoted in Scott, 1979: 71). In 1971 half the largest 200 industrial enterprises in France were family-controlled (Morin, 1974, quoted in Scott, 1979: 70). In West Germany it has been estimated that families such as Krupp, Siemens, Klöckner, Flick and Quandt were dominant in 47 of the top 115 enterprises (Marans, 1970 and Krejc, 1976, quoted in Scott: 1979: 71).[3]

Scott's review of the available evidence also questions the significance which has been attached to the passing of control to professional managers. Many of the enterprises which other studies have designated as subject to management control, he argues, are better thought of as being controlled by 'a constellation of interests' (Scott, 1979: 73–4). Fundamentally important in these 'constellations of interests' are the institutional shareholders. In Britain it is the insurance companies, the investment trusts and the pension funds which tend to be predominant;

[3] Only in Japan has there been a significant decline in family ownership of the large enterprises. In practice, the ending of the family control of the pre-war Zaibatsu or conglomerates was the only major change in their operation after the Second World War. For further details, see Scott (1979: 92–3).

in West Germany and Japan it is the banks. But it would be wrong, suggests Scott (1979: 174), to see this simply in terms of the dominance of finance capital. The financial institutions are themselves controlled by very similar 'constellations of interests'. Indeed, the same individuals are often to be found sitting on the boards of both industrial and financial enterprises. In brief, a picture emerges of a complex system of interlocking shareholding and credit relations. The precise details may be different from one country to another, but the pattern is broadly similar.

The same also appears to be true of the organizational structures through which the control is actually exercised in the large multi-establishment enterprise. Increasingly, it seems that these large enterprises are moving away from the highly-centralized functional organizations or loose holding organizations to the multi-divisional organizational structure (Chandler, 1962, 1977; Channon, 1973; Chandler and Daems, 1980) Crucially, the introduction of the multi-divisional organization structure denotes the drawing of a distinction between strategic and operating management. A small group of senior managers at central or divisional headquarters is given the responsibility for developing a corporate strategy for ratification by the board. This strategy, which continues to stress such important financial ratios as the return on capital and market share, is then passed on for implementation by the operating managers in the individual establishments. The performance of these operating managers is in turn closely monitored by the senior managers at central or divisional headquarters. Such have been the developments in information technology in recent years that this performance can now be monitored in the minutest detail at very short notice.

Summary and Conclusion

To summarize, then, there are large and small employers in each of the countries. In terms of the number and relative importance of the large enterprises, Britain is probably second only to the USA; it also has the lowest number of small enterprises and they employ a smaller proportion of the labour force than in the other countries. But the differences between Britain and the other countries are much less so far as establishments are concerned. Indeed, there are marked similarities from one country to another in the size and relative importance of establishments within each of the industries. For example, establishments in chemicals and the metalworking industries tend to be on the large side in all the countries, whereas those in clothing, construction and printing tend to be small. The evidence would also appear to suggest that the patterns of ownership and control are broadly similar from one country to another, especially in the case of the large enterprises. Increasingly, ownership is in the hands of what has been described as a 'constellation of interests'. Strategic management is separate from operating management; operating management is decentralized and its performance closely monitored from the centre. In conclusion, then, there are grounds for expecting differences in the collective bargaining behaviour of employers from one industry to another; the reasons why there are differences from one country to another in the same industry, and why these differences are mainly to be found in the chemical and metalworking industries, are less obvious.

References

Ammassari, G.P. 1976. *La Politica della* CONFINDUSTRIA. Napoli: Liguori Editore.

Amulree, *Baron* (W.W. Mackenzie). 1929. *Industrial Arbitration in Great Britain*. Oxford: Oxford University Press.

Anderman, S.D. 1967. 'Central Wage Negotiations in Sweden: Recent Problems and Developments'. *British Journal of Industrial Relations*, Vol. 5, November, 322–37.

Armstrong, E.G.A. 1984. 'Employers' Associations in Great Britain'. *Employers' Associations and Industrial Relations*. Ed. J.P. Windmueller and A. Gladstone. Oxford: Clarendon Press, 44–78.

Bachy, J.-P., F. Dupuy and D. Martin. 1974. *Représentation et Négociation dans l'Entreprise*. Paris: Éditions du CRESST.

Baglioni, G. 1974. *L'Ideologia della Borghesia Industriale nell'Italia Industriale*. Torino: Giulio Einaudi Editore.

Bain, G.S. and H.A. Clegg. 1974. 'A Strategy for Industrial Relations Research in Great Britain'. *British Journal of Industrial Relations*, Vol. 12, March, 91–113.

Bain, J.S. 1966. *International Differences in Industrial Structure: Eight Nations in the 1950s*. New Haven, Conn.: University of Yale Press.

Banfield, P. 1976. 'Industrial Relations in the UK Clothing Industry: An Analysis of the Employers' Role'. MA dissertation, University of Warwick.

Batstone, E.V. 1978. 'Arms' Length Bargaining: Industrial Relations in a French Company'. Unpublished manuscript.

Bendix, R. 1956. *Work and Authority in Industry*. New York: Wiley.

Bergmann, J. and W. Müller-Jentsch. 1975. 'The Federal Republic of Germany: Cooperative Unionism and Dual Bargaining System Challenged'. *Worker Militancy and Its Consequences, 1965–75*. Ed. S. Barkin. New York: Praeger, 235–76.

Berle, A.A. and G.C. Means. 1932. *The Modern Corporation and Private Property*. New York: Macmillan.

Bezard-Falgaz, P. 1922. *Les Syndicats Patronaux de l'Industrie Métallurgique en France*. Paris.

Bieda, K. 1970. *The Structure and Operation of the Japanese Economy*. London: Wiley.

Bisson, T.A. 1945a. 'Increase of Zaibatsu Predominance in Wartime Japan'. *Pacific Affairs*, Vol. 18, March, 55–9.

—— 1945b. 'The Zaibatsu's Wartime Role'. *Pacific Affairs*, Vol. 18, December, 355–64.

Blanc-Jouvan, X. 1971. 'The Settlement of Labor Disputes in France'. *Labor Courts and Grievance Settlement in Western Europe*. Ed. B. Aaron. Berkeley and Los Angeles: University of California Press, 3–82.

Bonnett, C.E. 1922. *Employers' Associations in the United States: A Study of Typical Associations*. New York: Macmillan.

Braun, A. 1908. *Die Tarifverträge und die Deutschen Gewerkschaften*. Stuttgart. Quoted in R. Hilferding. 1974. *Das Finanzkapital*. Bd II. Frankfurt a.M.: Europäische Verlagsanstalt.

Braverman, H. 1974. *Labor and Monopoly Capital: The Degradation of Work in the Twentieth Century*. New York: Monthly Review Press.

Brizay, B. 1975. *Le Patronat*. Paris: Seuil.

Brogan, D.W. 1949. *The Development of Modern France*. 8th impression. London: Hamish Hamilton.

Brown, W.A. (ed.). 1981. *The Changing Contours of British Industrial Relations: A Survey of Manufacturing Industry*. Oxford: Blackwell.

—— and M. Terry. 1978. 'The Changing Nature of National Wage Agreements'. *Scottish Journal of Political Economy*, Vol. 25, June, 119–33.

Brun, A. 1965. 'Collective Agreements in France'. *Labour Relations and the Law: A Comparative Study*. Ed. O. Kahn-Freund. London: Stevens, 78–83.

Buchholz, E. 1969. *Die Wirtschaftsverbände in der Wirtschaftsgesellschaft*. Tübingen: Mohr and Siebeck.

Bunel, J. and J. Saglio. 1976. *La Société des Patrons*. Lyon: Groupe Lyonnais de Sociologie Industrielle.

—— and J. Saglio. 1984. 'Employers' Associations in France'. *Employers' Associations and Industrial Relations*. Ed. J.P. Windmueller and A. Gladstone. Oxford: Clarendon Press, 169–201.

Bunn, R.F. 1984. 'Employers' Associations in the Federal Republic of Germany'. *Employers' Associations and Industrial Relations*. Ed. J.P. Windmueller and A. Gladstone. Oxford: Clarendon Press, 232–63.

Burawoy, M. 1979. *Manufacturing Consent: Changes in the Labor Process under Monopoly Capitalism*. Chicago: University of Chicago Press.

—— 1985. *The Politics of Production*. London: Verso.

Butler, M. 1980. 'Bargaining, Industrial Conflict and Union–Employer Relations in the Federal Republic of Germany 1978–80'. MA dissertation, University of Warwick.

Cabrini, A. 1905. *La Resistenza nell'Europa Giovane*. Quoted in D.L. Horowitz. 1963. *The Italian Labor Movement*. Cambridge, Mass.: Harvard University Press, 62.

Caire, G. 1984. 'Recent Trends in Collective Bargaining in France'. *International Labour Review*, Vol. 123, November/December, 723–43.

Casparsson, R. 1966. *LO – Backgrund, Utveckling, Verksamhet*. Stockholm: Prisma.

Cassau, Jeanette. 1927. *Die Arbeitergewerkschaften: eine Einführung*. Halberstadt: H. Meyer's Buchdr., Abt. Verlag.

Castronovo, V. 1971. *Agnelli*. Torino: Unione Tipografico-Editrice Torinese.

Chamberlain, N.W. and J.W. Kuhn. 1965. *Collective Bargaining*. 2nd edn. New York: McGraw-Hill.

Chandler, A.D. 1962. *Strategy and Structure: Chapters in the History of the Industrial Enterprise*. Cambridge, Mass.: MIT Press.

—— 1977. *The Visible Hand: The Managerial Revolution in American Business*. Cambridge, Mass.: Harvard University Press.

—— 1978. 'The United States: Evolution of Enterprise'. *Cambridge Economic History of Europe. The Industrial Economies: Capital, Labour and Enterprise*. Vol. 7, Part II. Ed. P. Mathias and M.M. Postan. Cambridge: Cambridge University Press, 70–131.

—— and H. Daems. 1980. *Managerial Hierarchies: Comparative Perspectives on the Rise of the Modern Industrial Enterprise*. Cambridge, Mass.: Harvard University Press.

Channon, D. 1973. *The Strategy and Structure of British Enterprise*. London: Macmillan.

Charles, S.T.R. 1973. *The Development of Industrial Relations in Britain, 1911–39: Studies in the Evolution of Collective Bargaining*. London: Hutchinson.

Chotard, Y. 1976. 'Une Politique Sociale pour une Année de Transition'. *Patronat: La Revue des Entreprises*. No. hors série, février. Paris: CNPF.

Clapham, J.H. 1968. *Economic Development of France and Germany 1815–1914*. 4th edn. Cambridge: Cambridge University Press.

Clark, J. 1979. 'Concerted Action in the Federal Republic of Germany'. *British Journal of Industrial Relations*, Vol. 17, July, 242–57.

—— H. Hartman, C. Lau and D. Winchester. 1980. *Trade Unions, National Politics and Economic Management: A Comparative Study of the TUC and the DGB*. London: Anglo-German Foundation.

Clegg, H.A. 1976. *Trade Unionism under Collective Bargaining: A Theory Based on Comparisons of Six Countries*. Oxford: Blackwell.

—— 1979. *The Changing System of Industrial Relations in Great Britain*. Oxford: Blackwell.

—— A. Fox and A.F. Thompson. 1964. *A History of British Trade Unions Since 1889*. Vol. 1. Oxford: Clarendon Press.

Collida, A., L. De Carlini, G. Mossetto and R. Stefanelli. 1972. *La Politica del Padronato Italiano*. Bari: De Donato Editore.

Commission of Inquiry into Industrial and Commercial Representation. 1972. *Report by the Chairman, Lord Devlin*. London: Association of British Chambers of Commerce and the Confederation of British Industry.

Commission on Industrial Relations. 1974a. *Clothing Wages Councils*. Report No. 77. London: HMSO.

—— 1974b. *Worker Participation and Collective Bargaining in Europe*. Study No. 4. London: HMSO.

Commons, J.R. and Associates. 1961. *History of Labor in the United States*. Vol. 2. 9th printing. New York: Macmillan.

Confederation of British Industry. 1965. *Evidence to the Royal Commission on Trade Unions and Employers' Associations*. London: CBI.

CONFINDUSTRIA. 1972. *An Outline of Provisions Governing Labour Relations in Italy*. Roma: CONFINDUSTRIA.

—— 1973. *Le Rappresentanze dei Lavoratori in Fabbrica*. Roma: CONFINDUSTRIA.

—— 1975. *La Contrattazione Aziendale nell'Industria Chimica*. Roma: CONFIN-DUSTRIA.

Conseil National Économique. 1934. *Les Conventions Collectives du Travail*. Paris.

Cronan, G.P. 1976. 'An Investigation into Employer Organisation in the Printing Industry'. MA dissertation, University of Warwick.

Daniel, W.W. and N. Millward. 1983. *Workplace Industrial Relations in Britain: The DE/PSI/SSRC Survey*. London: Heinemann.

Delamotte, Y. 1971. 'Recent Collective Bargaining Trends in France'. *International Labour Review*, Vol. 103, April, 351–77.

—— 1985. 'Recent Trends in the Statutory Regulation of Industrial Relations in France'. *Labour and Society*, Vol. 10, January, 7–26.

Department of Employment. 1981. *Trade Union Immunities*. Cmnd 8128. London: HMSO.

Derber, M. 1984. 'Employers' Associations in the United States'. *Employers' Associations and Industrial Relations*. Ed. J.P. Windmueller and A. Gladstone. Oxford: Clarendon Press, 79–114.

Donovan, *Lord*. 1968. Royal Commission on Trade Unions and Employers' Associations. *Report*. Cmnd 3623. London: HMSO.

Dore, R.P. 1973. *British Factory–Japanese Factory: The Origins of National Diversity in Industrial Relations*. London: Allen & Unwin.

Duchemin, R. 1940. *Organisation Syndicale Patronale en France*. Paris.

Durand, P. 1956. 'The Evolution of Industrial Relations Law in France since the Liberation'. *International Labour Review*, Vol. 74, December, 515–40.

Edelman, M. and R.W. Fleming. 1965. *The Politics of Wage-Price Decisions*. Urbana: University of Illinois Press.

Edgren, G., K.-O. Faxen and C.-E. Odhner. 1973. *Wage Formation and the Economy*. London: Allen & Unwin.

Edwards, P.K. 1981. *Strikes in the United States 1881–1974*. Oxford: Blackwell.

Edwards, R. 1979. *Contested Terrain: The Transformation of the Workplace in the Twentieth Century*. London: Heinemann.

Ehrmann, H. 1957. *Organised Business in France*. Princeton, NJ: Princeton University Press.

Engineering Employers' Federation. 1965. *Evidence to the Royal Commission on Trade Unions and Employers' Associations*. London: EEF.

Erdmann, E.G. 1958. 'Organization and Work of Employers' Associations in the Federal Republic of Germany'. *International Labour Review*, Vol. 78, December, 539–51.

—— 1966. *Die Deutschen Arbeitgeberverbände im Sozialgeschichtlichen Wandel der Zeit*. Neuwied u. Berlin: Luchterland.

Eyraud, F. and R. Tchobanian. 1985. 'The Auroux Reforms and Company Level Industrial Relations in France'. *British Journal of Industrial Relations*, Vol. 23, July, 241–60.

Farley, M. 1947. 'Labor Policy in Occupied Japan'. *Pacific Affairs*, Vol. 20, June, 131–4.

—— 1950. *Aspects of Japan's Labor Problems*. New York: John Day.

FEDERMECCANICA. 1972. *La Contrattazione Articolata a Livello Aziendale*. Roma: FEDERMECCANICA.

Flanders, A.D. 1970a. 'Collective Bargaining: A Theoretical Analysis'. *Management and Unions: The Theory and Reform of Industrial Relations*. London: Faber, 213–40.

—— 1970b. 'Industrial Relations: What is Wrong with the System?' *Management and Unions: The Theory and Reform of Industrial Relations*. London: Faber, 83–128.

—— 1970c. 'Collective Bargaining: Prescription for Change'. *Management and Unions: The Theory and Reform of Industrial Relations*. London: Faber, 155–211.

—— 1974. 'The Tradition of Voluntarism'. *British Journal of Industrial Relations*, Vol. 12, November, 352–70.

Fohlen, C. 1973. 'The Industrial Revolution in France'. *The Fontana Economic History of Europe: The Emergence of Industrial Societies*. Vol. 1. Ed. C.M. Cipolla. London: Fontana, 7–75.

Forseback, L. 1980. *Industrial Relations and Employment in Sweden*. Uppsala: Swedish Institute.

François-Poncet, F. 1927. *La Vie et l'Oeuvre de Robert Pinot*. Paris: Armand Colin.

Freeman, R.B. and J.L. Medoff. 1984. *What Do Unions Do?* New York: Basic Books.

Friedberg, E. 1974. 'Administration et Entreprises'. *Où Va l'Administration Française?* Paris: Les Éditions d'Organisation.

Friedman, A.L. 1977. *Industry and Labour: Class Struggle at Work and Monopoly Capitalism*. London: Macmillan.

Fulcher, J. 1976. 'Joint Regulation and its Decline'. *Readings in Swedish Class Structure*. Ed. R. Scase. Oxford: Pergamon, 51–99.

Funahashi, N. 1973. 'The Industrial Reward System: Wages and Benefits'. *Workers and Employers in Japan: The Japanese Employment System*. Ed K. Okochi, B. Karsh and S.B. Levine. Tokyo: University of Tokyo Press, 361–99.

Galenson, W. 1969. *The Danish System of Industrial Relations: A Study in Industrial Peace*. New York: Russell & Russell.

George, K.D. and T.S. Ward. 1975. *The Structure of Industry in the EEC: An International Comparison*. Cambridge: Cambridge University Press.

Gershenkon, A. 1955. 'Notes on the Rate of Industrial Growth in Italy, 1881–1913'. *Journal of Economic History*, Vol. 15, December, 360–75.

Giddens, A. 1973. *The Class Structure of the Advanced Societies*. London: Hutchinson.

Giugni, G. 1957. 'Bargaining Units and Labor Organisation in Italy'. *Industrial and Labor Relations Review*, Vol. 10, April, 424–39.

—— 1965a. 'Recent Developments in Collective Bargaining in Italy'. *International Labour Review*, Vol. 91, April, 273–91.

—— 1965b. 'The Legal Status of Collective Bargaining in Italy'. *Labour Relations and the Law: A Comparative Study*. Ed. O. Kahn-Freund. London: Stevens, 92–100.

—— 1965c. 'The Right to Strike and to Lockout under Italian Law'. *Labour Relations and the Law: A Comparative Study*. Ed. O. Kahn-Freund. London: Stevens, 211–19.

—— 1971a. 'Recent Trends in Collective Bargaining in Italy'. *International Labour Review*, Vol. 104, October, 307–28.

—— 1971b. 'The Settlement of Labor Disputes in Italy'. *Labor Courts and Grievance Settlement in Western Europe*. Ed. B. Aaron. Berkeley and Los Angeles: University of California Press, 249–338.

—— 1976. *Il Sindacato fra Contratti e Riforme, 1969–1973*. Bari: De Donato Editore.

Goll, U. 1980. 'Staat und Aussperrung: Zum Verfahren und den Masstäben einer Rechtlichen Entscheidung'. *Recht der Arbeit*, Vol. 33, January/February, 22–5.

Gouldner, A. 1954. *Patterns of Industrial Bureaucracy*. New York: Free Press.

Grant, W.P. 1979. 'Employers' Associations in Britain'. Paper presented to the International Institute of Management Workshop on 'Employers' Associations as Organisations', Berlin, November.

—— 1983. 'The Organisation of Business Interests in the UK Food Processing Industry'. Discussion Paper. Berlin: International Institute of Management.

—— and D. Marsh. 1977. *The Confederation of British Industry*. London: Hodder & Stoughton.

Guidi, E., D. Valcavi, G. Salvarani, E. Giambamba, A. La Porta, F. Drago and G. Vinan. 1974. *Movimento Sindacale e Contrattazione Colletiva, 1945–1973*. Milano: Franco Angeli Editore.

Hadley, E. 1970. *Antitrust in Japan*. Princeton, NJ: Princeton University Press.

Hallendorff, C. 1927. *Svenska Arbetsgivare Föreningen*. Stockholm.

Hansson, S. 1927. *The Trade Union Movement in Sweden*. Amsterdam: International Federation of Trade Unions.

Hart, H. and C. Von Otter. 1973. *Lonebilding pa Arbetsplatsen*. Stockholm: Swedish Institute for Social Research and Prisma.

Hartwich, H. 1967. *Arbeitsmarkt, Verbände und Staat, 1918–1933*. Berlin: de Gruyter.

Hawes, W.R. and D. Smith. 1981. 'Employee Involvement Outside Manufacturing'. *Employment Gazette*, Vol. 89, June, 265–71.

Hepple, B.A. 1980. 'Lockouts in Great Britain'. *Recht der Arbeit*, Vol. 33, January/February, 25–32.

Horowitz, D.L. 1963. *The Italian Labor Movement*. Cambridge, Mass.: Harvard University Press.

Howe, E. and H.E. Waite. 1948. *The London Society of Compositors: A Centenary History*. London: Cassell.

Hyman, R. 1972. *Disputes Procedure in Action: A Study of the Engineering Disputes Procedure in Coventry*. London: Heinemann.

Ingham, G.K. 1974. *Strikes and Industrial Conflict*. London: Macmillan.

International Labour Office. 1959a. 'Wage Negotiations and Wage Policies in Sweden I'. *International Labour Review*, Vol. 80, October, 319–30.

—— 1959b. 'Wage Negotiations and Wage Policies in Sweden II'. *International Labour Review*, Vol. 80, November, 391–401.

—— 1960. 'Works Agreements of the Renault Type'. *International Labour Review*, Vol. 81, March, 205–32.

INTERSIND. 1968. *Dieci anni di Attività Contrattuale, 1958–1967*. Roma: INTERSIND.

Iwao, A. 1966. *A History of Labor in Modern Japan*. Honolulu: East–West Center Press, University of Hawaii.

Jackson, P. and K. Sisson. 1976. 'Employers' Confederations in Sweden and the UK and the Significance of Industrial Infrastructure'. *British Journal of Industrial Relations*, Vol. 14, November, 306–23.

Johnston, T.L. 1962. *Collective Bargaining in Sweden*. London: Allen & Unwin.

Jölberg, L. 1961. *Growth and Fluctuations of Swedish Industry 1869–1912*. Stockholm: Almquist & Wiksell.

—— 1973. 'The Industrial Revolution in the Nordic Countries'. *The Fontana Economic History of Europe: The Emergence of Industrial Societies.* Vol. 2. Ed. C.M. Cipolla. London: Fontana, 375–486.

Kahn-Freund, O. 1954a. 'Intergroup Conflicts and their Settlement'. *British Journal of Sociology*, Vol. 5, September, 193–227.

—— 1954b. 'The Legal Framework'. *The System of Industrial Relations in Great Britain.* Ed. A.D. Flanders and H.A. Clegg. Oxford: Blackwell, 42–127.

—— 1959. 'Labour Law'. *Law and Opinion in England in the 20th Century.* Ed. M. Ginsberg. London: Stevens, 215–63.

—— 1965a. 'Introduction'. *Labour Relations and the Law: A Comparative Study.* Ed. O. Kahn-Freund. London: Stevens, 1–18.

—— 1965b. 'Report on the Legal Status of Collective Bargaining and Collective Agreements in Great Britain'. *Labour Relations and the Law: A Comparative Study*, 21–39.

—— 1977. *Labour and the Law.* 2nd edn. London: Stevens.

Kassalow, E.M. 1969. *Trade Unions and Industrial Relations: An International Comparison.* New York: Random House.

Kawada, H. 1973. 'Workers and their Organisations'. *Workers and Employers in Japan: The Japanese Employment System.* Ed. K. Okochi, B. Karsh and S.B. Levine. Tokyo: Tokyo University Press, 217–69.

Kendall, W. 1975. *The Labour Movement in Europe.* London: Allen Lane Penguin Books.

Keohane, D. 1976. 'An Account and an Assessment of Two Employers' Associations in Building and Civil Engineering, with Special Reference to Industrial Relations in the Two Sectors'. MA dissertation, University of Warwick.

Kerr, C., J.T. Dunlop, F. Harbison and C.A. Myers. 1973. *Industrialism and Industrial Man.* 2nd British edn. Harmondsworth: Penguin.

Kirsch, M. 1980. 'Le Lock-out en Droit Français'. *Recht der Arbeit*, Vol. 33, January/February, 32–9.

Kochan, T.A. 1980. *Collective Bargaining and Industrial Relations: From Theory to Policy and Practice.* Homewood, Ill.: Irwin.

Kocka, J. 1978. 'Entrepreneurs and Managers in German Industrialisation'. *Cambridge Economic History of Europe. The Industrial Economies: Capital, Labour and Enterprise.* Vol. 7, Part I. Ed. P. Mathias and M.M. Postan. Cambridge: Cambridge University Press, 442–89.

Korpi, W. 1978a. 'Shop-Floor Bargaining and Industrial Democracy: Unofficial Strikes in Sweden'. *Industrial Democracy: International Views.* Coventry: SSRC Industrial Relations Research Unit, University of Warwick, 265–82.

—— 1978b. 'Workplace Bargaining, the Law and Unofficial Strikes: The Case of Sweden'. *British Journal of Industrial Relations*, Vol. 16, November, 355–68.

Krusche, R. and D. Pfeiffer. 1975. *Betriebliche Gewerkschaftsorgane und Interessenvertretung: Betriebsräte- und Vertrauensleutepolitik der I.G. Metall.* Berlin: Verlag Die Arbeitswelt.

Kugelberg, B. 1951. 'Centralised or Decentralised Wage Negotiations?' *Scandinaviska Banken Quarterly Review*, Vol. 25, October, 91–8.

—— 1953. 'The Saltsjöbaden Agreements between the Federation of Swedish Employers and the Confederation of Swedish Trade Unions'. *Scandinaviska Banken Quarterly Review*, Vol. 27, October, 94–103.

Lambert, J. 1969. *Le Patron*. Paris: Bloud & Gay.

Landes, D.S. 1972. *The Unbound Prometheus*. Cambridge: Cambridge University Press.

Laroque, P. 1938. *Les Rapports entre Patron et Ouvriers*. Paris: Aubier.

Lash, S. 1985. 'The End of Neo-Corporatism? The Breakdown of Centralised Bargaining in Sweden'. *British Journal of Industrial Relations*, Vol. 23, July, 215–40.

Lazonick, W. 1983. 'Technological Change and the Control of Work: The Development of Capital-Labour Relations in Mass Production Industries'. *Managerial Strategies and Industrial Relations: An Historical and Comparative Study*. Ed. H.F. Gospel and C. Littler. London: Heinemann, 111–36.

Leckebusch, R. 1966. *Entstehung und Wandlungen der Zielsetzungen, der Struktur und der Wirkungen von Arbeitgeberverbänden*. Berlin: Duncker & Humblot.

Lee, J.J. 1978. 'Labour in German Industrialisation'. *Cambridge Economic History of Europe. The Industrial Economies: Capital, Labour and Enterprise*. Vol. 7, Part II. Ed. P. Mathias and M.M. Postan. Cambridge: Cambridge University Press.

Lefranc, G. 1976. *Les Organisations Patronales en France*. Paris: Payot.

Levine, L. 1924. *The Women's Garment Workers*. New York: B.W. Huebsch.

Levine, S.B. 1958. *Industrial Relations in Post-War Japan*. Urbana: University of Illinois Press.

—— 1984. 'Employers' Associations in Japan'. *Employers' Associations and Industrial Relations: A Comparative Study*. Ed. J.P. Windmueller and A. Gladstone. Oxford: Clarendon Press.

Lewis, R. 1970. 'The Legal Enforceability of Collective Agreements'. *British Journal of Industrial Relations*, Vol. 8, November, 313–33.

—— 1979. 'Collective Agreements: The Kahn-Freund Legacy'. *Modern Law Review*, Vol. 42, November, 613–22.

Livingston, J., J. Moore and F. Oldfather. 1976. *Postwar Japan: 1945 to the Present Day. The Japan Reader*. Vol. 2. Harmondsworth: Penguin.

Lockwood, W. 1964. *The Economic Development of Japan*. Princeton, NJ: Princeton University Press.

Lohse, L. 1958. 'Centralisation of Bargaining in Sweden since 1939'. *Monthly Labor Review*, November, 1230–5.

Lorwin, V. 1954. *The French Labor Movement*. Cambridge, Mass.: Harvard University Press.

Löwisch, M. 1980. 'Besteht ein Grund, die Rechtsprechung des Bundesarbeitsgerichts zur Aussperrung zu ändern?'. *Recht der Arbeit*, Vol. 33, January/February, 1–14.

Mann, M. 1973. *Consciousness and Action among the Western Working Class*. London: Macmillan.

Marsh, A.I. 1965. *Industrial Relations in Engineering*. Oxford: Pergamon.

—— and W.E.J. McCarthy. 1968. *Disputes Procedures in Britain*. Research Paper 2, Part 2, Royal Commission on Trade Unions and Employers' Associations. London: HMSO.

Meidner, R. 1973. 'Samordning och Solidarisk Lönepolitik under Tre Decennier'. *Tvarsnit*. Stockholm: Prisma.

Merli Brandini, P. 1971. 'Sindacati e Struttura Contrattuale'. *Rassegna Sindacale Quaderni*, Vol. 31/32, July/October, 62–74.

Miller, D. 1978. 'Trade Union Workplace Representation in the Federal Republic of Germany: An Analysis of the Post War Vertrauensleute Policy of the German Metalworkers' Union 1952–77'. *British Journal of Industrial Relations*, Vol. 16, November, 335–54.

Mills, H. and R. Montgomery. 1945. *Organised Labor.* New York: McGraw-Hill.

Mitsufuji, T. and K. Hagisawa. 1972. 'Recent Trends in Collective Bargaining in Japan'. *International Labour Review*, Vol. 105, February, 135–53.

Montgomery, D. 1980. *Workers' Control in America: Studies in the History of Work, Technology and Labour Struggles.* Cambridge: Cambridge University Press.

Mortillaro, F. and B. Fernex. 1976. 'FEDERMECCANICA e FLM sul Ruolo della Contrattazione Colletiva Nazionale'. *I Diritti dei Lavatori.* Ed. P.A. Varesi. Milano: Gabriele Mazzotta Editore, 74–83.

Mouly, J. 1967. 'Wage Policy in Sweden'. *International Labour Review*, Vol. 95, February, 166–201.

Müller-Jentsch, W. 1984. 'The Changing Balance between Workplace Representation and Industrywide Representation in West Germany'. *Industrial Relations in Transition: The Cases of Japan and the Federal Republic of Germany.* Ed. T. Shigeyosni and J. Bergmann. Tokyo: University of Tokyo Press/Campus-Verlag, 197–208.

Musson, A.E. 1954. *The Typographical Association.* London: Oxford University Press.

National Board for Prices and Incomes (NBPI). 1968. 'A Further Note on Wage Drift'. Supplement to *Payment by Results Systems.* Report 65, Cmnd 3627. London: HMSO.

Neufeld, M.F. 1961. *Italy: School for Awakening Countries.* New York: Cornell University Press.

Noé, C. 1970. *Gebändigter Klassenkampf: Tarifautonomie in der Bundesrepublik Deutschland.* Berlin: Duncker & Humblot.

Norgren, P.H. 1941. *The Swedish Collective Bargaining System.* Cambridge, Mass.: Harvard University Press.

Oechslin, J.-J. 1972. 'The Role of Employers' Organisations in France'. *International Labour Review*, Vol. 106, November, 391–412.

Offe, C. and H. Wiesenthal. 1980. 'Two Logics of Collective Action: Theoretical Notes on Social Class and Organisational Form'. *Political Power and Social Theory.* Ed. M. Zeitlin. New York: JAI Press, 67–115.

Okamoto, H. 1973. 'Management and their Organisations'. *Workers and Employers in Japan: The Japanese Employment System.* Ed. K. Okochi, B. Karsh and S.B. Levine. Tokyo: University of Tokyo Press, 163–217.

Olivetti, G. 1922. 'Collective Agreements in Italy'. *International Labour Review*, Vol. 5, February.

Olsen, M. 1969. *The Logic of Collective Action.* New York: Shocken Books.

Pera, G. 1980. 'Die Aussperrung im Italienischen Recht'. *Recht der Arbeit*, Vol. 33, January/February, 39–43.

Phelps Brown, E.H. 1959. *The Growth of British Industrial Relations: A Study from the Standpoint of 1906–14.* London: Macmillan.

—— 1962: 'Wage Drift'. *Economica* (new series) Vol. 29, November, 339–56.

Pierson, F.C. 1950. 'Prospects for Industry-Wide Bargaining'. *Industrial and Labor Relations Review*, Vol. 3, April, 341–61.

—— 1960. 'Cooperation among Managements in Collective Bargaining'. *Labor Law Journal*, Vol. 11, July, 621–8.

—— 1961. 'Recent Employer Alliances in Perspective'. *Industrial Relations*, Vol. 1, October, 39–57.

Prais, S.J. 1981. *The Evolution of Giant Firms in Britain: A Study of the Growth of Concentration in Manufacturing Industry in Britain, 1909–70.* 2nd impression. Cambridge: Cambridge University Press.

Price, R. 1980. *Masters, Unions and Men: Work Control in Building and the Rise of Labour 1830–1914.* Cambridge: Cambridge University Press.

Priouret, R. 1963. *Origines du Patronat Français.* Paris: Les Éditions Bernard Grasset.

Pugh. A. 1951. *Men of Steel: A Chronicle of Eighty-Eight Years of Trade Unionism in the British Iron and Steel Industry, by One of Them.* London: Iron and Steel Trades Confederation.

Ramm, T. 1965a. 'The German Law of Collective Agreements: Its Development and Problems'. *Labour Relations and the Law: A Comparative Study.* Ed. O. Kahn-Freund. London: Stevens, 84–91.

—— 1965b. 'The Restriction of the Freedom to Strike in the Federal Republic of Germany'. *Labour Relations and the Law: A Comparative Study.* Ed. O. Kahn-Freund. London: Stevens, 201–10.

—— 1971. 'Labor Courts and Grievance Settlement in West Germany'. *Labor Courts and Grievance Settlement in Western Europe.* Ed. B. Aaron. Berkeley and Los Angeles: University of California Press, 83–100.

Ratner, G., J.H. Soltow and R. Sylla. 1979. *The Evolution of the American Economy.* New York: Basic Books.

Reader, W.J. 1973. *The First Quarter Century, 1926–1952. Imperial Chemical Industries: A History.* Vol. 2. Oxford: Oxford University Press.

Reindl, R. 1922. *Die Deutsche Gewerkschaftsbewegung.* Altenburg: Geibel.

Reynaud, J.-D. 1975a. *Les Syndicats en France.* Vol. 1. Paris: Éditions du Seuil.

—— 1975b. 'France: Elitist Society Inhibits Articulated Bargaining'. *Worker Militancy and Its Consequences.* Ed. S. Barkin. New York: Praeger, 277–317.

Rice, M. 1980. 'The 1979 Engineering Dispute'. MA dissertation, University of Warwick.

Robbins, J.S. 1942. *The Government of Labor Relations in Sweden.* Chapel Hill: University of North Carolina Press.

Roberts, B.C. 1958. *National Wages Policy in War and Peace.* London: Allen & Unwin.

Roberts, D.D. 1979. *The Syndicalist Tradition in Italian Fascism.* Manchester: Manchester University Press.

Robinson, B. 1976. 'The Nature and Extent of Employer Organisation: The British Chemical Industry and Its Multi-Nationals'. MA dissertation, University of Warwick.

Ross, A.M. 1962. 'Prosperity and Labor Relations in Europe: The Case of West Germany'. *Quarterly Journal of Economics*, Vol. 76, August, 331–59.

Sales, H. 1967. *Les Relations Industrielles dans l'Imprimerie Française.* Paris.

Sasaki, N. 1981. *Management and Industrial Structure in Japan.* Oxford: Pergamon.

Schmidt, F. 1971. 'The Settlement of Employment Grievances in Sweden'. *Labor Courts and Grievance Settlement in Western Europe.* Ed. B. Aaron. Berkeley and Los Angeles: University of California Press, 161–248.

Schmitter, P.C. and W. Streeck. 1981. 'The Organisation of Business Interests: A Research Design to Study the Associative Action of Business in the Advanced Industrial Societies of Western Europe'. Discussion Paper. Berlin: International Institute of Management.

Schmölders, G. 1965. *Das Selbstbild der Verbände: Schriften des Vereins für Sozialpolitik*. Berlin: Duncker & Humblot.

Scott, J. 1979. *Corporations, Classes and Capitalism*. London: Hutchinson.

Seidman, J. 1942. *The Needle Trades*. New York: Farrar & Rinehart.

Sellier, F. 1960. 'La Cohésion Patronale dans les Négociations Sociales'. *Droit Social*, July/August.

—— 1961. *La Stratégie de la Lutte Sociale*. Paris: Les Éditions Ouvrières.

—— 1970. 'L'Évolution des Négociations Collectives dans la Sidérurgie et la Métallurgie en France (1950–69)'. *Droit Social*, September/October.

—— 1976. 'Les Problèmes du Travail en France: 1920–1974'. Paper for the Conference of the International Industrial Relations Association, Geneva, September.

Sharp, I.G. 1950. *Industrial Conciliation and Arbitration in Great Britain*. London: Allen & Unwin.

Shirai, T. 1973. 'Collective Bargaining'. *Workers and Employers in Japan: The Japanese Employment System*. Ed. K. Okochi, B. Karsh and S.B. Levine. Tokyo: University of Tokyo Press, 269–309.

Simon, W. 1976. *Macht und Herrschaft der Unternehmerverbände*. Cologne: Pahl-Rugenstein.

Skogh, G. 1984. 'Employers' Associations in Sweden'. *Employers' Associations and Industrial Relations*. Ed. J.P. Windmueller and A. Gladstone. Oxford: Clarendon Press, 149–68.

Slichter, S.H. 1941. *Union Policies and Industrial Management*. Washington, DC: Brookings Institute.

Söllner, A. 1980. 'Zur Zulässigkeit der Aussperrung nach Geltendem Recht aus Rechtsgeschichtlicher Sicht'. *Recht der Arbeit*, Vol. 33, January/February, 14–22.

Stearns, P.N. 1971. *Revolutionary Syndicalism and French Labor: A Cause without Rebels*. New Brunswick, NJ: Rutgers University Press.

Stein, J. 1969. *Die Geschichte des Ersten Fachlichen Wirtschaftsverbandes in Deutschland*.

Streeck, W. 1978. 'Organisational Consequences of Corporatist Cooperation in West German Labour Unions: A Case Study'. Discussion Paper. Berlin: International Institute of Management.

Stryman, G. 1946. *Verkstadsföreningen 1896–1945*. Stockholm: Norstedt.

Sturmthal, A. 1951. 'Collective Bargaining in France'. *Industrial and Labor Relations Review*, Vol. 4, January, 236–48.

Sumiya, M. 1973. 'The Emergence of Modern Japan'. *Workers and Employers in Japan: The Japanese Employment System*. Ed. K. Okochi, B. Karsh and S.B. Levine. Tokyo: University of Tokyo Press, 49–89.

Summerfield, P.H. 1976. 'The Role of the West Midlands Engineering Employers' Association'. MSc dissertation, University of Warwick.

Sunesson, S. 1974. *Politik och Organisation*. Arkiv Avhandlingsserie 1, Kristianstad.

Von Sydow, H. 1931. 'Om den Svenska Arbetsgivareorganisation, dess Verksamhet och Betydelse'. Speech delivered to the Swedish Institute of Foremen, November.

Taira, K. 1970. *Economic Development and the Labor Market in Japan*. New York: Columbia University Press.

—— 1978. 'Factory Labour and the Industrial Revolution in Japan'. *Cambridge Economic History of Europe. The Industrial Economies: Capital, Labour and Enterprise*. Vol. 7. Part II. Ed. P. Mathias and M.M. Postan. Cambridge: Cambridge University Press, 166–213.

Treu, T. and A. Martinelli. 1984. 'Employers' Associations in Italy'. *Employers' Associations and Industrial Relations*. Ed. J.P. Windmueller and A. Gladstone. Oxford: Clarendon Press, 264–93.

Ulman, L. 1961a. 'The Development of Trades and Labor Unions'. *American Economic History*. Ed. S.E. Harris. New York: McGraw-Hill.

—— 1961b. *The Rise of the National Trade Unions*. Cambridge, Mass.: Harvard University Press.

—— 1974. 'Collective Bargaining and Competitive Bargaining'. *Scottish Journal of Political Economy*, Vol. 21, June, 97–109.

Union des Industries Métallurgiques et Minières. 1968. *Année Métallurgique*. Paris: UIMM.

Victorin, A. 1974. 'Lonebildingsprocessen'. *Kibflict pa Arbetsmasknaden*. Ed. L. Branntgarde. Lund.

Villey, E. 1923. *L'Organisation Professionelle des Employeurs dans l'Industrie Française*. Paris: Felix Alcan.

Waline, P. 1951. 'Le Patronat Français et les Conventions Collectives'. *Revue Économique*, February.

Webb, S. and B. Webb. 1920. *The History of Trade Unionism 1666–1920*. London: Longman.

Weber, A. 1954. *Der Kampf zwischen Kapital und Arbeit*. Tübingen: J.C.B. Mohr.

Wedderburn, K.W. *Lord*. 1971. *The Worker and the Law*. 2nd edn. Harmondsworth: Penguin.

Werner, K.G. 1968. *Organisation und Politik der Gewerkschaften und Arbeitgeberverbände in der Deutschen Bauwirtschaft*. Berlin: Duncker & Humblot.

Westerståhl, J. 1945. *Svensk Fackföreningsrörelse*. Stockholm: Tidens.

Wigham, E. 1973. *The Power to Manage: A History of the Engineering Employers' Federation*. London: Macmillan.

Wolman, L. 1936. *The Ebb and Flow in Trade Unionism*. New York: National Bureau of Economic Research.

Wright Mills, C. 1948. *The New Men of Power*. New York: Harcourt Brace.

Wunderlich, F. 1940. *Labor under German Democracy*. New York: New School for Social Research.

Zeitlin, J. 1983. 'The Labour Strategies of British Engineering Employers, 1890–1914'. *Managerial Strategies and Industrial Relations: An Historical and Comparative Study*. Ed. H.F. Gospel and C. Littler. London: Heinemann, 25–54.

Zirano, B. 1962. 'Origini e Sviluppi dell'Organizzazione Industriale'. Paper presented to internal conference organized by CONFINDUSTRIA

Author Index

General Index

AC (W. Germany), 88, 104
  internal structure of, 58
  membership coverage of, 49
  membership density of, 67
accord(s) (France), 102–4
Act for the Promotion of Stability
  and Growth (W. Germany), 105
'adhesion contracts' (Sweden), 132
AES (W. Germany), membership
  coverage of, 52
AG (Sweden)
  internal structure of, 58
  membership coverage of, 49, 57
  membership density of, 67
Agnelli, 98n.20, 151, 152, 177n.8, 192
Agricultural Wages Acts (Britain), 131
AIE (Italy), membership coverage of,
  53
AIIA (Italy)
  internal structure of, 59
  membership coverage of, 50
AIIGCT (Italy)
  internal structure of, 64
  membership coverage of, 53
Akarp Law 1899 (Sweden), 157
Alfa Romeo, 50
Alfa-Laval, 198
Amalgamated Engineering Union
  (AEU) (Britain), 123n.15
American Federation of Labor (AFL),
  175, 177, 178

  membership of, 177
ANCE (Italy)
  constitutional arrangements of, 78
  internal structure of, 60, 61, 65
  membership coverage of, 51
  membership density of, 67
  negotiations between trade unions
  and, 84
ANIC (Italy)
  internal structure of, 58
  membership coverage of, 49
  membership density of, 67
Ansoldo, 151
Anti-Socialist Law 1879 (Germany),
  147, 148n.9
arbitration
  in Britain, 164, 166–7n.27
  in France, 112n.6
  in Germany, 104, 149, 150
'aristocratic revolution' 1868 (Japan),
  179–80
'arms length' bargaining, 39
'articulated bargaining' (Italy), 23,
  100, 113
Asano, 180
ASAP (Italy), 113
  membership coverage of, 47, 48, 50
ASE (Britain), 82n.1, 110n.3, 158, 162,
  163, 164, 165, 168, 169, 175n.7,
  187
Askwith, 82n.1, 166–7n.27